BASKETBALL

BASKETBALL

THE COMPLETE HANDBOOK OF INDIVIDUAL SKILLS

ROBERT A. FOX
John Jay College of Criminal Justice
City University of New York

Prentice Hall, Englewood Cliffs, New Jersey 07632

Library of Congress Cataloging-in-Publication Data

Fox, Robert A.
    Basketball: the complete handbook of individual
skills.

    Includes index.
    1. Basketball—Training.   I. Title.
GV885.35.F69 1987   796.32′3′07   87-14560
ISBN 0-13-066796-X

Editorial/production supervision and
    interior design: Joe O'Donnell Jr.
Cover design: Bruce Kenselaar
Cover photo: George Kalinsky, Major League Graphics
Manufacturing buyer: Margaret Rizzi

 © 1988 by Robert A. Fox

Printed in the United States of America

10 9 8 7 6 5 4 3 2 1

ISBN 0-13-066796-X 01

Prentice-Hall International (UK) Limited, *London*
Prentice-Hall of Australia Pty. Limited, *Sydney*
Prentice-Hall Canada Inc., *Toronto*
Prentice-Hall Hispanoamericana, S.A., *Mexico*
Prentice-Hall of India Private Limited, *New Delhi*
Prentice-Hall of Japan, Inc., *Tokyo*
Simon & Schuster Asia Pte. Ltd., *Singapore*
Editora Prentice-Hall do Brasil, Ltda., *Rio de Janeiro*

Dad

CONTENTS

FOREWORD

There never can be enough books on fundamental basketball as far as I am concerned. As time goes on, the game changes and it is important for all players and coaches to update their approach to the strategy and the application of the basics.

It's a sport that requires fresh viewpoints to match the infusion of the different type players each generation supplies. While the fundamentals never change, it still takes an incisive mind to take all the parts and put them together in a manner that makes it easy to understand.

Bob Fox has done just that in his comprehensive presentation. He has taken all his experiences as a player and coach and put them between these pages. I have found him to be an avid student of the game during those times that our paths have crossed when he was Director of Basketball at the Kutsher's Sports Academy.

It's one thing to have natural talent. It's another to know what to do with that talent. There are proper ways to shoot, pass, and rebound. Bob has helped players grow by passing on the things he learned. And now he has put it all in this book, an all-encompassing one.

He describes various basketball drills that are of great value to improving skills. He has put a lot of work and effort into transferring his learning experiences into written explanations that are easy to understand.

Bob Fox has touched all the bases in this total approach to the game of basektball. It all helps no matter at what level of basketball people are involved. I have seen players come into the NBA sometimes lacking in fundamentals. There isn't a coach alive who doesn't have to remind players of and go back to the fundamentals at one time or another.

I believe this book will make it a lot easier for a lot of people.

William (Red) Holzman

PREFACE

Natural ability is the promise of potential, but fundamentals are the foundation of excellence. It is on this premise that this text has been written. All basketball coaches need a handbook to assist them in developing the basic skills for their players. *Basketball: The Complete Handbook of Individual Skills* is written to the player because the material, to be effective, must be communicated to the player. For clarity and simplicity, the text addresses the player as "you," in the way that the coach should address him or her in passing on the information. In choreographic fashion, footwork, dribbling, passing, shooting, one-on-one moves, post moves, advanced scoring, and rebounding are carefully broken down into their essentials and presented with step-by-step instruction and skill-specific drills. Each section contains diagrams, photographs, points of emphasis for each skill, suggested workouts, a self-evaluation and improvement test, a personal progress chart, and many advanced tips and secrets that reinforce and extend the basics.

While there have been countless articles and books written on team concepts, relatively few have been devoted to individual skills. Moreover, none of those on individual skills has systematically broken down each skill sufficiently so that a coach or player can understand and learn each component fully.

Coaches at every level will find this a valuable, practical reference for planning practices, working camps, giving clinics, and preparing lectures. Individual skills must be mastered by each player to execute any team concept satisfactorily. A basketball team can be likened to an orchestra, where each member must master his or her own instrument before a symphony is possible.

HOW TO USE THIS BOOK

This book is not meant to be read in long stretches. Rather, a short section should be studied and then the drills performed. The body must learn along with the mind, so that the movements become semiautomatic. In a game situation, a player decides what to do, but the execution must, of course, be second nature. Only drill and repetition will make this possible.

The coach, the player, or the interested parent can use this handbook as a programmed guide, progressing at his or her own speed. For the beginning player, the manual should be followed in order and to the letter. For more advanced players, sections can be excerpted. For coaches, this handbook can be used in many ways:

To teach individual fundamentals in a logical progression with all the necessary discussion, description, drills, photographs, diagrams, workouts, self-evaluation and improvement charts, and progress charts.

To review areas of individual skills and integrate some new ideas, drills, and tests into your own system.

For specialization in a specific area, for example, to develop low-post moves for an unusually tall player or ball-handling skills for a talented point guard.

As a diagnostic tool. Often, a coach becomes frustrated because a specific area of his or her team game is not being executed at the level he or she expects. In such cases, the problem often lies in deficient individual skills, and this handbook can help to analyze and correct the problem.

ACKNOWLEDGMENTS

If I have learned anything from my basketball playing and coaching career it is that success is most meaningful when it comes from the combination of "gift and grit." You can't succeed without any talent, but ability is often wasted for lack of perseverence and perspicacity—that dogged determination and self-discipline to work to be as good as your talent will permit you to be. And although it is cliche, the success you attain, regardless of the level, when you have actualized your ability, is deeply satisfying and personal. It elevates your self-esteem and becomes permanently embedded in your character.

This book is written to the individual—the coach and the player. Work diligently and, hopefully, you will enjoy and grow from this marvelous game as much as I have.

Many people provided me with help on this project and I want to thank them: Rich Alin, Barry Bergen, John Davis, Bob Dukiet, Peter Dodenhoff, Michael Fox, Ted Hurwitz, Linda Vonlumm, John Makuch, Herman Masin, Nick McNickle, Ray Rankis, Marie Rosen, Mike Saunders, and Ed Stanford. But especially, I am indebted to Wes Meltzer for his tireless energies field testing the drills, Bob Phillips for his editorial supervision, Chuck Durang for his wide-ranging advice and support, and Susie Silvan for her emotional support and photographic assistance.

The photographs for the book were taken by Paul Dodenhoff, Susie Silvan, and myself; illustrations were prepared by Tiina Kangur; and models for the photographs were Courtney Callender, Gladys Chaves, Gerald Henderson, Brett Howard, Wes Meltzer, Stuart Roth, and Curtis White. Finally, my thanks to Cliff Lispon, who took the photograph for the inside of the book jacket.

Robert A. Fox

BASKETBALL

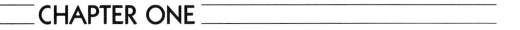

CHAPTER ONE

INTRODUCTION

ORGANIZATION OF THE BOOK

This book is a manual. Unlike the typically theoretical approach of most other technical material, this handbook begins at the beginning—with footwork—and builds block by block, skill by skill, in a logical progression, integrating the most basic skills into the more complex areas of dribbling, passing and receiving, shooting, one-on-one moves, post moves, advanced scoring, and rebounding. Each skill is described and discussed, talked and walked through, and drilled before it is integrated into more complex skills.

In addition, each drill is followed by "Points of Emphasis," where the most important aspects of the skill's acquisition are reinforced and the most commonly committed errors associated with that skill are addressed. Each section culminates in suggested workouts for that specific skills area, a self-evaluation and improvement test, and a personal progress chart.

1

TO THE PLAYER

Drills Instructions

Read through each drill thoroughly *before* you begin practicing the skill. This includes the introduction to the skill and the Points of Emphasis.

Walk through the drill, without the ball if necessary, concentrating on following the directions and developing the proper form.

Young players should use a smaller basketball and lower basket. In addition, distances may have to be modified to suit the player.

For example, for young players, wall passing may require lowering the wall targets and shortening some of the passing distances. Shooting spots may have to be moved in, and distances pertaining to how far apart the feet should be or how long a step should be taken for certain skills might have to be shortened.

Practice as often as possible. Remember that several short practice sessions are better than one long one. It is far better to practice for a half hour four times than once for two hours.

Concentrate on each drill and learn to do each perfectly. First, learn the skill with *form*. After form is mastered, concentrate on the skill's *rhythm*. After form and rhythm have been mastered, *speed* is practiced.

Each chapter of the book concentrates on one skill area. The drills in one chapter progress from easy to more difficult skills.

Be your own worst critic. That does not mean that you should downgrade yourself. Rather, your self-appraisal should be completely honest. This will develop your confidence by allowing you to become the best player you can possibly be.

THE "OFF," OR NONDOMINANT, HAND

For simplicity, this text will assume that you are a righty. If your left hand is your dominant hand, you will have to reverse all the directions in the drills when learning the skills.

Learn to use your nondominant or "off" hand. This will be very frustrating at times, but in the long run will be worth the effort. Sometimes you will have to spend two, three, or even four times the amount of effort to get the "off" hand just to become functional, while the dominant hand will seem to come naturally. Stay with it. Once you master a few skills with the "off" hand, others will start to come more easily.

But why, you might ask, is it so important to be able to use both hands? It is important because you are learning to use more than both hands, you are learning to control your whole body.

Soon, you will be able to balance and control yourself jumping off either foot, sliding, and changing course equally well in any direction. You will be able to shoot from close range, pass in any direction, and dribble proficiently with either hand. In short, you will become a *complete* player! A player who cannot dribble with the left hand, for example, can be defensed easily and rendered ineffective most of the time.

It is easier to learn skills involving your "off" hand at an early age. As you mature, it will be harder and harder to master.

PRACTICING WITH A FRIEND

The skills and drills in this book are designed to be learned and taught individually. However, at some point, you will want to apply them competitively or cooperatively with a friend. You will benefit most by choosing a friend who is close to you in ability, especially when playing against one another one-on-one. It does not do much good to play against someone who is too much better or worse than you.

COMPETITION

DRIBBLING

1. Two players, each with a ball, in one of the three circles—at midcourt or the two foul lines. Each player keeps his or her dribble alive and tries to bat the opponent's ball out of the circle. Play this game using right hand only, left hand only, and using either hand.
2. Set up obstacle courses and see who can dribble through them in the least amount of time.

PASSING

1. Practice each of the passes—with proper reception—at various distances passing the ball back and forth.
2. See how many of each of the passes the two of you can do in one minute.
3. Use the wall targets and see who can pass into the target square the most out of ten for each type of pass.

SHOOTING

1. Shooting contests are terrific motivation for improving concentration and form. See who can make the most out of five or ten shots from each spot for each shot. You can use this for spot shots, jumpers, hooks, and layups.

2. Play "Horse." One player shoots any shot from any place he or she chooses. If the first player makes the shot, the second player must make that shot also or receive a letter. If the first player misses the shot, the second player gets to shoot any shot he chooses and, if the second player makes it, the first player must make the shot or receive a letter. This pattern continues and the player who misses five shots first, after his opponent has made his shot, loses.

3. Play "Around the World." Each player begins at SS (shot spot) #1 and must make two shots in a row from each shooting spot to progress from SS #1 to 17. (For a layout of the spot shots, see Figure 5-1.) For example, player A makes two in a row from SS #1. Player A continues and makes one shot from SS #2 but misses the second shot. Player B misses the first shot at SS #1. Now it is player A's turn, and he or she begins from SS #2 because he or she has already made two in a row from SS #1. This pattern continues until one player finishes by making two in a row at SS #17. You can play this game with spot shots and jump shots. Use only the left hand and use SS #1–10. In addition, play the same game with bank shots only using SS #1, 2, 4, 5, 7, 9, 12, and 16.

4. Play "One-on-One." How much this game contributes to the development of your five-on-five full-court game will depend on the rules you develop:
   a. Start play from different spots.
   b. Allow only one to three dribbles per move, and set a five-second time limit for each possession.
   c. Devise the game so that you will both have to learn to play and defend against facing-the-basket and back-to-the-basket moves.
   d. Play a special series where one player begins his or her possession at midcourt dribbling toward the defender who begins at the top of the foul circle.

WARMUP

It is important that you get into the habit of warming up to begin each workout. A warmup prepares the heart and blood vessels for the increased workload experienced while exercising. If you don't warm up, you may feel tired very quickly. A warmup is also needed to stretch the muscles and tendons so they are less likely to be injured. This habit may seem to be a waste of time, but it becomes more important as you get older.

As you get older you need to warm up longer because your body will be bigger, stronger, and more powerful. This means you will run faster and jump higher, but you will also place more stress on your joints and muscles. Athletic trainers assure us that if we get into the habit of warming up properly when we are young, our bodies will stay more flexible and be less susceptible to injury as we get older.

Guidelines for Warmup

Begin each warmup with an exercise that will get your blood circulating faster in preparation for your workout. For example, jumping jacks and running in place are good exercises to begin with.

Always breathe rhythmically when you exercise. Never hold your breath. When you are doing pushups and situps, exhale as you are coming up and inhale as you are returning to the floor.

All stretches are done without forcing. Let the weight of the body naturally stretch the joint. Never stretch to the point of pain. Stretch until you feel resistance, or pull, hold, then stretch in the opposite direction. This will stretch the joint to its maximum in time and with repeated stretches. Never bounce or use a rapid or sudden movement when you stretch. Muscles stretch best when warm and in a relaxed state.

Warm up until you feel loose and have broken into a sweat. The colder it is, the longer it will take you to warm up.

Be in touch with your own body—learn to listen to it. Warm up and stretch at your own pace and never force a joint. Each person has muscles and joints that take a little longer to stretch out. The larger a muscle or muscle group is, the longer it will take to stretch it. For example, the thighs, hamstrings, and calves (lower-body muscles) usually take longer to stretch than do the arms (upper-body muscles). The following is a modest warmup routine that should take between five and ten minutes to complete:

1. Run in place for one minute. Begin slowly picking your feet up at least four inches off the floor. Increase your pace every fifteen seconds.
2. Jumping Jacks: Stand with your legs together and your hands at your sides. Jump two or three inches off the floor and spread your feet out a little more than shoulder width while bringing your hands together over your head. On the next jump, bring your feet together again and your hands back to your sides. Repeat this twenty-five times (Figs. 1-1a and 1-1b).
   Hold for a count of eight in each of the following stretches where it says "*Hold.*"
3. Head Hang: Let your head hang down so your chin is almost on your chest. *Hold.* Let your head fall back as far as it will go. *Hold.* Repeat twice more (Figs. 1-2a, 1-2b, and 1-2c). Let your head fall to the right with your ear almost resting on your right shoulder. *Hold.* Repeat on the other side so your left ear is nearly touching your left shoulder. *Hold.* Repeat twice more. (Figs. 1-2d and 1-2e).
4. Arms and Shoulder Stretch: Reach both arms straight up over your head and reach for the sky. *Hold.* Alternate arms reaching as far as you can with the right arm and holding and then with the left arm. Repeat twice more (Figs. 1-3a, 1-3b, and 1-3c).

(a)   (b)

Figures 1-1a and 1-1b   Jumping Jacks

5. Waist and Side Stretch: Keeping your legs straight, bend forward at the
    waist and let your head and arms fall toward the floor. *Hold.* Straighten
    up and let your head roll back, arms relaxed by your side. Lean back-
    ward and hold. Repeat twice more (Figs. 1-4a and 1-4b). Raise your right
    arm straight over your head, with your left arm across your body, and
    lean to your left. *Hold.* Repeat with your left arm raised, right arm across
    your body, leaning to your right. Repeat twice more (Figs. 1-5a and
    1-5b).

6. Thigh Stretch: Stand on your left foot by holding your right ankle with
    your right hand. Be sure you are standing straight, and *gently* pull on
    your ankle until you feel the stretch in your right thigh. *Hold.* Repeat
    with the other leg. Repeat twice more. Be sure that when you pull on
    your ankle you do not pull so hard that you feel pain in the knee. This
    means you pulled too tight. (See Figure 1-6.)

7. Hamstring Stretch: Squat down and reach both hands between your
    legs, placing all five fingers on the floor behind each heel. Slowly raise
    your rear end up until you feel the stretch in your hamstrings. *Hold.* Re-
    peat this twice, and on the last time, swing your rear end from side to
    side five times. (See Figure 1-7.)

(a)

(b)

(c)

Figures 1-2a, 1-2b, and 1-2c Head Hang

(d)

(e)

Figures 1-2d and 1-2e Head Hang

| (a) | (b) | (c) |

Figures 1-3a, 1-3b, and 1-3c Arms and Shoulders Stretch

Figures 1-4a and 1-4b Waist Stretch

| (a) | (b) |

(a)

(b)

Figures 1-5a and 1-5b Side Stretch

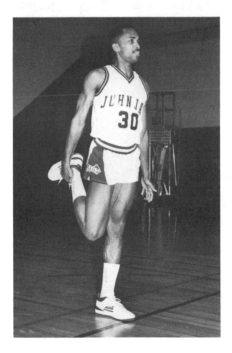

Figure 1-6 Thigh Stretch

Figure 1-7 Hamstring Stretch

8. Groin Stretch (Butterfly): Sit with the soles of your feet pressed together, with your knees out and your forearms resting on the insides of the knees. Gently lean forward and press down with your forearms until you feel the stretch in your groin. *Hold.* Repeat twice more. (See Figure 1-8.)

9. Achilles Tendon Stretch: Stand twelve inches from a wall, facing it. Place both hands on the wall directly in front of you and stretch your right leg behind you as far as possible without straining so that your foot is flat on the floor. Gently press forward until you feel the stretch in your calf and Achilles tendon. *Hold.* Repeat with the other leg. Repeat twice more. (See Figure 1-9.)

10. Abdominals: Lie on your back with your knees bent as much as possible and your arms across your chest with your left hand in your right armpit and your right hand in your left armpit. Do as many situps as possible without straining. Be sure that when you come up you bring your elbows between your knees and go as far as possible without straining. Exhale as

Figure 1-8 Groin Stretch

Figure 1-9   Achilles Tendon Stretch

you come up and inhale as you return to the floor. (See Figures 1-10a and 1-10b.)

11. Arms, Chest, Fingers, and Hands: Lie on your stomach and keep the back as straight as possible. Push yourself up on your *fingertips*. Be sure your fingers are as spread as possible. At first, you may only do one or two, but you will improve rapidly. Every two or three days, change your arm position by moving the hands wider apart or closer together. This will strengthen your fingers, arms, and chest all at the same time. Remember to exhale as you push up from the floor and inhale as you return to the floor. (See Figure 1-11.)

Figures 1-10a and 1-10b   Situp

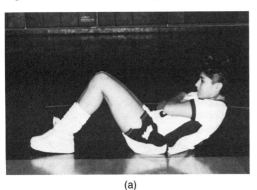

(a)

(b)

Figure 1-11 Fingertip Pushup

COOLDOWN

After you finish your workout, it is important that you do a cooldown. You may feel loose after a good workout, but you have actually tightened many of your muscles and tendons even though they may feel good. To cool down, do each of the stretches in the warmup twice and walk around until you are breathing normally. Cooling down with a lot of stretching will decrease the stiffness and soreness you might feel later and the next day.

It is important that you take a shower after each workout when-

Figure 1-12 Wall Sit

ever possible and, if you are working out indoors, do not go out into the cold immediately after your workout.

SPECIAL STRENGTH EXERCISES

The game of basketball demands a great deal of strength and endurance in certain specific areas. If you are not naturally strong in these areas, it might be a good idea for you to do some extra strength exercising:

- Wrists, hands and fingers—fingertip pushups and squeezing rubber or tennis balls.
- Arms and chest—pushups with hands six to twelve inches apart for arms and pushups with hands out wide apart for chest.
- Thighs—wall sitting (Fig. 1-12).
- Legs—rope skipping, stair climbing, and jumping back and forth over a stick two to four feet off the floor.

CHAPTER TWO

FOOTWORK

This basketball skills manual starts with no basketball in hand, or even in sight, for the good, simple reason that a player must have firm control over his or her own body before he or she can hope to control the ball effectively. Therein lies a major challenge to a coach, or to an individual player's self-control. Most players would like to start with shooting work. A few might be interested in dribbling, and fewer still in the passing and rebounding chapters of this book.

Why should you make the effort to practice footwork first? Whether you are playing defense, rebounding, handling the basketball, or moving into different offensive positions, your ability to use proper footwork will be of great importance. In fact, it can be argued convincingly that good dribbling, passing and receiving, shooting, rebounding, and defensive skills are impossible without sound footwork. Good footwork is the basis for developing good timing, yet despite the fact that basketball is a game in which ten players are in almost constant motion, footwork is often over-looked or underemphasized in most basketball literature and programs.

The goal of sound footwork is the easiest and most efficient way to move, getting where you want to go in the least amount of time, using the least amount of energy, and maintaining good body balance and position. Its importance is underscored by the fact that coaches have studied ballet, fencing, and boxing to learn more about the principles of good footwork.

In this chapter you will learn and practice the basic stance, change of pace, change of direction, sliding, backpedaling, the advance step, the retreat step, stopping, pivoting, the drop step, jumping, and falling. All this will be done first without the basketball in your hands. Before you begin dribbling, passing and receiving, and shooting a basketball, you should spend fifteen minutes a day for at least the first two weeks doing the workouts in this section to ensure that you develop sound footwork. It will make all the other individual skills easier to learn and help prevent you from learning them incorrectly and developing bad habits.

THE BASIC STANCE

This is the position from which you will make most footwork movements. It is particularly useful when playing defense because it represents the position from which you are able to move most easily in any direction:

- Feet are comfortably spread apart slightly more than shoulder width.
- Weight is equally distributed on both feet.
- Although both feet are flat on the floor, weight should be forward on the balls of the feet to allow for quick movement.
- Knees and waist are bent. Your back is straight but not tense.
- Elbows are bent and hands are in your sight with the fingers spread and palms facing away from you. The precise position of the arms and hands will vary according to the situation. For our purposes we will drill with the elbows in—two to six inches from the body—and the hands at about waist level with the fingers pointing upward.
- Head and chin are up. You are looking straight ahead. Do not lean your head forward, backward, or to the side, as this will throw off your balance.
- Be comfortable. Every joint should be at least a little bent. You should feel low to the ground and be ready to move quickly in any direction. (See Figures 2-1a and 2-1b.)

The Basic Stance will be a little different for each player, depending on what is comfortable and effective. The purpose of the Basic Stance is to find a body position from which you can move, stop, jump, and change direction most easily. As you practice and play basketball, you will learn a great deal about yourself and how you move. The following are important principles of movement:

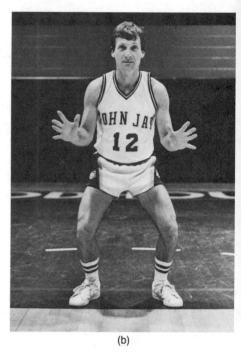

(a)   (b)

Figures 2-1a and 2-1b Basic Stance

1. Sound footwork and movement from the Basic Stance is generated from the legs. You will probably discover that certain muscles need to be stronger for you to improve. For example, the calf muscles, the back of the upper legs (hamstrings), and the thigh muscles must be strong to move quickly in the Basic Stance for any length of time. Weak muscles in the legs cause many players to develop poor habits. This occurs because they are not strong enough to work from a good Basic Stance. If you find yourself getting tired in the legs after being in the Basic Stance for a short time or leaning with your upper body instead of moving your feet first when you make a movement, it is an indication that you need to strengthen your leg muscles. Do the extra strengthening exercises at the end of this section for those muscles you know are weak.

2. There are applications of the laws of motion, stability, and force from physics and mechanics:
   a. Stability is a function of base of support and center and line of gravity. This means that you should keep your feet spread, knees bent, and body balanced and centered.
   b. The law of inertia says a body at rest resists initiation of motion. This means it is easier to make a move off a move than from a still position. Basketball is a game of movement, and like a good boxer or fencer, you should always be moving, on offense and defense, to be able to react quickly. A player who stands still cannot react as quickly as can one who is in motion.

c. Quick, explosive movements are easier to make off small steps. Large steps distribute the body weight over too large an area, and still bodies must overcome inertia. The small step creates momentum to help the movement. Whenever possible, avoid a large step and use a small step before you change direction, stop, or jump.

3. The position and movement of the head is too often overlooked. A great deal of your balance and rhythm will depend on your head position. As you learn and practice footwork, jumping, dribbling, and shooting, remember that keeping your head centered and balanced will be crucial to your body control. If your head leans or is not balanced on your shoulders, it will be almost impossible to change direction quickly and smoothly, maintain body balance and control, or shoot consistently. A good maxim to remember in every basketball situation is: Keep your chin up and your head under control.

Use the following patter drill to develop foot quickness and stamina (endurance):

Drill F-1

1. Begin in your Basic Stance.
2. Patter your feet by picking up one foot two to three inches off the floor, putting it down, and picking up the other foot two or three inches and replacing it on the floor.
3. Your weight should be on the balls of your feet, and your head is up.
4. Continue pattering as quickly as possible for fifteen seconds while maintaining your Basic Stance, constant rhythm of your feet, and good body balance.
5. Repeat this three more times with fifteen-second rest periods in between.

POINTS OF EMPHASIS

- Patter your feet as quickly as you can with as little movement as possible above the waist. Keep your head and shoulders steady.
- Maintain your Basic Stance.

The next two skills are the change of pace and change of direction. Before beginning, it should be noted that you will probably be able to execute these maneuvers quite easily. You might even think to yourself: "This is a waste of time because it's too easy." The importance of these two skills, however, cannot be stressed enough.

Many great coaches have said that the change of pace and change of direction are the most important moves in basketball! Defense, dribbling, and getting free on offense cannot be mastered without excellent changes of pace and direction. While it is true that every player can execute these moves, the difference is that the great players do their changes of pace and direction sharpest, quickest, and most deceptively and with the best timing. The secrets in the changes of pace and direction are in the words *timing* and *change*.

Many players run around on the basketball court aimlessly, expending a lot of energy and not understanding why they are ineffective. The smart player is constantly on the move, but moving with a purpose and in the flow of the game. The smart player picks the spots for changes of pace and direction to improve either the team's position or his or her position for a shot, pass, or rebound. This is called timing—making the right move at the right time.

The smart player understands that quickness is not simply the rate of speed of a move. Quickness is the difference between the two speeds and directions of a move. For example, a move is quick when it goes from a quarter speed to full speed with a sharp 90-degree change of direction and good acceleration. A change of direction without a change of pace, even at a high rate of speed, is not quick and is easy for an opponent to time. The difference between pace and direction of a move and the rate at which the changes are made are the keys to the quickness of the move. You do not have to be the fastest player in the world to be quick if you learn to change your pace and direction effectively.

Skill: Change of Pace

The ability to change your speed or pace is important in almost every facet of basketball. Always maintain good body balance with your head up. You will notice how much longer your steps are when you run at faster speeds. Smaller steps give you more control, quickness, and mobility, but larger steps cover more ground, giving you more speed.

Drill F-2 (Figure 2-2)

1. Begin running at point A at half speed around the basketball court to your right (counterclockwise).
2. After ten steps, speed up (accelerate) to three quarters of your maximum speed.
3. Continue at this pace for ten strides and slow down quickly to your original pace of half speed.
4. Your head is up and you are looking straight ahead.
5. Repeat this five times as you run around the court.
6. Repeat steps 1–5 running in the other direction, to your left or clockwise, around the court.

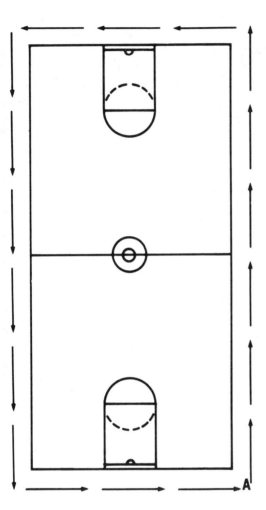

Figure 2-2 Drill F-2

7. Repeat steps 1–6 changing from one quarter speed to three quarters speed, half speed to full speed, and one quarter speed to full speed.

POINTS OF EMPHASIS

- When speeding up (accelerating), bend your knees and push hard off the back foot on the first step. Then increase the length of your stride.
- When you change pace slowing down (decelerating) quickly, it is helpful to bend your knees and cut the length of your stride.

Skill: Change of Direction—45 Degrees

Like the change of pace, the change of direction is important in almost every facet of basketball.

You will make a sharper change of direction if you bend your knees a step or two before you pivot. The resultant lower-body position will give you better balance. Always remember that lowering your body position (center of gravity) makes it easier to change direction.

Another helpful tip on the change of direction is to point the toe of the lead foot in the direction you want to go after each pivot. For example, after pivoting on the ball of the right foot, point the toe of the left foot in the direction you want to go, and after pivoting on the ball of the left foot, point the toe of the right foot in the direction you want to go.

Notice that as you increase your speed, it is more difficult to maintain good balance when changing direction. You can increase your stability by shortening the length of your steps and lowering your center of gravity by bending your knees just before you change direction.

The effectiveness of the change of direction is based on the sharpness of the pivot. The change should be done smoothly and quickly going from one speed to another.

Drill F-3 (Figure 2-3)

1. Begin at point A and, stepping with your left foot first, run at half speed up the right side line for ten steps.

2. On your tenth step, plant your right foot firmly and pivot on the ball of your right foot one-eighth of a turn to your left.

3. Push off hard on your right foot and continue running on that diagonal line for nine steps.

4. When your left foot lands on the ninth step, plant it firmly and pivot on the ball of that foot one-eighth of a turn to your right.

5. Push off hard on your left foot and continue running at half speed for another nine steps.

6. Now pivot again on your right foot and continue running.

7. Your head is up and you are looking straight ahead.

8. Repeat this up and down the court five times.

9. Repeat steps 1–8 changing your speeds and the number of steps between changes of direction.

POINTS OF EMPHASIS

- Maintain good balance and body control.
- Your head should be up, and you should be looking straight ahead of you.
- Shorten your steps and bend your knees before each change.
- Push off hard on your back foot on the first step after your change of direction.
- Make your changes of direction sharp and smooth.

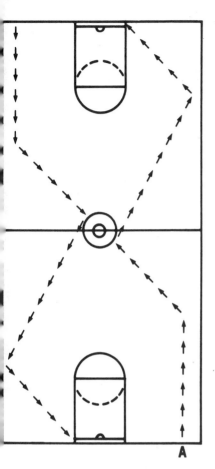

Figure 2-3 Drill F-3

A

Skill: Change of Direction—90 Degrees

The 90-degree change of direction is sharper and, therefore, more difficult to accomplish than is the 45-degree change of direction.

1. You should slow down and concentrate on balance and body control.
2. Review the discussion and Points of Emphasis in Change of Direction—45 Degrees.

Drill F-4 (Figure 2-4)

     1. Begin at point A and, stepping with your left foot first, run at half speed up the right side line for ten steps.

     2. On your tenth step, plant your right foot firmly, and pivot on the ball of your right foot one quarter of a turn to the left.

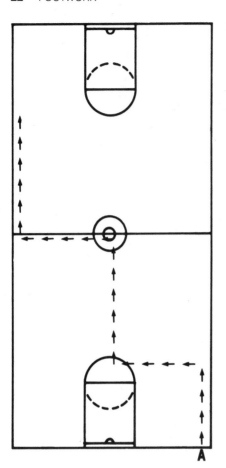

Figure 2-4 Drill F-4

3. Push off and continue running cross court for nine steps.

4. When your left foot lands on the ninth step, plant it firmly and pivot on the ball of that foot one quarter of a turn to your right and continue running at half speed.

5. Keep your head up and look straight ahead.

6. Repeat this up and down the court five times.

7. Repeat steps 1–6 changing your speeds and the number of steps between changes of direction.

POINTS OF EMPHASIS

You should be able to answer each of the following questions with a "yes" if you executed the drill correctly:

- Were your pivots and changes of direction sharp and smooth?
- Did you keep your balance and body control during the drill?

- Did you shorten your steps and lower your center of gravity just before pivoting?
- Did you accelerate after the pivot by bending your knees and pushing hard off the pivot foot?
- Was your head up at all times?

Skill: Cutting

There are many types of cuts you will have to learn to be a complete basketball player. The ability to cut is a very important part of any half-court offense against man-to-man defense. Too many players run around in circles on offense with no sense of purpose. This makes the job of the defense easy. The intelligent player, while always in motion, moves with a purpose and uses *well-timed* cuts to free himself or herself for easy scoring opportunities. Cutting is based on using changes of pace and direction, sudden stops and starts, pivots, and hard drives to the basket at the right time within the context of an offensive pattern.

Cutting is the offensive weapon that allows you to get free from your defender. It usually consists of a fake or movement in the opposite direction from where you want to go followed by a quick change of direction. In most cases, this involves taking one or more steps in one direction and either pushing off on the lead foot or using a crossover step to change direction. The step or steps taken in the opposite direction before a cut is called "dropping your man" or "setting up your man."

- *Timing* is the single most important aspect of a good cut. With experience, you will learn when and at what rate of speed to make your cuts in various situations so that you arrive in the right place at the right time for a good scoring opportunity.
- Most cuts involve changes of pace and direction.

Note: The angles of cuts are based on the position of the defense and, to some extent, the particular types of scoring opportunities an offense is designed to get. The angles in the following drills are only for the purpose of understanding the concepts of proper cutting. They will vary according to different offensive situations.

Drill F-5 (Figure 2-5)

　　　1. Begin at point A and face the basket from about twenty-one feet out.
　　　2. Take one walking step with the right foot followed by one walking step with the left foot toward the center of the midcourt circle.
　　　3. Bend your knees and pivot off the ball of your left foot, cutting toward

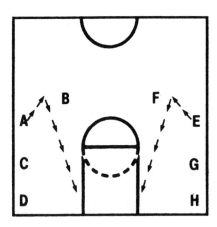

Figure 2-5 Drill F-5, Steps 1–6

the basket. Accelerate your speed but stay under control. Extend your right hand as a target, with the palm open, fingers spread and relaxed, in anticipation of a pass. Your head is up.

4. Cut to the block on the right side of the basket.

5. Repeat this V cut five times each from points A, B, C, and D.

6. Repeat steps 1–5 from the other side of the court, from points E, F, G, and H, pivoting off the right foot on your cuts.

(Figure 2-6)

7. Begin at point A, facing the basket.

8. Take one walking step with the left foot followed by one walking step with the right foot toward the base line and the corner of the backboard on your side of the basket.

9. Bend your knees and pivot off the ball of your right foot and cut toward the top of the circle above the foul line. Repeat five times.

10. Repeat steps 7–9 from points B, C, and D.

11. Repeat steps 7–9 from the other side of the basket, from points E, F, G, and H, using the left foot as your pivot.

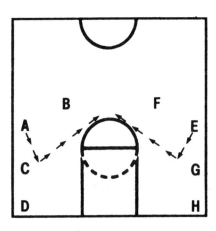

Figure 2-6 Drill F-5, Steps 7–11

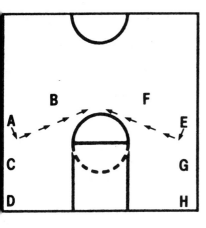

Figure 2-7   Drill F-5, Step 12 and Drill F-6, Steps 1–5

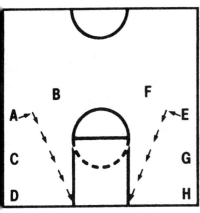

Figure 2-8   Driff F-5, Step 12 and Drill F-6, Steps 6–9

(Figures 2-7 and 2-8)

12. Repeat steps 1–11 using only one step instead of two before your change of direction. This means that you must take a step with your right foot to the right before you pivot and cut to the left. (Fig. 2-7), and you must take a step with your left foot to the left before you pivot and cut to the right. (Fig. 2-8).

Drill F-6 (Figure 2-7)

1. Begin at point A, facing the basket.

2. Take one step to your right with your right foot, but do not lift your left foot off the floor. Shift your weight back to your left leg and cross over by bringing your right leg over and in front of your left leg so that you are moving to your left.

Be sure that the original step to your right is not too long and you bend your knees. Remember to keep your head up and maintain good body position and balance.

3. Accelerate your speed as you run toward the top of the circle above the foul line.

4. Repeat this cut with the crossover step five times from points A, B, C, and D.

5. Repeat steps 1–4 from points E, F, G, and H, crossing over from left to right.

(Figure 2-8)

6. Begin at point A, facing the basket.

7. Take one step to your left with your left foot and crossover to your right cutting to the box on the right side of the basket.

8. Repeat this maneuver five times from points A, B, C, and D.

9. Repeat steps 6–8 from points E, F, G, and H, crossing over from right to left.

POINTS OF EMPHASIS

- Besides timing, the keys to good cutting are the changes of pace and direction. Be sure that you make the changes smoothly and accelerate quickly. Bend your knees, push off the pivot foot on your changes, and point the nonpivot foot in the direction you want to go.
- Keep your head up and stay under control.

Skill: Sliding

The slide is the basic movement a defensive player uses to move from side to side. Whether your opponent has the ball or not, you must be able to slide and change direction quickly when necessary.

In the open court, farther than twenty-five feet from the basket you are defending, sliding is often done with long side steps. However, in close to the basket, within about twenty-one feet, you must learn to slide with short, quick steps so that you maintain good body control and balance and can change direction quickly. The sliding techniques we will learn and practice are those especially important for developing good defensive habits within twenty-one feet of the opponents' basket.

SLIDING CHECKPOINTS

1. Begin in a good Basic Stance.
2. Your feet and legs are the key to good sliding movements. Keep your feet wide and under your body. Do not lead a slide with your head, arms, or shoulders, or your balance will be poor. Move your legs when you slide and keep your body balanced and centered.
3. When sliding right, your first step to your right is made with the right foot. As the first step with the right foot is completed, the left foot slides

SLIDE STEP TO LEFT **SLIDING** SLIDE STEP TO RIGHT **Figure 2-9** Sliding

right after it. Pretend that there is a rubber band attached from your right foot to your left foot and after the right foot slides to the right, the left foot follows. Reverse the procedure when sliding left. (See Figure 2-9.)

4. Your feet should *not* come together when sliding, and only one foot should be off the floor at a time. Your feet should always be at least six to twelve inches apart depending on your size. This will enable you to maintain good balance and change direction more easily. Once your feet come together or get too close to each other, you cannot change direction easily.

5. Slides are made with short, quick, low-to-the-floor side steps, not long steps. There should be no hopping or foot dragging.

6. Keep your body balanced and low. Your knees and waist are bent, but your back is straight. All your joints should be at least a little bent.

7. Your head and chin are up and not leaning. (See Figures 2-10a, 2-10b, and 2-10c.)

Figures 2-10a, 2-10b, and 2-10c Sliding Right

(a)

(b)

(c)

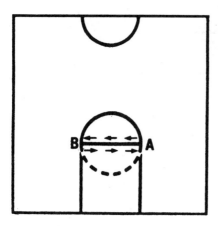

Figure 2-11 Drill F-7

Drill F-7 (Figure 2-11)

Do this drill slowly at first and increase your speed only when you have mastered the form and rhythm.

1. Begin at point A, facing midcourt, with your right foot on the lane line and your left foot inside the three-second area.

2. From your Basic Stance, slide across the lane until your left foot touches the lane line to your left, point B.

3. Push off on the left foot and slide back until your right foot touches the line on the right side of the lane, point A.

4. Continue sliding back and forth for fifteen seconds.

5. Repeat the drill until you have done it four times with fifteen-second rest periods in between.

Note: After sliding to your left, you will find it helpful to lower your body position by bending your knees a little more as you get to the line on your left. Plant your left foot firmly on the line and push off as you change direction. As you approach the line on your right, you should again lower your body position for balance, plant your right foot firmly on the line, and push off as you change direction.

POINTS OF EMPHASIS

- Maintain your Basic Stance as much as possible while sliding.
- Keep your feet low to the floor and spread apart.
- Always step with the left foot first when sliding left and with the right foot first when sliding right.
- As you increase your sliding speed and stamina, do not sacrifice your form.

Skill: Backpedaling

Backpedaling is commonly used on defense when you wish to retreat quickly but not lose sight of the ball.

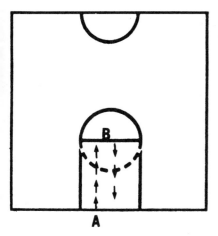

Figure 2-12 Drill F-8 and Drill F-9

1. When you backpedal, your momentum tends to force your weight to shift into your heels. You should counter this tendency by bending forward at the waist to stay on the balls of your feet.
2. Practice this drill slowly at first to adjust to balancing your body position during backward movement.

Drill F-8 (Figure 2-12)

     1. Begin at point A, facing the foul line with both feet on the base line in the three-second area under the basket.
     2. Sprint to the foul line, point B, and touch the floor with both hands.
     3. Backpedal to the base line and touch the floor with both hands.
     4. Continue this for fifteen seconds, and repeat the drill until you have completed it four times with fifteen-second rest periods in between.

POINTS OF EMPHASIS

- Work on bending your knees a little more one or two steps before you get to the foul line and base line. This will help you to stop and change direction more smoothly.
- When you are backpedaling, keep your head up and shoulders steady.
- To counterbalance your backward motion while backpedaling, remember that you must bend more at the waist to stay on the balls of your feet.

Skill: Advance Step

    The advance step is similar to the slide except that you will move forward instead of sideways (Fig. 2-13). Many of the same principles for the slide apply to the advance step.

LEFT FOOT FORWARD **ADVANCE STEP** **RIGHT FOOT FORWARD** **Figure 2-13** Advance Step

1. Your feet should not cross.
2. You should try to advance with many little steps instead of big steps.
3. You should maintain good body balance with a low center of gravity and your head up.

Drill F-9 (Figure 2-12)

1. Begin at point A on the base line, facing the foul line in the three-second area.

2. You are in your Basic Stance with your left foot forward so that the tip of your right toe is even with the back of your left heel.

3. Your feet are still at least a shoulder width apart.

4. Your first step forward is with the forward or left foot. The step should not be too long, or you will lose good body position and balance.

5. After the left foot steps forward, the right foot turns naturally so that the instep faces the heel of the left foot and your weight shifts onto the left foot.

6. After your weight shifts forward onto the left foot, the right foot, as though on a string attached to the left foot, slides forward so that your feet are back in their original position.

7. Advance step to the foul line, point B, and stop.

8. When you reach the foul line you must turn your back foot, in this case the right, so that your toe is pointing straight ahead before retreating.

9. Backpedal to the base line.
10. Continue this for thirty seconds.
11. Repeat steps 1–10 with the right foot as the forward foot.

POINTS OF EMPHASIS

- Maintain good, low, balanced body position with your head up.
- Your feet must slide low to the floor without hopping, coming together, or dragging.

Skill: Retreat Step

The retreat step is mechanically the same step as the advance step done in reverse. The first step is with the back foot, and, as you make that step, the foot turns so that the instep of the back foot faces the heel of the front foot when it lands. (See Figure 2-14.)

1. Your feet should not cross.
2. Try to retreat step with many little steps instead of big steps.
3. Maintain good body balance with a low center of gravity and your head up.

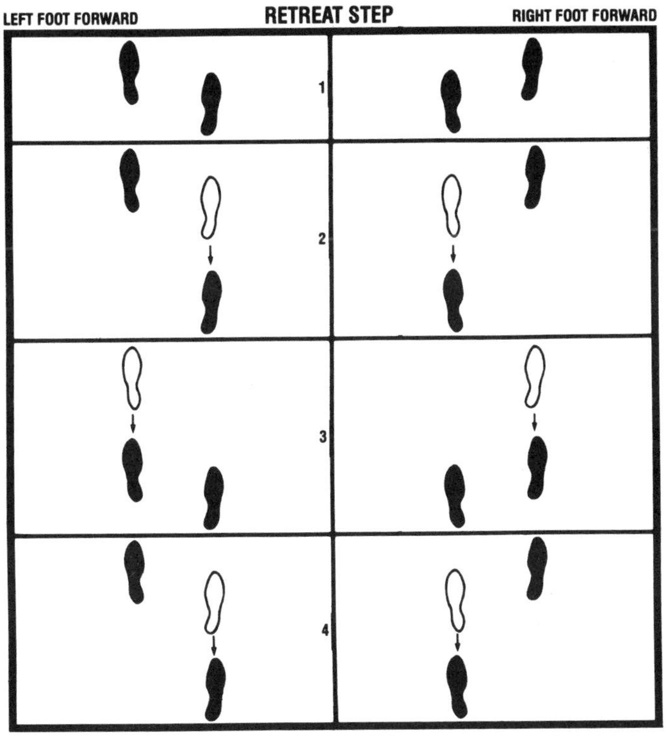

LEFT FOOT FORWARD　　**RETREAT STEP**　　**RIGHT FOOT FORWARD**

Figure 2-14 Retreat Step

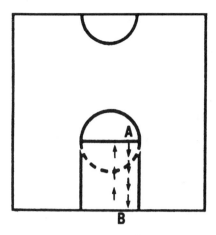

Figure 2-15 Drill F-10

Drill F-10 (Figure 2-15)

1. Begin on the foul line at point A with your back to the basket in the three-second area.

2. You are in your Basic Stance with your left foot forward so that the tip of your right toe is even with the back of your left heel.

3. Your feet are still at least a shoulder width apart.

4. Your first step backward is with the rear or right foot. The step should not be too long, or you will lose good body position and balance.

5. As the right foot steps backward, it turns naturally so that when it lands, the instep faces the heel of the left foot and your weight shifts onto the right foot.

6. After your weight shifts backward onto the right foot, the left foot, as though a rubber band were attached to the right foot, slides backward so that your feet are back in their original position.

7. Retreat step to the base line, point B, and stop.

8. When you reach the base line, you must turn your back foot, in this case the right, so that both your toes are pointing straight ahead.

9. Jog to the foul line.

10. Continue this for thirty seconds.

11. Repeat steps 1–10 with the right foot as the forward foot.

POINTS OF EMPHASIS

- Maintain good, low, balanced body position with your head up.
- Your feet must slide low to the floor without hopping, coming together, or dragging.
- When retreating, your backward momentum may have to be counterbalanced by bending forward a little more at the waist to remain on the balls of your feet.

STOPPING

There are two basic types of stops:

1. The jump stop.
2. The stride stop.

The jump stop is executed with both feet landing simultaneously. When this maneuver is done with the ball, either foot can then be used as a pivot.

The stride stop is done with one foot landing before the other, and, if the player is in possession of the ball, only the foot that lands first can be used as a pivot.

For numerous situations on both defense and offense, with or without the ball, stops are important. Proper stopping technique is particularly important off the dribble and after catching a pass.

Although you will not use both stops in conjunction with every skill you learn, we will practice them to increase your stopping proficiency and overall body control.

Skill: Jump Stop

Although you land almost flat on both feet on the jump stop, you should be aware that at faster running speeds, your greater forward momentum must be considered. This means that at slower speeds, your weight on your landings should be slightly forward on the balls of your feet. At faster paces, you will have to shift your weight back on your feet a little as you land, or your forward momentum will carry you too far forward. Beware that landing too far back on your heels will result in a "shock" up the back of your legs and spine as well as a poorly balanced body position.

Land flat-footed but keep your weight on the balls of your feet as much as possible. At faster speeds, you will have to land with your weight farther back to compensate for your forward momentum. (See Figure 2-16.)

Drill F-11

1. Walk straight ahead for ten steps.
2. As you get to the last step of your walk, bend your knees so you are lower and make that last step a little shorter. This will improve your balance and body control.

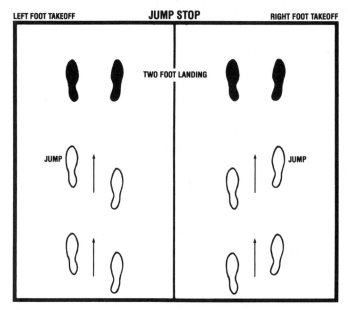

Figure 2-16   Jump Stop

3. Jump in the air off your left foot and land flat on your two feet at the same time without taking another step. (Do not try to jump too high or far.)

4. Upon landing, your head should be up, knees bent and feet parallel, at least a shoulder width apart.

5. At first, practice this with as slow a walk as you need to be able to land firmly, with your head up, and in perfect balance and control.

6. Repeat steps 1–5 taking off on the right foot.

7. Increase your speed to a run only after you can do the drill perfectly five times in a row jumping off each foot.

8. Practice the jump stop at many speeds with right- and left-footed takeoffs. You will learn to adjust your weight shift on landings to your speed.

POINTS OF EMPHASIS

- The key to this move is low, balanced body position.
- When you land, be sure your feet are spread and parallel, your tail is down, and your head is up.
- Jump stops off faster running speeds require a lower body position on landing with the weight shifted farther back on the feet.

Skill: Stride Stop

A second method of stopping is called the stride stop. This is enacted by one foot landing before the other. Many of the principles in terms of forward momentum that were discussed concerning the jump stop will also apply to the stride stop.

Your forward momentum must be considered. The faster your running speed, the more you will have to lower your center of gravity and shift your weight back. (See Figure 2-17.)

Drill F-12

1. Walk straight ahead for ten steps.

2. As you get to the last step of your walk, bend your knees so you are lower and make that last step a little shorter. This will improve your balance and body control.

3. Jump off your left foot. While you are in the air your right foot will be in front of your left foot. Both knees will be bent, with your legs tucked under your body. You will land with your rear foot, in this case the left, first. This maneuver should feel like a "hop" and a "scoot." (You should not try to jump too high or far.)

4. When you land, the back of your right heel should be just ahead of the toes on your left foot. You should otherwise be in a good Basic Stance with your knees and waist bent, feet spread at least a foot apart, and your head up.

5. At first, practice this with as slow a walk as you need to be able to land firmly and in perfect balance and control.

6. Repeat steps 1–5 taking off on the right foot.

7. Increase your speed to a run only after you can do the drill perfectly five times in a row taking off on each foot.

8. Practice the stride stop at many speeds with right- and left-footed takeoffs and you will learn to adjust your weight shift on landings to your speed.

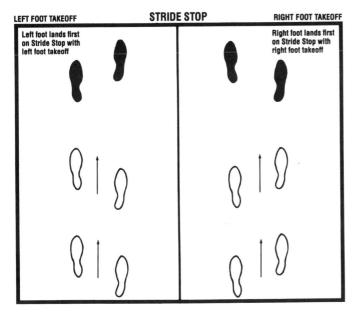

Figure 2-17 Stride Stop

POINTS OF EMPHASIS

- As you increase your running speed you will notice that the stride stop becomes more difficult. The secret of the stride stop is getting into a low, balanced body position on the last steps before your jump and, especially at faster speeds, while you are in the air, throwing your weight back by "sitting" on the heel of your rear foot. This will help you land with more balance and control.
- When you land, be sure your feet are spread, your tail is down, and your head is up.

PIVOTING

Pivoting is a critical skill for every aspect of the game. It may appear easy, but in pressure situations you will have to be able to pivot with the basketball in your hands while protecting the ball from the defense. Simultaneously, you must also decide whether to shoot, pass, or dribble.

In addition, pivoting is just one part of more complex skills. We will learn and practice the forward and reverse pivots, and in later chapters we will integrate pivoting into more complex skills such as changing direction on the dribble, shooting and passing off the dribble, one-on-one moves facing the basket and posting, and rebounding.

Skill: Forward, or Front, Pivot (Figure 2-18)

Drill F-13

1. Walk straight ahead for ten steps and jump stop.

2. Be sure that after you land on your jump stop, you are in a good Basic Stance with your feet spread at least a shoulder width apart and parallel, knees bent, and head up.

3. Forward or front pivot clockwise on the ball of your right foot 90 degrees or one quarter turn to your right. (In other words, after you have landed on your two feet, pick up your left foot and swing it around in front of you so you are facing to the right.)

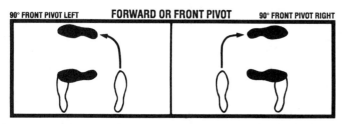

90° FRONT PIVOT LEFT   **FORWARD OR FRONT PIVOT**   **90° FRONT PIVOT RIGHT**

Figure 2-18   Forward Pivot

4. Practice this ten times and repeat using the left foot as your pivot.

5. Repeat steps 1–4 pivoting 180 degrees or a half turn on your pivots. (In other words, after your jump stop, your turn will be halfway around so you will be facing in the opposite direction.)

POINTS OF EMPHASIS

- You should be in a low, balanced, body position with your feet spread at least a shoulder width apart and parallel, knees bent, and head up.
- Pivots of a half turn will require an even lower center of gravity than will pivots of a quarter turn.

Skill: Reverse Pivot (Figure 2-19)

The reverse pivot is especially important when playing man-to-man defense, boxing out and turning during rebounding, and executing posting moves. The reverse pivot is a little more difficult than the forward pivot because it requires better balance and greater body control.

Do this pivoting drill more slowly at first.

Drill F-14

1. Walk straight ahead for ten steps and jump stop.

2. Be sure that after you land you are in a good Basic Stance, with your feet spread at least a shoulder width apart and parallel, knees bent, and head up.

3. Reverse pivot counterclockwise on the ball of your right foot 90 degrees or one quarter turn to your left. (In other words, after you have landed on your two feet, pick up your left foot and swing it around behind you so you are facing to the left.)

4. Practice this ten times and repeat using the left foot as your pivot.

5. Repeat steps 1–4 pivoting 180 degrees or a half turn on your pivots. (In other words, your turn will be halfway around, so you will be facing in the opposite direction.)

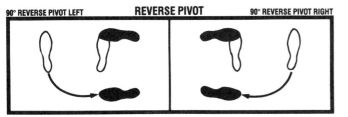

90° REVERSE PIVOT LEFT   **REVERSE PIVOT**   90° REVERSE PIVOT RIGHT

Figure 2-19   Reverse Pivot

POINTS OF EMPHASIS

- Reverse pivots require a little more balance and body control than forward pivots, so be sure that before you pivot, you are in a low, balanced, body position with your feet spread at least a shoulder width apart and parallel. Your knees and waist should be bent with your head up.
- Reverse pivots of a half turn will require an even lower center of gravity than reverse pivots of a quarter turn.

Skill: Drop Step—45 Degrees

The drop step is an important fundamental of defensive movement and post moves. (See Figure 2-20.)

Drill F-15 (Figure 2-21)

1. Begin at point A in your Basic Stance with your back to the basket.
2. Slowly slide to your left along the foul line.
3. When your left foot reaches the elbow, point B, stop, pick up your right foot, and reverse pivot on the ball of your left foot one-eighth of a turn to your right. You should bend your knees a little more just before you pivot to get better balance on the pivot.
4. Now slide diagonally across the three-second area to where the lane line meets the base line, point C.
5. When your right foot reaches this junction, reverse pivot one-eighth of a turn to your left.
6. Continue sliding to your left along the base line until you get to the lane line, point D.
7. Advance step up the lane line and jump stop into your Basic Stance at the elbow, point B. Your back is still to the basket.

(Figure 2-22)

8. Slide to your right until your right foot reaches the elbow, point A.
9. Pick up your left foot and reverse pivot one-eighth of a turn to your left.
10. Slide diagonally across the three-second area to where the lane line meets the base line, point D.
11. Reverse pivot on your left foot one-eighth of a turn to your right.

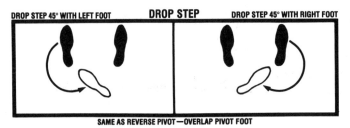

DROP STEP 45° WITH LEFT FOOT   **DROP STEP**   DROP STEP 45° WITH RIGHT FOOT

SAME AS REVERSE PIVOT—OVERLAP PIVOT FOOT

Figure 2-20 Drop Step

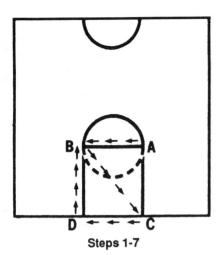

Figure 2-21 Drill F-15, Steps 1–7

Steps 1-7

12. Continue sliding to your right until you get to the foul lane line, point C.

13. Advance step up the lane line to the elbow and jump stop into your Basic Stance at point A.

14. Do this drill for one minute, but do it slowly, concentrating on the form of your slides, drop steps, and jump stops.

When you slide, always step first with the left foot when sliding left and step first with the right foot when sliding right.

When advance stepping always step with the lead foot first.

POINTS OF EMPHASIS

- Keep your body position low by bending your knees and waist and keeping your tail low to the floor.
- Your head is up, looking in the direction of your movement.
- Bend your knees a little more before each pivot.

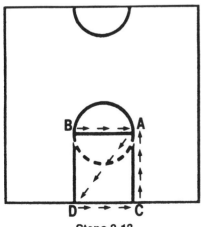

Steps 8-13

Figure 2-22 Drill F-15, Steps 8–13

Skill: Drop Step—90 Degrees

Drill F-16 (Figure 2-23)

      1. Begin in your Basic Stance at the elbow, point A, with your back to the basket.

      2. Slowly slide to your left along the foul line.

      3. When your left foot reaches the elbow, point B, stop, pick up your right foot, and reverse pivot on the ball of your left foot one quarter of a turn to your right.

      4. Slide down the lane line to the base line, point C.

      5. Jog diagonally back to the elbow, point A.

      6. Repeat ten times.

(Figure 2-24)

      7. Get into your Basic Stance at point A with your back to the basket.

      8. Slide across the foul line to the elbow, point B.

      9. Drop step on the ball of your right foot one quarter turn.

      10. Slide down the foul lane line to the base line, point C.

      11. Jog diagonally back to point A.

      12. Repeat ten times.

POINTS OF EMPHASIS

- Maintain a good Basic Stance during the drill.
- Lower your center of gravity by bending your knees more on the pivots to achieve better balance.

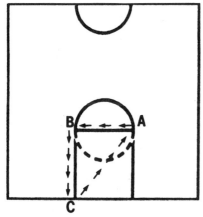

Steps 1-5   **Figure 2-23** Drill F-16, Steps 1–5

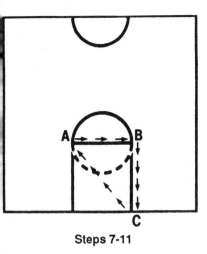

Figure 2-24 Drill F-16, Steps 7–11

Steps 7-11

THE FOX BOX FOOTWORK DRILLS

The Fox Box Footwork Drills (FBFD) are designed to combine different footwork skills that you have learned. Each drill will be done in the three-second lane (see Fox Box Footwork Drill diagram).

- Practice these skills for *form* and *rhythm* until you can do them mechanically perfectly with your head up before you attempt to increase your speed.

Fox Box Footwork Drill I (Figure 2-25)

    1. Begin at point A and advance step to point B and jump stop.
    2. Turn your head to the left and slide left, making sure that your first step is with your left foot, to point C.
    3. Retreat step to point D and jump stop.
    4. Turn your head to the right and slide right to point A. Make sure that your first step is with your right foot.
    5. Repeat twice for a total of three times around the three-second area.

(Figure 2-26)

    6. Repeat steps 1–5, but begin from point D advance stepping to point C and reversing the directions.
    7. Repeat steps 1–6 replacing jump stops with stride stops, advance stepping with forward sprints, and retreat stepping with backpedaling.

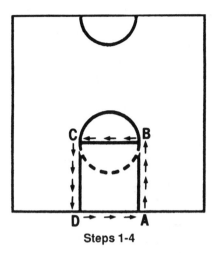

Figure 2-25 Fox Box Footwork Drill I, Steps 1–4

Steps 1-4

Fox Box Footwork Drill II (Figure 2-27)

1. Sprint from point A to point B and jump stop.

2. Turn your head to the left and execute a 45-degree drop step with your left leg and slide diagonally down and across the three-second area to point D. Be sure that your first slide step to your left is with your left foot.

3. When your left foot reaches point D, stop, turn your head to the right, do a 45-degree drop step with your right leg, and slide right along the base line to point A. Be sure that your first step sliding to your right is done with the right foot.

4. Repeat twice for a total of three times around the three-second area.

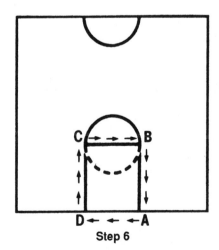

Step 6

Figure 2-26 Fox Box Footwork Drill I, Step 6

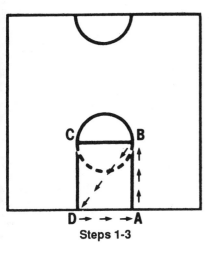

Figure 2-27 Fox Box Footwork Drill II, Steps 1–3

Steps 1-3

(Figure 2-28)

     5. Repeat steps 1–4, but begin from point D sprinting to point C and reversing the directions.

POINTS OF EMPHASIS

- Your head must be up, and you must be able to maintain good body control and balance throughout the drills.
- When you drop step, you should first look in the direction of your step.
- When you slide, your head must be turned in the direction of the slide, and your first step must be with your right when sliding right and your left when sliding left. Pointing your front foot in the direction of the

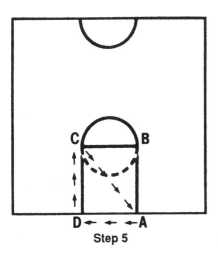

Step 5

Figure 2-28 Fox Box Footwork Drill II, Step 5

slide is optional. For some players this makes the slides easier, but for some it makes it more difficult.

JUMPING

Jumping is obviously a very important part of basketball. But aside from your God-given ability to jump high, there is a lot more to jumping. Hard work can maximize your natural potential and improve your agility, power, balance, stamina, and timing. The height of a jump is only one element. How quickly did you get to that height? Many coaches feel that a quick jump is better than a high jump. How stable are you at the top of your jump? Are you balanced?

Did you get to that rebound first? Were you able to grab the ball at the top of your jump? Did you block that shot? What good is it to get up high if your balance is so poor that it restricts you from accomplishing these fundamental tasks? Timing has proven to be equally as important as natural ability in the effectiveness of great rebounders and shot blockers. For these reasons, we cover jumping in the footwork section of our text. It is helpful to think of jumping as "footwork in the air." Many of the principles of footwork governing body position, balance, and control apply to a body in the air as well as a body on the ground.

Types of Jumps

There are two basic types of jumps:

1. The one-foot takeoff jump.
2. The two-foot takeoff jump.

The one-foot takeoff jump should primarily be used when jumping off of movement. Driving layups are good examples of when the one-foot takeoff jump is preferred because it would take too much time for a player on a driving layup to stop, collect himself, and shoot. The one-foot takeoff jump is quicker when the player is on the move and has to cover distance on his jump. For example, in many cases a player will have to move to block an opponent's shot or tap or grab an offensive rebound. If the player has to cover distance on his jump, the one-foot takeoff jump is quicker and often the only one that will get the job done. However, the one-foot takeoff jump often provides less stability and control for the jumper. Because the jumper is getting both height and distance on his jump, he is more liable to foul, collide with another player, or be injured because of poor balance on his landing. The one-foot takeoff jump usually requires the jumper to land on the opposite foot from that which he took off, and that is less stable than jumping off of two feet and landing on two feet.

The two-foot takeoff jump, on the other hand, is preferred when the player is not on the move and does not have to cover any distance on his jump. Most two-foot takeoff jumps enable the jumper to land on both feet with good balance and body control. The two-foot takeoff jump is the primary jump for rebounding and jump shooting. Most coaches prefer their players to use the two-foot jump whenever possible because it is quicker and more powerful when standing still. It is easier to jump straight up off of two feet than one and gives the player more body control and stability in the air. This can help prevent unnecessary injury as well as cut down on the number of turnovers and offensive and defensive fouls a player might commit.

The following points are a few applications of the laws of physics and mechanics that generally relate to jumping and are of particular relevance to the two-foot takeoff jump:

1. You will jump better with a balanced, low center of gravity. In other words, you will jump higher and straighter and be more stable and quicker if you "gather" or "collect" yourself before your jump. This means your feet are spread, you knees and waist are bent, and your arms are close into your body with the elbows bent and the fingers spread.
2. The more force you can exert against the floor before jumping, the higher and more explosive your propulsion. To improve your explosive force upward, lower your body position at the last moment before you jump by bending your knees and waist and, when possible, take a short step or small hop as you bend.
3. You will increase your upward thrust if you throw your arms and hands straight up as you jump.

Jumping plays an especially important part in rebounding, blocking or changing the trajectory (arc) of a shot, and shooting off the floor. However, timing, readiness, anticipation, aggressiveness, and concentration also play important roles. To rebound and block shots effectively, you must concentrate at all times and try to anticipate what will happen next. Timing is a result of a combination of skills: readiness and anticipation, natural rhythm and judgment, and practice and experience. Aggressiveness is a combination of desire, anticipation, and confidence. All these qualities must be tempered in time with the judgment that only comes with hard work and experience.

JUMPING CHECKPOINTS

1. The last step before you jump should be small enough so that the momentum of your body is straight up (not out or at an angle that will adversely affect your balance and body control). Be sure that your feet are spread (not together) and are under you when you take off.
2. "Gather" or "collect" yourself before your jump.
3. For most jumps without the ball, you should throw your arms and hands straight up as you jump.
4. Keep your head up and centered between your shoulders. If your head is down or leaning one way, it will throw your balance off.
5. Your feet should be spread on landing. You should land evenly on the balls of your feet and give at the knees to absorb some of the shock of landing.

Vertical Jump Test

You can measure your vertical jump with a two-foot takeoff by following this procedure:

1. Stand with your right shoulder to a wall.
2. Put some chalk on the tips of the fingers on your right hand.
3. Reach as high as you can with your right hand and touch the wall with your fingertips leaving a mark.
4. Taking off on two feet, jump as high as you can and touch the wall with the fingertips on your right hand at the top of your leap. You are allowed one small step or hop before you jump.
5. Measure the distance between the two chalk marks.
6. Repeat steps 1–5 standing with your left shoulder to the wall and using your left hand.
7. Repeat steps 1–5 facing the wall and using both hands.

Jumping drills are especially effective in improving your jumping stamina, balance, agility, quickness, power, and timing. However, they will only be meaningful if you practice by jumping as high as you can on each jump. Also notice that the drills focus on the two-foot takeoff jump. This is because the two-foot takeoff jump is more important than the one-foot takeoff jump, and most gains from these drills will transfer to the one-foot takeoff jump.

Drill F-17: Jumping Stamina

　　1. Stand under the backboard, and, taking no steps and using a two-foot takeoff, jump as high as you can reaching as high as you can with both hands.

2. Continue jumping for fifteen seconds.

3. Repeat the drill until you have done it four times with fifteen-second rest periods in between.

4. Repeat steps 1–3 taking one step before you jump, alternating the step with the right and left foot.

Drill F-18: Jumping Stamina, Quickness, and Agility

1. Standing to the right of the basket facing the backboard and base line, jump off both feet as high as you can, touching the backboard if possible.

2. As soon as you land on both feet, slide, stepping with the left foot first, to the left of the basket and jump again off both feet as high as you can.

3. As soon as you land on both feet, slide back to the right of the basket and jump again off both feet as high as you can.

4. Continue for fifteen seconds and repeat until you have completed four fifteen-second periods with fifteen-second rest periods in between.

Drill F-19: Jumping Agility

1. With your feet together and a basketball to the right of your right foot, begin jumping over the ball from side to side.

2. Continue for fifteen seconds and repeat until you have completed four fifteen-second periods with fifteen-second rest periods in between.

3. Repeat steps 1 and 2 facing the basketball and jumping back and forth over the ball.

Drill F-20: Jumping Agility and Quickness

1. Use tape or chalk to make the jumping box shown in Figure 2-29.

2. Using two-foot jumps, jump from 1 to 2 to 3 to 4 to 1 and so on for fifteen seconds.

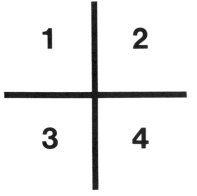

Figure 2-29 Jumping Box

3. Repeat until you have completed four fifteen-second periods with fifteen-second rest periods in between.

4. Repeat steps 1–3 using the following sequences: 4,3,2,1; 1,3,2,4; and 2,4,3,1.

FALLING

In the course of a basketball game, there will be times when you fall down. Most falls are the result of losing your balance:

- Driving to the basket.
- Shooting off balance.
- Running into or being run into by another player.
- Jumping for a rebound.
- Jumping to block a shot or pass.
- Going or diving for a loose ball.
- Taking a charge on defense.
- Being fouled by a defensive player while shooting, dribbling, or moving without the ball.
- Saving a ball from going out of bounds.

Falling is a necessary part of the game, but you can minimize the number and severity of falls necessary:

- Always keep your head up.
- Maintain as much balance and body control as possible.
- Keep your speed under control—slow down as you approach the defense and make your moves under control.
- Anticipate other players' movements.
- Always try to jump straight up and under control and land properly on both feet.

When you know that you are going to fall, it is important that you attempt to do the following to minimize the chance of being injured:

- Relax and go in the direction that you are falling by leaning that way—do not brace yourself against the force.
- Lower your body position by bending your knees so the shock of impact is reduced by decreasing the distance of the fall.
- When possible, especially on falls forward, turn your head and shoulders in the direction of the fall.
- When you break your fall with your hands, try to do it with the elbows bent instead of arms straight.

- When hit from the front, lean back on your heels, relax, and roll with the force by bending your knees and waist, tucking your chin and breaking your fall with your hands.

The best way to avoid injury is to learn to keep your head up, keep your speed under control, and maintain as much balance and body control as possible at all times, but when falling is inevitable, do not fight it. Relax and roll with the momentum of the fall. Falling can be drilled most effectively by tumbling on a mat practicing forward, backward, and shoulder rolls.

WORKOUT, EVALUATION, AND PROGRESS CHARTS

Table 2-1   Footwork Workout—15 Minutes

Warmup		
DRILL	*TIME*	*INSTRUCTIONS*
F-1	1 minute	Patter for two 15-second periods with 15-second rests in between.
F-2	1 "	
F-3	1 "	
F-5	1 "	
F-6	1 "	
F-7	1 "	Slide for two 15-second periods with 15-second rests in between.
F-9	1 "	
F-10	1 "	
F-11	1 "	
F-12	1 "	
F-13	1 "	
F-14	1 "	
F-15	1 "	
F-17	1 "	Each jump must be to maximum; two 15-second periods with 15-second rests in between.
F-19	1 "	
Cooldown		

Table 2-2 Footwork Workout—30 Minutes

Warmup		
DRILL	TIME	INSTRUCTIONS
F-1	1 minute(s)	Patter for two 15-second periods with 15-second rests in between.
F-2	1 "	
F-3	1 "	
F-4	1 "	
F-5	1 "	
F-6	1 "	
F-7	2 "	Slide for four 15-second periods with 15-second rests in between.
F-8	1 "	
F-9	1 "	
F-10	1 "	
F-11	2 "	
F-12	2 "	
F-13	1 "	
F-14	2 "	
F-15	1 "	
F-16	1 "	
FBFDI	1 "	30 seconds in each direction with 15-second rest in between.
FBFDII	1 "	" "
F-17	2 "	Each jump must be to a maximum; four 15-second periods with 15-second rests in between.
F-18	2 "	" "
F-19	2 "	Jump for two 45-second periods with 15-second rests in between.
F-20	2 "	" "
Cooldown		

Table 2-3 Footwork Self-Evaluation and Improvement Test

DRILL	TIME	SCORE
F-1	Patter for four 15-second periods with 15-second rests in between.	Total number of patters
F-7	Slide for four 15-second periods with 15-second rests in between.	Total number of slides
F-8	30 seconds.	Total number
F-9	30 seconds.	Total number
F-10	30 seconds.	Total number
FBFDI	1 minute, 30 seconds in each direction.	Total number of circuits
FBFDII	1 minute, 30 seconds in each direction.	" "
Vertical Jump Test:	Three Trials	Best jump
F-17	15 seconds.	Total number of jumps
F-18	30 seconds.	" "
F-19	30 seconds.	" "
F-20	30 seconds.	" "

Drill										
F-1										
F-7										
F-8										
F-9										
F-10										
FBFDI										
FBFDII										
Vertical Jump Test										
F-17										
F-18										
F-19										
F-20										

EXTRA EXERCISES

The development of sound footwork habits is very demanding and requires considerable muscle strength and endurance, especially in the legs. For many young players, the workouts will be enough to develop both the muscle strength and endurance and the footwork skills.

However, some players will want to do some special exercises:

Rope skipping. This will increase footwork timing, agility, and stamina.

Line hopping. See how many times you can hop back and forth over a line in one minute. Do this on the right foot, the left foot, and both feet together. This will increase your footwork agility and stamina.

Heel raises. This will strengthen your calf muscles.

Stair climbing. This will strengthen your thigh muscles.

Wall sitting. Place your back flat against a wall with both feet flat on the floor. Slide your back down the wall until your knees are bent at 90 degrees. This means your thighs are parallel to the floor. Your feet must remain flat on the floor. Begin holding this position for fifteen seconds at a time and increase until you can hold for two minutes.

Running backward. This will increase the strength of your hamstrings.

CHAPTER THREE

DRIBBLING

In basketball, a player with the ball may not take more than a step and a half without dribbling. For this reason, it is important that every basketball player master some dribbling skills. Guards are required to develop excellent dribbling skills because players at that position usually handle the ball on the fast break and are responsible for most of the ball-handling in the half-court offense. In a team situation where guards are further designated as "point" guard and "off," "shooting," or "two" guard, the "point" guard must be an *outstanding* dribbler.

Forwards and centers, who usually fill fast-break lanes and, in half-court offenses, are often stationed close to the basket and are required to dribble less than guards. However, more and more bigger players are developing their dribbling skills to increase the number of roles they can play on a basketball team.

While dribbling skills are essential for guards, especially "point" guards, they are great assets for forwards.

DRIBBLING WITH A PURPOSE

Dribbling is fun and an attention-getter. Maybe for these reasons, many inexperienced players dribble unnecessarily. While dribbling can be a powerful and valuable weapon in any offensive system, it is too often overdone and abused by players who dribble when a shot or a pass would be more appropriate. Overdribbling demoralizes teammates, leads to unnecessary turnovers, and limits offensive opportunities.

Each time you gain possession of the ball in a game situation, you should immediately look up in the direction of the offensive basket. Your first options are to shoot if a good shot is there, or option to pass to a teammate who is in better offensive position. The dribble is the third option. Too many players get into the deadly habit of dribbling before they look up. Each player, after receiving the ball, must automatically look up and ask:

1. Do I have a good shot?
2. Is a teammate open in a better offensive position than I am?
3. If I do not have a good shot or a teammate open for a pass, I may elect to dribble *with a purpose*:
   a. To drive to the basket if there is an open or unguarded lane.
   b. To improve a passing angle, move into shooting position or set up the offense.
   c. To escape defensive pressure.
   d. To advance the ball on the fast break.
   e. As a special part of a stall.

Once you receive the ball, you are only allowed to start and stop your dribble once. Therefore, it is important that you learn not to put the ball down without a purpose, and you do not pick up your dribble (stop dribbling) until you can pass or shoot.

THE GOOD DRIBBLER

Red Auerbach, the winningest coach in NBA history, is fond of saying: "The ground is flat, the ball is round. You don't have to worry, it will always come back to your hand." But no matter how well you dribble, you must keep your head up to be effective in a game situation.

It is imperative to practice and master each dribbling skill to the point where dribbling becomes second nature. Once it does, you can concentrate solely on what opportunities are open off the dribble. If you are looking at the ball while dribbling, or if you are concerned about your dribbling skills, how can you find your open teammate cutting to the basket, pick up a double team from the defense, or find an open driving lane?

The necessity to make quick decisions in game situations demands that the dribbler be able to devote his or her full concentration on keeping the ball safe from the opposition and seeing the whole floor to execute the precise move at the right time. The best play at any given time might be a pass to an open teammate, a drive to the basket or down an open lane, a shot, or a retreat from defensive pressure.

THE FUNDAMENTALS OF DRIBBLING

Mechanically, dribbling can be broken down as follows:

1. Dribbling involves moving your arm from the shoulder, the elbow, the wrist, and the fingers. You control the basketball with your fingertips. Fingertips do not necessarily mean the tips of the fingers, but rather the padded area of each finger between the tip of the finger and the first joint on the palm side of the hand.
2. Your fingers are comfortably spread and relaxed when dribbling. Push the ball down with the finger tips and keep the hand slightly cupped to avoid slapping the ball. The fingertips control the ball but don't worry if the ball brushes against the palm of the hand. (See Figure 3-1.)
3. Keep your head up. You should not have to look at the ball while dribbling. If it is necessary to look at the ball during a drill, it means that you have not mastered that skill. Practice it more.
4. The higher the dribble, the more you will use your shoulder and elbow. The lower the dribble, the more you will use your wrist and fingers to control the ball.

Notice that we have not discussed body position or protecting the ball yet. The game situation and type of dribble dictate different body positions and techniques of protecting the ball, so these aspects will be integrated into the individual skills and drills where they apply.

Figure 3-1 Proper Position of Hand on the Ball While Dribbling

However, it should be noted that the lower the dribble, the more you protect the ball from the opposition. This controlled dribble is done in close to the body, and your knees and waist should be well bent. The higher dribble is better used when running at high speed. The ball is bounced considerably farther away from the body, which is fairly erect while running.

There are two general areas a dribbler must master:

1. The mechanical or individual dribbling skills.
2. The mental or conceptual aspects of dribbling: dribbling with a purpose.

As far as dribbling mechanics are concerned, you must be totally confident in your ability to:

- Execute each of the skills with either hand.
- Keep your head up and protect the ball from the defense.
- Make quick moves and changes of direction and pace while dribbling.
- Pass and shoot well off the dribble.
- Keep the dribble alive (do not pick up or stop your dribble) until you can shoot or pass the ball to a teammate.

Drill D-1

1. Take the basketball in your right hand and begin bouncing it to waist level. Your knees are bent, and you should be dribbling the ball about three to six inches in front of and to the right of your right foot.

2. Continue this for one minute.

3. Repeat steps 1 and 2 looking straight ahead and not at the ball. Concentrate on controlling the dribble with your finger tips by pushing the ball down to the floor and almost catching it in your cupped hand as it returns to you. Your fingers are spread, your hand is relaxed, and your forearm absorbs the shock or force of the ball as it bounces up to you. Most important, do not slap the ball. Concentrate on maintaining contact with the ball on your fingertips on the downstroke.

4. Repeat steps 1–3 using the left hand. Remember to keep your head up and do not slap at the ball.

POINTS OF EMPHASIS

- Your head is up.
- Your fingertips control the ball.
- Your dribble should be in a smooth rhythm.

Skill: Low Dribble

The low dribble is used to protect the basketball from a nearby defender.

The lower the dribble, the closer the ball is to your body and the more you control it with your wrist and fingers. The higher the dribble, the farther it is from your body, and the more you will use your shoulder and elbow.

Drill D-2

1. Get down on both knees and begin dribbling with your right hand. Dribble the ball waist high about three to six inches in front and to the right of your right knee. Your head should be up, and you should be able to feel the ball bouncing in a steady rhythm.

Keep your forearm parallel or even with the floor. In this drill the forearm should move up and down about two to four inches while you are dribbling, enabling you to feel the ball on your finger tips. (See Figure 3-2.)

To help you concentrate on the skill, it might be useful to fix your eyes on a spot at eye level about ten or fifteen feet away. Continue dribbling for one minute.

2. Repeat step 1 with the left hand.

3. Remain on your knees dribbling with the right hand and your head up. Look to your right for fifteen seconds, then to your left for fifteen seconds. Repeat.

4. Repeat step 3 using your left hand.

5. Remain on your knees dribbling with your right hand and slowly lower your dribble until you are dribbling only a few inches off the floor. Keep your head up and maintain rhythm and control in your dribble. You should be using mostly fingertips and a little wrist on this very low dribble. Continue for one minute.

6. Raise your dribble to shoulder level and notice how much more

Figure 3-2 Dribbling on Knees

shoulder and elbow action is needed. Maintain rhythm and control in your dribble. Continue for one minute.

7. Repeat steps 5 and 6 with your left hand.

8. Remain on your knees, dribbling at waist level with the right hand. Push the ball across the body on one bounce to your left hand and continue dribbling with the left hand. Now repeat this pushing the ball across your body on one bounce from the left hand to the right hand. The ball should bounce in the middle of your body on each crossover.

Push the ball firmly off the dribbling hand so the bounce from hand to hand is in the same rhythm as the dribble.

Note: The catching or receiving hand should be cupped and relaxed, with fingers comfortably spread and slightly turned with the palm facing the ball as it comes up off the floor.

The hand and arm of the receiving hand should "give" as the ball bounces into it and you continue dribbling. Keep your head up and practice this from the low, medium, and high dribbling levels. This move is called a crossover dribble.

9. Repeat steps 1–8 squatting where your rear end is just above knee level.

10. Repeat steps 1–8 standing with knees and waist bent.

POINTS OF EMPHASIS

- Your head is up.
- The ball is controlled by your wrist and fingertips.
- Your joints are bent, especially your knees, waist, and elbow, keeping the ball close to your body and under control.
- Dribbling is a rhythmic activity. You should always be able to feel a musical rhythm and timing in your head as you dribble. (See Figures 3-3, 3-4, and 3-5.)

Figure 3-3 Low (Protected) Dribble

Figure 3-4 Medium Dribble

Skill: Speed Dribble

The speed dribble is used in the open court while running. It must be mastered with either hand, with the head up at all times and under enough control so that stops, changes of pace, and changes of direction are possible according to the situation. The speed dribble is executed by bouncing the ball farther in front of you as you increase your running speed. It involves a higher bounce as you increase your foot speed. The

Figure 3-5 High (Speed) Dribble

higher the dribble, the more arm and shoulder action is required to control the ball.

Drill D-3

1. While walking, dribble with your right hand at waist level. The dribble should be in front and about six inches to the right of the right foot. Your head is up, and you are not looking at the ball. Continue for one minute.

2. Repeat step 1 with the left hand.

3. Repeat step 1 and slowly increase your foot speed until you are dribbling at one-half running speed.

Notice that the faster you run, the farther you must push the ball out in front of you and the higher the dribble becomes. While walking, the dribble was comfortable at waist level. As you begin to run, however, the dribble reaches chest height.

4. Repeat step 3 using your left hand.

POINTS OF EMPHASIS

- The ball must be pushed farther in front of you on the bounce as you increase your running speed.
- The faster the dribble, the higher the bounce. At full speed, the ball should bounce to your upper chest, and you should be using considerable shoulder and arm movement to control the dribble.

Skill: Change-of-Pace Dribble

It is important that you have the ability to change your pace on the dribble to speed up or slow down on the court. This must be accomplished with maximum control and quickness. Anticipate each change of pace by bending your knees a little more to lower your center of gravity and lean forward when increasing pace and leaning slightly to the rear just before you slow your speed.

Drill D-4

1. Begin dribbling with your right hand (to your right at one-fourth speed) with your right hand in a large circle around the outside of the basketball court. Every five seconds, change your speed, going from one-fourth speed to one-half speed, back to one-fourth speed, and so on. Continue for one minute.

2. Repeat step 1 using your left hand dribbling around the court to your left.

3. Repeat steps 1 and 2 using different one-fourth, one-half, and three-fourths dribbling speeds.

POINTS OF EMPHASIS

- Your head is up.
- The ball is always under control.
- Your knees are more bent and your lean forward is increased just before you increase your dribbling speed. When changing pace to a slower speed, bend your knees a little more and shift your weight slightly to the rear.

Skill: Jump Stopping and Stride Stopping Off the Dribble

Drill D-5

1. Dribble with your right hand at half speed for five dribbles and come to a two-foot jump stop grabbing the ball firmly with both hands before you land on your two feet. (See Footwork Drill F-11.) You should be in the air when you grab the ball, with your fingers spread on the sides of the ball.

Land with your head up, knees bent, elbows out, and the bottom of the ball at waist level with your feet spread at least shoulder width apart. Repeat this five times.

2. Repeat step 1, but *do not* pick up your dribble on the jump stop. In other words, do the jump stop, but keep your dribble alive (continue dribbling the ball). Do this five times.

3. Increase your speed to almost a full run and repeat steps 1 and 2 until you are able to jump stop off the dribble, grabbing the ball and keeping your dribble alive at any speed.

4. Repeat steps 1–3 using the left hand.

5. Dribble with your right hand at half speed and do a jump stop practicing the following pivots (review Footwork Drills F-13 and F-14):

    a. *Front pivot*—Quarter turn to your right off the ball of your right foot.

    b. *Front pivot*—Quarter turn to your left off the ball of your left foot.

    c. *Reverse pivot*—Quarter turn to your left off the ball of your right foot.

    d. *Reverse pivot*—Quarter turn to your right off the ball of your left foot.

6. Repeat Step 5, dribbling with the left hand.

7. Repeat steps 5 and 6, at various dribbling speeds until you have mastered the jump stop off both feet, dribbling with either hand and pivoting off either foot, at any speed.

8. Repeat Dribbling Drill D-5, steps 1–4, using the stride stop in place of the jump stop. Review Footwork Drill F-12 before you begin.

POINTS OF EMPHASIS

- Your head must be up at all times, and your dribble must be completely under control.
- As you increase your dribbling speed, you must cut the length of your steps before your stop or you will lose your body control.

- Bend your knees more on your last dribble or two and bend them even more on your landing. This lower center of gravity will improve your balance and body control.

PROTECTING THE BASKETBALL

At this point, before we begin learning crossover dribbles, it is important to discuss protection of the basketball. When you are dribbling, the defense will constantly try to disrupt you and your attempt to progress or better your position. For this reason, you must keep your head up at all times so that you know where the defense is and what measures of action are most appropriate.

When a defensive player is within six feet of you when you are dribbling, you must use your body position to provide extra protection of the ball:

Place your body between the defender and the ball. This means that you dribble with the hand away from the defender. The closer the defensive player is to you, the lower your dribble and body position.

Your knees and waist are bent, your feet are spread comfortably apart, your head is up, and your nondribbling arm is extended naturally three to six inches away from your side with the forearm parallel to the floor. (See Figure 3-6.)

Drill D-6

1. Dribble with your right hand at half speed from the base line to the foul line and come to a stride stop without picking up your dribble.

Figure 3-6 Protecting the Dribble

2. Get into a good protective dribbling stance by:

a. Lowering your dribble.

b. Bending your knees and waist and stepping across with your left foot so that your lowered left shoulder is facing midcourt. Your dribble should be directly in front of the toes of your right foot.

c. Keeping your feet comfortably spread apart, your head up, and your left arm extended naturally three to six inches away from your side with the forearm parallel to the floor.

3. Remain in your protective dribbling stance for five dribbles and then dribble to midcourt.

4. Come to a jump stop and get into a good protective dribbling stance.

5. Remain in your protective dribbling stance for five dribbles and then continue dribbling to the foul line.

6. Come to a stride stop and repeat step 2.

7. Repeat step 5 dribbling to the baseline and come to a jump stop.

8. Repeat steps 1–7, dribbling with the left hand and reversing the directions for hands and feet.

9. Repeat steps 1–8 three times.

10. Repeat steps 1–8 dribbling at three quarter speed.

Skill: Front Crossover Dribble

Crossover dribbling moves are used to move the ball from one hand to the other to change direction. Because the defense usually dictates the crossover move, it is imperative that during the crossover you always:

- Keep your head up so that you can see the court at all times.
- Keep your dribble and body under control so that you can pass, change pace and direction, or shoot as the situation calls for.
- Protect the ball from your opponents.
- Execute each crossover smoothly and quickly.

Drill D-7

1. Begin dribbling with your right hand (while walking) at a 45-degree angle to your right.

2. After a few steps, as your right foot starts forward, push the ball on a bounce from your right hand across your body so it comes off the floor into your left hand.

3. As the ball comes across your body, swing your right leg across and in front of your body so that you are now dribbling with your left hand at a 45-degree angle to your left.

4. Continue dribbling at a walk, and use the crossover dribble from the left hand to the right by pushing the ball across your body, on a bounce, to your right hand as your left foot starts forward.

5. Continue this pattern zigzagging up and down the floor until you can do it without looking at the ball.

6. Dribble at one quarter speed with your head up, crossover after every five dribbles. In other words, dribble five times with your right hand and crossover to your left hand. Now dribble five times with your left hand and crossover to your right. Be sure the crossovers are done quickly and smoothly, your head is up, and the ball is protected. Continue this zigzagging up and down the court until you have completed twenty crossovers.

7. Repeat step 5 at one-half, three-fourths, and full speeds.

Remember: As you push the ball across your body, your right hand slides slightly to the outside (right) of the ball and, with your fingers comfortably spread, pushes the ball sharply, on a bounce, to the receiving (left) hand. The receiving hand meets and "catches" the ball at a lower level than where the ball was pushed from the right hand, with the left palm slightly turned in toward the body and the fingers comfortably spread.

Be sure that after your crossover dribble, you step across with your right leg and swing your right shoulder to protect the ball from the defense. Keep the ball in as close to your body as possible on the crossover dribble without letting it touch you. When dribbling with the left hand, your right arm should be three to six inches from your body with the forearm parallel to the floor for added protection of the ball.

You must learn to do crossovers at various speeds. For example, on a fast break, you will have to be able to crossover at a high rate of speed. Against a pressing defensive player, you must be able to crossover standing still, walking, moving at slow paces, and while changing speeds.

Notice that the crossover dribble is done at a low level (at the knee or below) when standing or walking slowly and at a higher level (above the waist) when running.

Points of Emphasis   It will take a great deal of practice and practical game experience to learn the correct timing of the front crossover move. In addition to mastering the dribbling mechanics, the three crucial aspects of this move are:

- The distance from the defender you choose to make your move.
- The height of the ball on the crossover (the closer the defender, the lower the crossover dribble must be).
- The ability to keep the ball close to your body and under control as the distance closes between you and your defender.

OPTIONAL CROSSOVER DRIBBLES

The following drills present optional methods of crossing over the dribble. Many high-level players, particularly guards, prefer to have several perfected skills of crossing over the dribble, using them according to the situation. However, it is only mandatory for each player to have one excellent move of crossing over on the dribble *each* way.

It is not uncommon for players to prefer one crossover going from the left-handed dribble to the right and another going from the right to the left. For example, you might perfect the front crossover dribble going from the right-handed dribble to the left and the between-the-legs crossover move going from the left to the right-handed dribble.

In my opinion, *every* player should master the front crossover dribble *both* ways because it can be executed at most dribbling speeds, keeps the dribbler facing his or her basket and the defense, and is the simplest, quickest and most easily learned. However, each of the other crossover moves can be effective in certain circumstances when mastered, and I strongly encourage young players, especially guards, to learn them after they have mastered the front crossovers.

Skill: Crossover Dribble—Between the Legs

Review Front Crossover Dribble (D-7) carefully before learning this skill. This will give you another method of changing dribbling direction.

Drill D-7A

1. Dribble with your right hand while walking at a 45-degree angle to your right. After several steps (when your left leg is forward), firmly push the ball from your right hand through your legs on one bounce to your left hand.

To push the ball firmly through your legs, you must bend your knees to lower your body position on the last dribble and slide your right hand slightly, with the fingers comfortably spread, to the outside (right) of the ball. Be sure the last step with the left leg is long enough to allow the ball to go through your legs.

Your left hand should be turned slightly in toward your body with the fingers comfortably spread, ready to receive the ball off the bounce from your right hand. The left hand should accept the ball at the same level or lower than where it left the right hand.

As the ball comes across your body from your right hand to your left hand, swing your right leg across and in front of your body so that you are now dribbling with your left hand at a 45-degree angle to your left. Be sure that immediately after you cross over, you step across with your right leg and swing your right shoulder to protect the ball from the defense. Your head should be up during this entire sequence.

2. Continue dribbling at a walk with your left hand and repeat the procedure in step 1 crossing over from left to right.

3. Continue zigzagging up and down the court, crossing over every five or seven steps with this crossover move. Continue this until you can execute these crossovers from right to left and left to right smoothly and quickly, without looking at the ball.

4. Repeat step 3 at one-fourth, one-half, three-fourths, and changing speeds.

Skill: Crossover Dribble—Spin Move

This has become one of the most popular change-of-direction moves off the dribble. Although once done only by daring guards, today it is not uncommon to see forwards executing this maneuver with great mastery.

Review Front Crossover Dribble (D-7) carefully before proceeding with this drill. This will provide you with another method of changing dribbling direction.

Drill D-7B

1. Dribble with your right hand while walking at a 45-degree angle to your right. Your knees are bent, your head is up, and you are protecting the ball with your body and left forearm. When your left foot is forward, you will simultaneously reverse pivot 180 degrees on the ball of your left foot and pull the ball around behind you with the right hand toward your right foot. This is the spin portion of the move.

The last dribble with the right hand before you spin should bounce in front of the right toe. As the ball comes up from that dribble, the right elbow rotates out, and the hand, with fingers comfortably spread, slides slightly to the inside or left of the ball. This causes the wrist to flex slightly in preparation of pulling the ball around behind you as you step back with your right foot.

As the right foot lands after the 180-degree reverse pivot, the ball should bounce immediately thereafter directly in front of the toes of the right foot from the right hand. The next part of the move is to swing your left leg around to complete the spin and continue dribbling with your left hand.

A simple way to remember the move is to think: "Plant, step and pull, and go." This refers to planting the left foot and stepping back with the right foot as you reverse pivot off of your left foot; "go" means to complete the momentum of the turn by swinging your left leg around and continue dribbling with your left hand.

2. Repeat this move starting your dribble with the left hand, walking at a 45-degree angle to your left, and spinning back to your left and crossing over to your right hand.

3. Practice this over and over spinning right and left and at different speeds. Remember, you must be able to execute this maneuver with your head up, under complete control and protecting the ball at all times.

Helpful Hints Begin practicing the spin move slowly and get a feeling for the rhythm of the spin. The plant step should be a hard step with the weight shifting almost entirely on that planted foot before the reverse pivot. Bend your knees a little bit more on the reverse pivot because it will improve your balance and smooth out the move. Last, bounce the ball hard on the last dribble and pull the ball around you by rotating the elbow in and wrist out without turning the palm over. The ball should bounce in front of the toes of the right foot when spinning right and in front of the toes of the left foot when spinning left.

If you are having trouble with the spin portion of this move, try this extra drill:

1. Stand sideways, dribbling the ball with your right hand in front of the toes of your left foot.
2. Bend your knees as the ball is going toward the floor on each dribble and, after several dribbles, pull the ball back as it is coming up while simultaneously stepping back with the right foot (reverse pivoting off the left foot). The first dribble after the spin should bounce in front of the toes of the right foot as it lands after you reverse pivot.
3. Repeat steps 1 and 2, dribbling the ball with your left hand in front of the toes of your right foot and reverse the directions for hands and feet.
4. Keep practicing this until you can spin smoothly with your head up and the ball well protected at all times.

MOST COMMON MISTAKES

1. Not pulling the ball around on the spin with the back hand. Too often, a player when dribbling to his or her right will plant the left foot, reverse pivot off the ball of that left foot, but instead of pulling the ball around him or herself with the right hand, will swing the left leg around and carry the ball around with the left hand. This leaves the ball unprotected, and either the defensive player will steal the ball or the dribbler will be called for a palming violation.
2. Looking at the ball and losing sight of the defense and teammates. Because this is a complex skill, many players try to execute it before they have mastered it completely. If the dribbler drops his head to see the ball, he may charge into a defensive player or miss an open teammate.
3. The spin move can be very effective, especially when being guarded closely, man-to-man, in the open court. However, the move takes more time than a front crossover and requires the dribbler to turn his back as he spins. Therefore, one should be careful choosing when to use the

spin move lest he be double teamed or miss an open teammate for an easy basket.

POINTS OF EMPHASIS

- This is a potentially very effective move, but it takes a great deal of practice before it can be used successfully in a game situation.
- The spin move is best used in the open court.
- The spin move is very difficult to execute when dribbling straight ahead where a front crossover or between-the-legs crossover dribble would be safer and easier to use. The spin move is best accomplished when dribbling on an angle.

Skill: Crossover Dribble—Behind the Back

Review Front Crossover Dribble (D-7) carefully before proceeding with this drill. The behind-the-back crossover dribble is another option of changing dribbling direction in the open court.

Drill D-7C

1. Dribble with your right hand while walking at a 45-degree angle to your right. As your left leg begins forward and the ball is slightly behind and at the level of your right hip, push the ball firmly behind your back angled toward the floor and the back of the knee of your left leg. You may arch your back slightly as you push the ball behind you.

Keep the ball in as close to your body as possible without allowing the ball to touch you when you push it behind your back. As the ball comes up from the last dribble with the right hand, the right elbow rotates out, and the hand, with fingers comfortably spread, slides slightly to the inside or left of the ball. This causes the wrist to flex slightly in preparation of pulling the ball around behind you. It should be noted that some players use a different method on this maneuver; they make the last dribble with the right hand *behind* their right hip, slide their right hand to the *outside* or *right* of the ball, and simply push the ball behind them.

After the ball leaves your right hand, quickly front pivot on the ball of the left foot, stepping over with your right leg, closing your right shoulder and arm to protect the ball as you pick the dribble up on one bounce with your left hand.

The move should be executed smoothly and quickly with your head up and the ball protected at all times.

2. Now you are dribbling with your left hand at a 45-degree angle to your left. Execute the behind-the-back crossover from left to right by reversing the move. As your right leg begins forward and the ball reaches your right hip, push the ball behind your back angled toward the floor and the back of the knee of your right leg.

3. Practice this off various dribbling speeds and hesitation dribbles.

Remember to keep your head up and protect the ball at all times by keeping your nondribbling arm and shoulder between the ball and where your defensive opponent will be.

POINTS OF EMPHASIS

- This maneuver needs a dribbling angle to be effective. It is a very difficult move to use when dribbling straight ahead (at a defender) where a front crossover or between-the-legs crossover dribble is easier and safer to use.
- The spin and behind-the-back crossover dribbles are best used in the open court and when dribbling at an angle.

Drill D-7D

1. Place one chair somewhere in the middle of the court.
2. Begin dribbling with your right hand at a walk toward the chair from twenty feet away.
3. Execute a front crossover dribble from your right hand to your left hand when you get in front of the chair and continue dribbling with your left hand for twenty feet past the chair.

Your head is up, the ball is well protected, and your body is under complete control.

4. Without picking up your dribble, turn and repeat steps 1–3 using the front crossover from your left hand to your right hand.
5. Repeat steps 1–4 ten times.
6. Repeat steps 1–5 using:
a. Between-the-legs crossover.
b. Spin move.
c. Behind-the-back crossover.
7. After you have mastered each of the foregoing crossover moves, repeat the drill at one-half and three-fourths running speeds.

POINTS OF EMPHASIS

- To be effective in a game situation, each crossover maneuver must be executed quickly and smoothly.
- Because the ball is bounced higher as you increase your dribbling speed, you will have to execute your crossovers further from the chair at higher speeds to protect the ball. At high dribbling speeds, most great players will use the front crossover. The spin move is almost exclusively employed at slow speeds, walking to one quarter, while the between-the-legs and behind-the-back moves are commonly used up to about half speed.
- Practice all the moves at various speeds because it will teach you both the

limitations of the moves and your own ability. You must master the front crossover dribble in both directions; however, in game situations you will ultimately select only the one or two other crossovers in each direction that you have the most confidence in to use.

Skill: Dribbling Change of Direction

Drill D-8

1. Set up an obstacle course with ten chairs, articles of clothing, or any other kind of marker. Place the markers in a circle five feet apart. You may begin the course at any marker dribbling to your right to the inside of the first marker, to the outside of the second marker, to the inside of the third marker, and so on around the circle until you have completed the circle three times.

First, dribble with the right hand only. Next, dribble with the left hand only. Finally, dribble with either hand using front crossovers. This is done by dribbling with your right hand as you are moving to your right. After you crossover to your left hand at the next marker, dribble with your left hand as you move to your left.

2. Repeat step 1 dribbling the circuit to the left.

3. Repeat steps 1 and 2, but change the distance between the markers to four feet, then three feet, then two feet, and finally to one foot apart.

4. Lay out another dribbling obstacle course by placing ten markers in a straight line five feet apart. Zigzag through the markers up and back three times using:

   a. Right-hand dribble only.
   b. Left-hand dribble only.
   c. Either hand with front crossovers.

As you master this, change the distance between the markers to four, three, two, and one foot apart.

5. Create your own obstacle course by laying out markers at different intervals and different angles to combine all the dribbling changes of direction you want to master.

6. After you have mastered the *form* and *rhythm* of these skills, you should begin timing yourself for each drill. Be sure that as you increase your speed:

   a. You are in perfect control of the dribble.
   b. You are balanced and have body control so that you can stop, change pace and direction, shoot, or pass at any time.
   c. Your head is up.
   d. The ball is well protected.

7. Repeat steps 1–6 using the other crossover maneuvers:

   a. Between the legs.
   b. Spin move.
   c. Behind the back.

POINTS OF EMPHASIS

- Take your time and practice these drills, concentrating on *form* and *rhythm*.

- Your head is up—you should not have to look at the ball. If you find yourself looking at the ball, slow down until you have mastered each pace.
- Protect the ball at all times.

Skill: Keeping the Ball Alive
Off Dribbling Moves

This skill is especially important for guards. It is critical that a guard have the ability to keep his or her dribble alive off any maneuver. This means that you should be able to continue your dribble (not pick the ball up) after a jump stop or stride stop or change of direction (crossovers) or pace at any speed.

Drill D-9

    1. Begin running at one-fourth speed and execute each of the following maneuvers that you have learned without picking up your dribble:
      a. Two-foot jump stop.
      b. Stride stops off both feet.
      c. Changes of direction (crossovers).
      d. Changes of pace.
    2. Practice these maneuvers at every speed and changing speeds and using either hand. In game situations you will have to do these things at different speeds so practice them. Dribble up and down the floor changing speeds, dribbling with each hand by doing each of the crossover dribbles and executing jump and stride stops every five seconds. Remember to keep the ball alive during the entire drill.

POINTS OF EMPHASIS

- Your head is up.
- The ball is well protected.
- You have your dribble under control. The slower the dribble, the lower it is and the closer it is to your body.
- You are balanced and your body is under control.

CONTROLLED DRIBBLE CHECKPOINTS

1. The dribbler's knees and waist are bent and he or she is on the balls of his or her feet.
2. The dribbler's head is up.
3. The dribbler's fingers are spread and relaxed, and the ball is under complete control, using the fingertips and wrist.

4. The ball is properly protected from the defense.

5. The dribbler is balanced and prepared to change direction and pace as well as stop, pass, or shoot off the dribble.

Skill: Laying the Ball Out

For guards and forwards who handle the ball on the fast break, the ability to catch the ball from either a rebound or an outlet pass and get into a high-speed dribble as quickly as possible is extremely important. Many players lose a half or full step when they begin their dribbles or lose the ball on a turnover because they have not learned and practiced the proper maneuvers of laying the ball out. Remember that the success of a fast break often depends on how quickly the ball is advanced to midcourt. The more quickly it gets to midcourt, the greater likelihood your team's attackers will outnumber your opponent's defenders.

Drill D-10

1. Begin facing the backboard at ten feet and about one foot to the left of the basket.

2. Throw the ball high off the backboard.

3. Meet the ball, jump and catch it in the air with both hands, landing squarely on both feet spread at least a shoulder width apart. You should land with good balance, your elbows out, your knees bent, and your head up. The ball should be held at the upper chest level (Fig. 3-7a).

4. Take a quick look over your left shoulder toward the near sideline to be sure that you are not closely guarded (Fig. 3-7b).

5. Front pivot on the ball of your left foot by swinging your right leg and shoulder around in front of you. Keep your knees bent and your head up as you turn toward the opposite basket.

6. Push the ball out in front of you with your right hand as you take a long first step with your right foot toward the opposite basket. This will enable you to begin your speed dribble very quickly (Fig. 3-7c).

7. Repeat steps 1–6 from the other side of the court using the front pivot off the right foot and laying the ball out with the left hand for the left-handed speed dribble.

Important Points The key to this maneuver is body balance: pivot with a comfortably wide base and low center of gravity with the head up. When you first practice this skill, you will have to look, pivot, and then lay the ball out. However, with practice, you will begin to smooth out the maneuver by looking, turning, and laying the ball out almost all in one motion.

As you practice, concentrate on using as few dribbles as possible to get to full speed. You should be able to reach your full-speed dribble,

(a)

(b)

(c)

Figures 3-7a, 3-7b, and 3-7c Laying the Ball Out on the Dribble

under control, by the time you get to the hash mark in the backcourt. It is important that you do not throw the ball but push it in front of you so that you can smoothly move into a high-speed dribble as quickly as possible without losing any control.

Optional Advanced Maneuver This inside pivot in the backcourt is risky because it often directs the dribbler into heavy defensive traffic. However, for the highly skilled dribbler on the fast break with good judgment, here is an advanced move:

---

8. Repeat steps 1–6, but after you look over the left shoulder, pretend that you see a defensive player there preventing you from pivoting out. With your knees still bent, feet spread comfortably apart, and elbows out, rotate your shoulders and arms enough to show that defensive player the ball with a quick one-fourth turn of your body.

Immediately thereafter, pivot inside off the ball of the right foot and lay the ball out with the left hand up the center of the court. Keep an extra low body position on this move.

9. Repeat step 7 from the other side of the court using the inside pivot off the left foot.

POINTS OF EMPHASIS

- When you receive the ball from either a rebound or outlet pass, it is important that you meet the ball and land in good body position after you catch it: your feet spread comfortably apart, knees bent, elbows out, and head up. This protects the ball from the defense and affords you maximum opportunity for an offensive maneuver.
- Be sure you take a quick glance over your outside shoulder (toward the near sideline) before you make any move.
- Pivot low and push off hard on the pivoting foot when laying the ball out.
- Push the ball out in front of you under control. Do not throw it.

Skill: Hesitation Dribble

Review the Change of Pace Dribble (D-4), Keeping the Ball Alive Off Dribbling Moves (D-9), Stride Stop (F-12), and Front Crossover Dribble (D-7), because the hesitation dribble is an advanced maneuver for highly skilled ballhandlers. This maneuver is very effective when you approach a defensive player in the open court, especially on a fast break. It involves slowing yourself quickly from one-fourth-, one-half-, or three-fourths-speed dribble to a stop or near stop while keeping the ball alive so that you can accelerate by your defender.

Your head is up and your dribble is completely under control. As you approach the defense, you must keep the ball close enough to your body so that it can't be swatted away by the defense.

Drill D-11

1. Dribble straight ahead at one-fourth speed with your right hand. Slow down quickly with a stride stop. Do not pick up your dribble. Now accelerate to a one-half-speed dribble. Repeat this ten times.

2. Repeat step 1 but add in a hand-and-shoulder fake by raising up your chin and shoulders after your stride stop, and then accelerate your dribble back to one-half speed.

3. Repeat step 1 and execute a front crossover dribble switching the ball from your right hand to your left before you accelerate and continue dribbling with your left hand.

4. Repeat steps 1–3, beginning each dribbling with the left hand.

POINT OF EMPHASIS

- It will take experience learning how to approach a defender in the open court, hesitation dribble, and accelerate past him. Aside from the dribbling mechanics, the three crucial aspects of this move are:

1. The speed at which you approach the defense.
2. The distance from the defender you select to make your move.
3. The ability to keep the ball close to your body and under control as you hesitation dribble by the defender.

Variations of the Hesitation Dribble   The hesitation dribble is one of the most effective moves in basketball and can be expanded with the use of other deceptive maneuvers. The following are advanced variations of the hesitation dribble:

Repeat Drill D-11, but do not do a stride stop. Instead slow down and:

1. Fake a front crossover dribble by sliding your dribbling hand over the top of the ball across the body with a little head and shoulder fake in the same direction, hesitate, and, instead of crossing over, push the ball out in the direction of your dribbling hand and accelerate.

2. Fake a spin move by stepping across your body with the leg opposite your dribbling hand. After that foot is planted, shift your weight back onto the foot of your dribbling side, and slide your hand over the top of the ball. This will give the impression that you are going to do a spin, hesitate, and step forward with the leg opposite your dribbling hand and accelerate. Be sure that you keep your head up during these maneuvers, and you have the ball well protected and under control at all times.

Skill: Stutter Step

The stutter step is another advanced change of pace dribbling maneuver. It will be helpful to review pattering (F-1), Jump Stop (F-11), Change of Pace Dribble (D-4), Front Crossover Dribble (D-7), Keeping the Ball Alive Off Dribbling Moves (D-9), and Hesitation Dribble (D-11). Because this move is interchangeable with the hesitation dribble, reread the introduction and Points of Emphasis in Drill D-11 before proceeding with the stutter step drill.

Drill D-12

1. Dribble straight ahead at one-fourth speed with your right hand. Slow down quickly (you may use a "soft" jump stop), but do not pick up your dribble. Patter your feet three or five times, push off hard on the ball of the left foot, and accelerate to one-half speed still using the right-hand dribble. Practice this ten times.
2. Repeat step 1, but execute a front crossover dribble, switching the ball from your right hand to your left before you accelerate by pushing off the ball of the left foot and continuing your dribble with the left hand. Be sure the ball is well protected at all times.
3. Repeat steps 1 and 2, beginning each dribbling with the left hand.

THE FOX BOX DRIBBLING DRILLS

The Fox Box Dribbling Drills (FBDD) are designed to combine different dribbling skills that you have learned. Each drill will be done in the three-second lane.

Practice them for *form* and *rhythm* until you can do them mechanically perfectly with your head up and the ball protected before you attempt to increase your speed.

Each drill should be done without picking up your dribble (keeping the ball alive).

Fox Box Dribbling Drill I (Figure 3-8)

1. Begin dribbling with the right hand at point A up the foul lane line and jump stop at point B.
2. Still dribbling with the right hand, slide left across the foul line to the elbow, point C. Always look in the direction in which you are sliding.
3. Retreat step, still dribbling with the right hand, to the base line, point D.

Figure 3-8 Fox Box Dribbling Drill Diagram

4. Execute a front crossover dribble from your right to your left hand and slide right along the base line to point A. Front crossover dribble from your left hand to your right.

5. Repeat this twice more.

6. Repeat steps 1–5, but begin from point D dribbling with the left hand and reverse the directions.

7. Repeat steps 1–6, using stride stops instead of jump stops.

Fox Box Dribbling Drill II

1. Begin at point A and dribble with your right hand up the foul lane line to point B and jump stop, maintaining your right-hand dribble.

2. Do a 45-degree drop step with your left leg and slide diagonally down and across the three-second area to point D, at the junction of the base line and the left lane line. Remember to look in the direction of your slide.

3. Do a front crossover dribble from your right to left hand, a 45-degree stop step with your right leg, and slide right along the base line to point A. Do a front crossover dribble from your left hand to your right.

4. Repeat twice for a total of three times around the three-second area.

5. Repeat steps 1–4, but begin from point D dribbling with the left hand and reverse the directions.

POINTS OF EMPHASIS

- You should be able to keep your dribble alive and under perfect control throughout each drill.
- Your head should be up and the ball well protected.
- When you do a drop step and slide while dribbling, you should have your head turned in the direction you are moving.

THE MECHANICS OF DRIBBLING

Now that you have learned the basic dribbling skills, the real work begins
To master the art of dribbling, you must not only learn these skills but
spend countless hours practicing them. Each dribbling skill must become
so familiar that you will be able to execute the maneuver perfectly without thinking. In other words, your skills must become a conditioned
reflex.

In the pressure of game situations, you have no time to think or
look at the ball to make sure you are performing the skill properly. You
must be able to react without hesitation. For this reason, you should practice each drill first for perfect form, then rhythm, and finally for speed

The following mechanical drills will help you to perfect your
dribbling skills if you do them regularly. They are designed to improve
form, rhythm, timing, speed, strength, and stamina.

MECHANICAL DRIBBLING DRILLS

Drill MD-1: Figure Eights

1. Dribble with your right hand while standing still. Your feet are a
shoulder width apart, your knees are bent, and your head is up.
2. Push the ball between your legs from front to back, on a bounce, to
your left hand and continue dribbling.
3. Dribble with your left hand around the outside of your left leg and push
the ball back between your legs, on a bounce, to your right hand and continue
dribbling.
4. With your right hand, dribble around the outside of your right leg and
again push the ball through your legs to the left hand.
5. Continue this pattern practicing dribbling at different heights.

Drill MD-2: Reverse Figure Eights

1. Begin dribbling with your right hand standing still. Your feet are a
shoulder width apart, your knees are bent, and your head is up.
2. Dribble around the outside of your right leg and push the ball through
your legs from behind you, on a bounce, to your left hand in front of you.
3. Continue dribbling with your left hand around your left leg and push the
ball, on a bounce, through your legs from behind to your right hand in front of you.
4. Continue this pattern, practicing your dribble at different heights.

Drill MD-3: Wall Dribbling

This drill is especially good for developing strength and stamina in the fingers, hands, wrists, and arms as well as timing and rhythm.

1. Using your right hand, dribble a ball against a wall at eye level (Fig. 3-9).

a. See how close you can dribble to the wall and keep control of the ball.

b. Next, see how far from the wall you can dribble and keep control of the ball.

2. Repeat step 1 with your left hand.

3. Use two balls, dribble them simultaneously (the two balls should bounce at the same time against the wall) and repeat (a) and (b) of step 1.

4. Repeat step 3 using an alternating dribble. This means that the two balls do not bounce simultaneously but alternate in a steady rhythm. Practice this until you can wall dribble each part of this drill for several minutes. For extra rhythm and timing practice, try this drill with your eyes closed.

Drill MD-4: Two-Ball Floor Dribble

1. Begin dribbling two balls, one with each hand, while standing still. The balls should be bouncing simultaneously (at the same time).

2. Pivot and turn to your left, pivot back to your right; pivot and turn to your right, and pivot back to your left.

3. Repeat step 2, with jump turns.

4. Walk straight ahead for fifty feet.

Figure 3-9 Wall Dribble

5. Increase your dribbling speed until you can dribble at almost full speed.

6. Practice jump and stride stops and 45-degree turns at each speed.

7. Zigzag up and down the court, adding head and shoulder fakes to your stops and changes of pace and direction.

8. Repeat steps 1–7 with an alternating dribble. This means that the two balls do not bounce simultaneously but alternate in a steady rhythm.

9. Do the Fox Box Dribbling Drills I and II (without crossovers) using two balls with both the simultaneous and alternating dribbles. Are you able to do all the above with your head up and the balls under your complete control?

WORKOUT, EVALUATION, AND PROGRESS CHARTS

Table 3-1 Dribbling Workout—15 Minutes

Warmup

DRILL	TIME	INSTRUCTIONS
D-4	1 minute(s)	Dribble with each hand.
D-7	1 "	
D-7D	1 "	
D-8	2 "	Circle at 3 feet apart and line at 2 feet.
D-9	1 "	
D-10	1 "	Both sides of court.
D-11	1 "	
D-12	1 "	
MD-1	1 "	Dribble right and left.
MD-2	1 "	Dribble right and left.
MD-3	1 "	Dribble with each hand and both hands.
MD-4	1 "	Complete simultaneous and alternate dribbles.
FBDDI	1 "	
FBDDII	1 "	
Cooldown		

Table 3-2 Dribbling Workout—30 Minutes

Warmup

DRILL	TIME	INSTRUCTIONS
D-2	1 minute(s)	Dribble on knees and squatting with each hand.
D-3	1 "	
D-4	2 "	
D-5	1 "	
D-6	1 "	
D-7	2 "	
D-7D	3 "	
D-8	2 "	Circle at 2 feet apart and line at 3 feet.
D-9	1 "	
D-10	2 "	Both sides of court.
D-11	1 "	
D-12	1 "	
MD-1	1 "	Dribble right and left.
MD-2	1 "	Dribble right and left.
MD-3	2 "	Dribble with each hand and both hands.
MD-4	2 "	Complete simultaneous and alternate dribbles.
FBDDI	3 "	
FBDDII	3 "	
Cooldown		

Table 3-3 Dribbling Self-Evaluation and Improvement Test

DRILL	TIME	SCORE
MD-1	1 minute	Total number of eights.
MD-2	1 "	Total number of eights.
MD-3a	1 "	Number of dribbles with right hand.
b	1 "	Number of dribbles with left hand.
c	—	Continuous time with right hand.
d	—	Continuous time with left hand.
e	1 "	Number of dribbles with two balls simultaneously.
f	—	Continuous time with two balls simultaneously.
D-8 a	1 "	Number of times around circle markers 3 feet apart, going right.
b	1 "	Number of times around circle markers 3 feet apart, going left.
c	1 "	Number of times through line of markers 2 feet apart.
FBDDIa	1 "	Total number around right.
b	1 "	Total number around left.
FBDDIIa	1 "	Total number around right.
b	1 "	Total number around left.

Table 3-4 Personal Dribbling Progress Chart

DATE

Drill											
MD-1											
MD-2											
MD-3											
a											
b											
c											
d											
e											
f											
D-8											
a											
b											
c											
FBDDI											
a											
b											
FBDDII											
a											
b											

CHAPTER FOUR

PASSING AND RECEIVING

For some unknown reason, passing and receiving are probably the least appreciated skills in the game of basketball. It is incredible how many otherwise talented and highly skilled players do not possess the most basic passing skills. Many coaches will tell you that good passing is a "lost art" and that it is the most underrated aspect of basketball. This is especially curious since learning proper passing and receiving techniques requires considerably less time and practice than does dribbling and shooting. However, once these skills are learned incorrectly, they are habits that are difficult to correct.

It is important that every coach and young player understand the importance of passing and receiving and practice these skills every day. Even when you are alone, there are many ways, which I will describe in this chapter, to practice passing and receiving.

You as a player want to be a good passer and receiver for selfish reasons. It is another way that you can be of value to your team and earn playing time. There are several situations where a coach must especially rely on his or her best passers to win a game:

- To execute the "delay" or "freeze" game.
- To beat full-court and half-court pressure defenses.
- To get the ball to particularly good scorers.

In this chapter you will learn and practice the basic passing skills. After perfecting these, you will be able to develop variations of these skills based on your size, strength, quickness, deceptiveness, judgment, and knowledge of and experience playing the game. However, the rudiments of the chest, bounce, baseball, overhead, jump, hook, and stride passes must be mastered first. Proper passing form and habits will allow you to develop passes that are efficient, deceptive (not "telegraphed"), varied, and accurate.

It is important that you develop strong hands and wrists to be a good passer. The stronger your hands and wrists, the crisper your passing will be. Players with weak hands and wrists are often not strong enough to throw crisp passes and must "wind up" and use their shoulders and arms for extra power. This "telegraphs" the passes and often allows alert defensive players to steal passes. Young players should do extra exercises such as squeezing tennis or rubber balls and fingertip pushups every day to strengthen their hands and wrists.

There are two major aspects of passing: physical and mental. The physical aspect refers to the individual skills of each type of pass and how to catch or receive the ball. The second aspect is mental and deals with judgment, discipline, responsibility, and concentration.

To execute the drills in this chapter, you will need an old basketball, a wall at least five or six feet high, and some tape or chalk for marking. The old ball should be used for several of the drills because a good ball will lose its shape if it is bounced off a wall too often.

Before we begin learning and practicing the individual skills of each pass, it is a good idea to list the General Rules of Good Passing and Receiving. These contain the basic ideas, concepts, and habits you must adopt to be an effective passer and receiver. You may not understand why some of these rules are important at this time, but, with more time and playing experience, the value of these concepts will prove themselves to you. Study them and refer back to them often after you play, and you will be able to analyze your mistakes and continue to improve your game in terms of skills and judgment.

GENERAL RULES OF GOOD PASSING

1. Concentrate on what you are doing—respect possession of the basketball and throw only 100 percent safe passes—fake all others.
2. Get into the habit of throwing crisp passes without "winding up" or "telegraphing" them. Passes must be released quickly so they are difficult to deflect or intercept.
3. See each pass into the receiver's hands—later, when you are more ad-

vanced, you can add deceptive looks and body moves in the other direction.

4. Usually pass the ball to the hand away from the receiver's defender—this means you pass to the outside hand of the receiver. The pass to the inside hand is appropriate when a teammate is clearly open, usually coming off a screen. This pass, to the inside hand, will put the ball in an easier position for your teammate to shoot, as long as there is no threat of a defender deflecting the pass.

5. When passing to a moving receiver (as in a cut to the basket), pass to the hand of the outstretched arm of the moving receiver rather than "leading" him or her with a pass.

6. Fake passes often to keep the defense from learning how to anticipate you. This keeps them "honest" so they won't be able to time your passes.

7. Attempt always to maintain good body balance when you pass, the same way you do when you shoot. It is much easier to be accurate with your passes when your balance is good.

8. Always be conscious of passing to a target on the receiver. This is usually above the waist and below the shoulders or to an outstretched hand. If the receiver is moving and does not give a target with the outstretched arm and hand, you must learn to imagine the target and hit it. A good rule of thumb is chest to chest on chest passes; bounce passes should come up to the receiver's waist.

9. Follow through toward the receiver on all passes the same way you do on your shots.

10. Try and use a bounce pass when a receiver is cutting to the basket.

11. Do not get into the habit of leading your receiver (throwing a pass in front of the receiver to where you think he or she will be when the ball arrives). This will lead to many turnovers as you try to anticipate where the receiver will or should move. Instead, a good receiver should always give a target with his or her outside hand (the hand away from the defender), and you should pass to that target. If the receiver does not provide a target, you must learn to imagine one and pass accurately to it. The exception to leading a receiver is the "head of the field" pass where a receiver is breaking toward your basket away from you and is wide open. However, even in this instance, it is better to be a little short than long on your pass.

12. Usually, you should pass to a teammate if he or she is in better position than you are. If you do not have a good opportunity to score and your teammate is in better position to score, pass your teammate the ball.

13. Always try to pass to a teammate at the right time. This usually means as soon as he or she is open and can do something with the ball.

14. When closely guarded, you must be deceptive and fake your passes. Against big players you will be most successful faking high and bounce passing low. Against smaller opponents fake low and pass over. Faking right and passing left and vice versa is also effective.

15. If you are in the Triple-Threat Position (discussed in Chapter 5) or have

not dribbled yet, avoid bouncing the ball before you pass. This is a common mistake and a poor habit to get into, as a smart defender can take advantage of it by attacking you as soon as you pick up the dribble.

16. Cross-court passes are dangerous but can be effective when used judiciously. Be sure that you fake the cross-court pass at least once (even on a prior possession) before you throw it and that the pass is quickly released and crisp. It if often a good idea to fake a pass in the opposite direction before throwing the cross-court pass and making sure that it is twice as open as other passes. Cross-court passes in front of your opponents' basket (in your backcourt) are doubly dangerous and never thrown unless 100 percent safe.

17. Always try to pass to players who are on the move either toward you or cutting into the open. Passes to receivers who are standing still and flat footed are easily intercepted.

18. Use a softer pass to a receiver who is very close to you, especially if the receiver is coming to meet the pass. If a receiver is close and well guarded, fake the pass to him or her and encourage the player to cut to the basket rather than make a quick, hard pass that he or she may not be able to handle.

19. Practice and perfect a variety of passes so you can mix your passes up. This will make it more difficult for the defense to anticipate or time your passes.

20. Avoid passing to a teammate going toward the sideline, or into a corner directly away from you and not to the basket. These are passes that gain little in terms of team position and often result in turnovers.

21. Incorporate eye and head fakes into your passing to increase your deceptiveness.

22. Encourage teammates to move without the ball by faking passes to them when they are not 100 percent open. This way they will know you saw them and will work harder to get more open for a good pass.

23. "Feather" your close passes. A good pass is catchable. Many short straight passes are difficult to handle. Learn to "feather" these passes by taking extra care to release the ball off your fingertips, and the pass will be softer and easier to handle for the receiver. This technique is particularly important when your receiver is on the move.

GENERAL RULES OF GOOD RECEIVING

1. Constantly work hard without the ball to receive a pass. This means you must be constantly moving and changing speeds and direction to get open.

2. See the ball at all times.

3. Always try to meet the pass. The exception is on a cut to the basket.

4. Give a target above your waist to the passer. Use a two-hand target when coming to the ball and one hand, the palm of the outside hand away from the defender, on cuts to the basket.

5. Always have at least one palm facing the passer. When coming to the

ball, both palms should be facing the passer with the fingers spread and pointing up.

6. Catch the ball with two hands and "soft" hands. You develop "soft" hands by spreading your fingers and relaxing them, slightly cupping your hands and giving a little when the pass arrives to absorb the shock.

7. Look to your basket each time after you receive a pass. This will give you all the information necessary to make your next decision correctly.

8. Be sure you catch the ball and attain good balance and ball protection before you look up, pivot, shoot, pass, or dribble.

9. See every pass into your hands.

10. If a pass is thrown low, below your waist, bend your knees and turn your hands so that your fingers are pointing toward the floor with the palms out to catch or block the ball.

11. If the ball is passed to your side where you can only reach it with one hand, block the ball with that hand and tuck the ball in securely by closing the other hand in on the other side of the ball.

In the following drills, we will learn the proper skills of passing and receiving. The first drill involves only receiving, while most of the subsequent drills focus on different individual passing skills. It is important that you apply and practice your receiving skills with each of the passing drills, even when doing so is not mentioned.

You can do this by stepping to the ball as it comes off the wall or backboard and applying all the rules of good pass reception. Sometimes you will have to catch the ball on one bounce, other times on the fly. Sometimes the ball will come off at unusual angles or on short hops. This will prepare you for the occasional bad pass you will receive in game situations. Review advanced receiving and how to block and catch these passes and practice them when passing drills offer the opportunity.

Skill: Receiving a Pass

You will receive more passes from your teammates if:

1. You constantly move without the ball and get open.
2. You demonstrate that you can catch a pass when it is thrown to you.
3. You prove that you will do the right thing with the ball after you catch it.

Above all, receiving a pass takes concentration. You must focus all of your attention on catching the basketball:

1. Always try to meet the ball except on a change of direction cut to the basket.

2. Meet the ball with your knees and waist bent, head up, elbows bent, and your palms facing the ball with your fingers spread and up. (See Figure 4-1.)

3. See the ball into your hands.

4. Catch the ball with two hands and make them "soft" by relaxing the fingers, slightly cupping your hands, and giving a little by bending your elbows when the pass arrives to absorb some of the shock.

5. After catching the ball, you should protect it and look toward your basket.

Important Note   There are two different schools of thought on the position of the elbows on the receipt of a pass. I teach catching the basketball with the knees bent, head up, and *elbows out* because it provides excellent protection from the defense. Many coaches like the elbows in so that the player can more easily shoot, pass, or dribble off the reception.

I find that the game of basketball is getting more and more aggressive with an increasing number of zone and man-to-man trap defenses. Because players often receive the ball off a rebound, posting up in the three-second area, or when there is defensive pressure, the first priority is to protect the basketball. Later, when I teach shooting off screens and other special situations, players learn when they can safely catch the ball with their elbows in, better prepared for a quicker release of their shot.

Drill PR-1

1. Stand at the foul line facing the basket, two feet to the right of the rim. Throw the ball, with either one or two hands, against the backboard above the rim level.

2. Step toward the ball as it comes off the backboard with knees and waist bent, weight slightly forward on the balls of your feet, head up, elbows out and bent, and palms facing the ball with the fingers spread and up.

3. See the ball into your hands. Make your hands "soft" by relaxing your fingers, slightly cupping your hands, and giving a little by bending your elbows when the ball, on the fly, arrives into your hands.

4. Do a short jump stop and pull the ball into your chest after the catch.

5. Repeat steps 1–4 twenty-five times.

POINTS OF EMPHASIS

• Come to the ball.

• See the ball into your hands or, in other words, *concentrate* on the ball.

• Catch the ball with your palms facing the ball and "soft" hands.

Figure 4-1 Receiving a Pass

- Protect the ball after catching it by pulling it into your chest with the elbows out.

PASSING LANES

A passing lane is the space directly between you, the passer, and the potential receiver, your teammate. If there are no defensive players in or near that space then the passing lane is open. If a defender is either in the lane or is close enough to the lane where he or she could steal or deflect a pass thrown in that lane, then the passing lane is closed and you, as the passer must either not throw the pass or find a way to overcome that obstacle.

There are four ways that you can pass the ball past a defender:

1. Over the top.
2. Under, usually with a bounce pass.
3. Around or to the side either right or left.
4. Through.

Depending on how close the defender is to you and his or her position to the passing lane, you may have to use various fakes or change your position to create a better passing lane. You might also wait until your receiver moves to create a better passing lane before you throw the pass. Experience will help teach you judgment in these areas. You will learn that passes must be generally crisp when they are thrown. Faking often in different directions keeps the defense from anticipating where and when you will actually pass. You will learn how to create passing lanes for your teammates and the proper pass depending on the relative positions of you, the defense, and your receiver on the court.

Passing over the top is used when a defender is directly in your passing lane and is almost always preceded by a fake low. Passing under is also used when the defender is directly in the passing lane and usually preceded by a fake high. If the passing lane is relatively open, passing to the side, either left or right, is used with a fake in the opposite direction if necessary.

Passing through the defender is an important concept when you are being guarded closely and cannot use any of the foregoing methods. In this case, you should understand that a defender can block your pass with any part of his or her moving arms or legs. However, the torso, or the trunk of the body, is capable of little movement. In these cases, pass *through* the defender by first giving a strong fake in one of the other directions and passing the ball by the defender with a crisp pass close to his or her body between his or her hips and upper chest. Make this pass quick and extend your arms as far as possible before you release the ball.

Important Note   When you first begin learning passing and shooting it is a good idea to learn it with the same grip each time. In a very short period of time, this grip will become automatic, and for the rest of your playing life, you will reflexively put the ball in that same position.

If you do not learn to grip the ball the same way each time you receive it, it will be very difficult to change that habit and learn to grip it the same way each time at a later date. My suggestion is that you learn to grip the ball with two hands on the natural sides of the ball with your thumbs behind the ball and the fingers comfortably spread each time you receive the basketball. From this position you will best be able to shoot or pass or dribble in any direction.

Skill: The Chest Pass

The chest pass is the most basic of all passes. The master of the chest pass usually has little trouble learning other passing skills. For this reason we will begin and spend more time on this pass.

FACTS OF THE CHEST PASS

1. The chest pass is ideally thrown six to twenty feet from its intended target.

2. The chest pass is thrown with two hands from the chest and should go straight to the receiver with backspin and little arc.

3. The chest pass wastes as little motion as possible using the hands and wrists. This makes it difficult for the defense to anticipate when and where the pass is going.

4. The chest pass can and should be faked often to add deceptiveness.

Drill PR-2: Grip and Release

1. Lie down on your back. Hold the ball with your hands on the sides and your thumbs behind the ball. If your hands are small, slide them slightly behind the ball for better leverage and control.

Be sure that your thumbs are pointing upward at an angle toward the other hand. The thumbs should not be pointing at each other. The thumb and forefinger of each hand should form a U.

Your hands should be relaxed and slightly cupped so that your palm only brushes against the ball. Your elbows are in and bent, and the ball is in front of your chest, held firmly by the pads of the fingertips (Fig. 4-2a).

2. As your arms extend directly upward, your palms should rotate away from you. When your arms are fully extended, snap your wrists outward. You should be able to feel the ball roll off the thumb, index, and middle fingers of both hands. The ball should go straight up with some backspin or rotation.

3. After the release of the ball, your arms should be fully extended, with the fingers pointing upward, the backs of your hands facing each other, and the thumbs pointing toward your feet (Fig. 4-2b). Catch the ball as it returns.

4. Repeat twenty times.

POINTS OF EMPHASIS

- Is there backspin on the ball? If not, check your grip and release.
- Is the ball rotating evenly? It should rotate a few times and come back into your hands in the same position as it left. The ball should not spin backward rapidly. This will result in a weak forward pass that is as hard to handle as a pass with no rotation. Too much spin on the ball usually means that the passer is using too much wrist and fingers and not enough extension from the arms.
- Is the ball going straight up and back down into your hands? If not, check and make sure that your elbows are in, your hands are evenly on the sides or slightly behind the ball, your arms are extending at the same time, your wrists are both snapping with equal strength, and you are following through with arms and hands. The most common fault is to slip the dominant hand slightly farther behind or under the ball to compensate for a weaker "off" hand.

CHEST PASS CHECKPOINTS

1. Feet are spread about a shoulder width apart, with the right foot slightly forward and both feet pointed straight ahead.

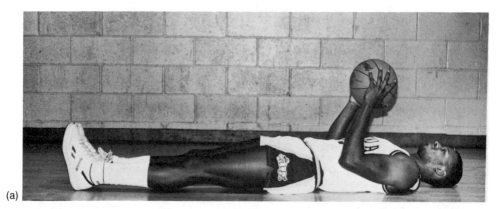

(a)

(b)

Figure 4-2 (a) Chest Pass Grip and (b) Chest Pass Release

2. Knees are bent comfortably.
3. Waist is bent slightly forward, back is straight but relaxed, and your weight is balanced on the balls of your feet.
4. Head is up and you are looking straight ahead.
5. Hands are on the sides and slightly behind the ball. The fingers are comfortably spread.
6. The thumbs are behind the ball and pointing upward at an angle toward the top of the opposite hand. The thumb and the index finger of each hand should form a U. The palms should only brush the ball.

7. The ball is held firmly by the pads of the fingertips and sometimes the heel of each hand.
8. The elbows are in close to the body and bent.

The chest pass is made from the wrists by quickly snapping the thumbs down and out at the same time the elbows fully extend and the passer steps forward with the right foot in the direction of the pass.

9. The ball should roll off the thumb and index and middle fingers, imparting backspin or rotation to the ball as the passer follows through.
10. The follow-through is completed by finishing the step forward as the arms continue to separate, fully extended with the palms facing outward with the thumbs down.
11. The pass should be crisp and straight and with little arc.
12. Most chest passes should be made from chest to chest. The receiver should receive the ball in the chest area, below the shoulders and above the waist.

CHEST PASS RELEASE AND FOLLOW-THROUGH CHECKPOINTS

1. The arms straighten as you step forward; the ball is released when the arms are fully extended in the direction of the receiver or target.
2. The wrists are snapped quickly, forcing the thumbs down and outward. The palms turn outward.
3. The ball rolls off the fingertips of the thumb and index and middle fingers, adding backspin or rotation to the pass.
4. The passer follows through by continuing to step toward the target as the arms continue to separate, fully extended, with the palms facing outward with the thumbs down.
5. The pass should be crisp and travel parallel to the floor.

Drill PR-3

The chest pass can be executed with either foot stepping forward. When appropriate, it can even be performed without stepping toward the target. We will first learn this pass using the left foot as the pivot foot because this is the most common case in game situations.

1. Make a six-inch-square target on a wall level to your chest (see Figure 4-3). Stand back ten feet facing the wall.

2. Execute the chest pass by stepping forward with the right foot and passing the ball to the target on the wall. (See Figures 4-4a, 4-4b, 4-4c, and 4-4d.)

Did the ball go into the square? Keep practicing.

Is the ball going straight? If not, check to see if you are stepping directly toward the target and following through to the target. Often a young player has a weak nondominant hand and arm. This may cause him unconsciously to slip the stronger (dominant) hand farther behind the ball to compensate for the weaker arm. Work on strengthening both arms and executing this pass correctly.

Figure 4-3 Six-Inch-Square Passing Target

Figure 4-4 (a) Chest Pass Stance and Grip, (b) Chest Pass Step, (c) Chest Pass Release, and (d) Chest Pass Follow-Through

(a)

(b)

(c)

(d)

Is there backspin on the ball? Make sure you snap the wrists so that the thumbs go down and outward and the ball rolls off the thumb and index and middle fingers.

Is the pass crisp and parallel to the floor? If not, you may need to strengthen your hands and wrists. Start doing fingertip pushups and squeezing rubber balls.

You may get a little extra snap on your passes if you extend your wrist a little forward and down just before you begin to extend your arms. This will cause your thumbs to rotate on top of the ball just before you extend your arms. Be careful that you do not allow your elbows to rotate out as you roll your wrists forward.

3. Practice your receiving by:

a. *Jumping to the ball* after you have stepped forward with your right foot and passed the ball.

b. *Bending your knees* and turning both palms out with fingers pointing up.

c. *Making your hands* "soft" as you catch the ball by spreading your fingers, and relaxing them, slightly cupping your hands and giving a little when the ball arrives to absorb the shock.

d. *Seeing the ball* into your hands. Do not take your eyes off the ball until it is in your hands.

4. Repeat fifty times or until you can pass the ball twenty times consecutively into the target square.

Skill: The Push Pass

The two-handed push pass is very similar to the chest pass. The big difference lies in the release. The push pass is used when the passer needs to get a pass to a teammate quickly. Therefore, the ball is released with a quick snap of the fingers and wrist. The elbows do not necessarily extend all the way on this pass.

The ball can be held anywhere from above the waist to eye level, and from the left, center, or right of the body. The fingers are comfortably spread on each side of the ball with the thumbs directly behind the ball. The body is balanced with the knees bent, elbows bent and in, and the head up.

The pass is accomplished by a quick snap of the fingers and wrists with the elbows not necessarily extended (fully). The palms should face the receiver after the release of the ball. Whenever possible, the passer should step toward the receiver as he or she releases the ball.

The pass is effective up to about twenty feet and can be used as either a straight or bounce pass.

A touch pass is a push pass that is executed very quickly. The ball is caught and passed in one quick motion. This is a pass only used by the most accomplished and experienced players because it takes great timing, skill, and judgment.

Drill PR-4

    1. Make a six-inch-square target on a wall at your chest level.

    2. Face the wall from ten feet and throw a two-handed push pass from chest level, stepping forward with the right foot, to the target square.

    3. Repeat twenty times or until you can pass the ball ten times consecutively into the target square.

    4. Repeat steps 1–3 using a two-handed push pass from:

    a. *Just to the right* of the right shoulder.

    b. *Just to the left* of the left shoulder.

    c. *Just below eye level* and center of the body.

    5. Repeat steps 1–4 by passing, using head and head-and-shoulder fakes in the opposite direction and alternate your pivot foot on each pass.

POINTS OF EMPHASIS

- Your head is up and the ball is well protected at all times.
- The pass is executed quickly with as little motion as possible.

Skill: The One-Handed Push Pass

The one-handed push pass is identical to the two-handed push pass except for the release. Usually the two-handed push pass becomes a one-handed push pass when it is released from the side of the body.

The passer, when using the one-handed push pass will rotate the right hand behind the ball when passing from his or her right side, and only use the left hand to support and protect the ball on the pass. From the left side, the passer will rotate the left hand behind the ball and use the right hand for support and protection.

Drill PR-5

    1. Make a six-inch-square target on a wall at your chest level.

    2. Face the wall from ten feet holding the ball at chest level with one hand on each side of the ball as though you were going to throw a two-handed chest pass.

    3. Take one side step to your right with your right foot while still facing the wall. At the same time, slide your right hand behind the ball. The ball should now be about a foot to the right and slightly above your right hip.

    4. Practice the right-handed push pass to the target until you can hit the target ten times in a row.

5. Repeat steps 1–4 stepping to the left and passing with the left hand.

POINT OF EMPHASIS

- The release of the ball may or may not involve full extension of the passing arm and backspin on the ball. This will depend on the circumstances under which the pass is thrown.

Skill: The Bounce Pass

Bounce passes can be thrown with one or two hands from the chest or from either side of the body at various heights.

Bounce passes should be aimed to bounce about two-thirds of the way between the passer to the receiver. The ball should reach the receiver at waist level. However, the passer must take into account the nature of the court surface, height from which the pass is thrown, and spin on the ball.

Some of the new synthetic surfaces "grab" the ball and cause it to bounce higher while other new surfaces are slick and cause the ball to skip and stay low off the bounce. If you are unfamiliar with a surface, take the time before the game to throw some different types of bounce passes so you will know how the ball will respond during the game. Also remember that outdoor surfaces like concrete and macadam usually "grab" the bounce, but if the surface is very well worn, it can become smooth so that the ball will skip or slide on a bounce pass.

If a ball is bounced too close to a receiver, it comes up fast and low, which makes it very difficult to handle. If the pass is bounced too far from the receiver, it may lose too much speed. This will cause it to float and make it easy to intercept. Even if the pass is not intercepted or deflected, it will be too high for the receiver to handle smoothly.

A bounce pass, when thrown correctly, will arrive at the same height as it was thrown. In other words, a bounce pass from waist level will come up to waist level on the receiver, if thrown properly. This is a particularly important point to remember when feeding the ball into the post.

Most bounce passes have spin on them. This is important because the ball will react with the floor, depending on what kind of spin it has. For example, two-handed chest passes usually have backspin on them. When the ball hits the floor, it will tend to slow down as the floor absorbs some of its energy and bounce up because of the backspin. Two-handed stride passes are usually released with overspin so the ball loses little momentum after it is bounced and tends to jump toward its target. Hook and baseball passes tend to have side spins and react somewhere in between the backspin and the overspin. However, one-handed passes tend to vary from player to player, and you will have to learn how your passes spin. Once learned and practiced, spin can give you greater control of your bounce passes.

Bounce passes should be thrown crisply, not too hard and not too softly. Bounce passes thrown too hard often bounce erratically and are difficult to control. Bounce passes thrown too softly may die as the floor absorbs their impact. Again, you must experiment to find the ideal speed for your bounce passes.

The bounce pass is particularly effective when thrown to a teammate cutting to the basket. The bounce gives the cutter an extra split second to time the pass, and it is easier to receive because it comes up from the floor and is softer after the bounce.

The bounce pass is also very effective when passing the ball into the post or three-second lane. In these situations, the defense is usually very tight. A fake high and a bounce pass is often the pass least likely to be deflected or stolen.

The bounce pass can most easily be pinpointed to a low target where a posting receiver can handle it easily. It is particularly useful when you are closely guarded, especially by a bigger player. When it is difficult to throw around or over an opponent, a strong ball fake high and a quick bounce pass is almost impossible to stop. This is because the taller a defensive player, the higher off the floor his or her hands will be. Therefore, there is usually an opening down low for a pass. (See Figure 4-5.)

Figure 4-5 Bounce Pass

Drill PR-6

    1. Make a six-inch-square target on a wall at your waist level.

    2. Face the wall from ten feet and throw a two-handed chest pass on one bounce so that the ball hits the wall in the target square.

    3. Repeat fifty times or until you can pass the ball twenty times consecutively into the target square. Alternate stepping forward with the left and right foot.

    4. Repeat steps 2 and 3 from a distance of fifteen feet from the wall.

    5. Perform Drill PR-3 using the bounce pass.

    6. Perform Drill PR-5 using the bounce pass.

POINTS OF EMPHASIS

- Use all the appropriate principles of good chest passing.
- The ball should bounce two-thirds of the way to the wall.

Skill: The Stride Pass

The stride pass is thrown with two hands after stepping to the right or left with either a side step or a crossover step. It is thrown with both hands, and most of the power is generated from the wrists, but the extension of the arms (straightening of the elbows) can provide some power.

The pass can be released anywhere from between knee and shoulder height depending on the positions of the passer's defender and the target of the receiver.

The pass is almost always a bounce pass with a range of between four and about fifteen feet. It can be very effective when you need to extend yourself to throw around a defender who is guarding you closely. Because the ball is held and passed with two hands, it is easy, safe, and effective to fake at least once before throwing the stride pass.

The crossover stride pass is particularly effective against pressure defenses. It is executed by stepping across and in front of your pivot foot and dropping your shoulder to protect the ball, thereby placing your body between your defender and the ball.

The stride pass is often used from the perimeter to feed the ball into the post.

Drill PR-7

    1. Face the wall ten feet away in the Triple-Threat Position (discussed in Chapter 5) with the left foot as your pivot. Hold the ball firmly with both hands on your right hip.

2. Take one step to your right with your right foot. As you step, lower the left shoulder and bend your knees. The ball remains on your right hip. Your right toe, after the step, should be pointing at a 45-degree angle to your right. Be sure that the step to your right is not so long that you could not, if necessary, return to the Triple-Threat Position.

3. Extend the ball out with both hands to your right by first raising your left elbow to protect the ball and then straightening your arms for the pass (Fig. 4-6a).

4. Bounce pass to the waist-high six-inch-square target on the wall by snapping your wrists and fingers toward the target when your arms are fully extended.

5. Practice this pass releasing the ball from knee, waist, and shoulder levels until you can hit your target ten times in a row from each level.

6. Repeat steps 1–5 using various fakes before you pass:

a. Fake high, pass low.

b. Fake low, pass low.

c. Fake low, fake high, pass low.

7. Repeat steps 1–6 using the right foot as your pivot foot and stepping to the left.

Drill PR-8

1. Face the wall ten feet away in the Triple-Threat Position with the left foot as your pivot. Hold the ball firmly with both hands on your left hip.

2. Take a crossover step with your right foot in front of your left, dropping your right shoulder as you step. Do not make the step so long that you could not, if necessary, return to your Triple-Threat Position. Your head is up, looking at the wall.

3. Extend the ball out with both hands to your left by first raising your right elbow to protect the ball and then straightening your arms for the pass (Fig. 4-6b).

4. Bounce pass to the waist-high six-inch-square target on the wall by snapping your wrist and fingers toward the target when your arms are fully extended.

5. Practice this pass releasing the ball from knee, waist, and shoulder levels until you can hit your target ten times in a row from each level. Depending on the situation, this pass can be thrown with the arms at less than full extension.

6. Repeat steps 1–5 using various fakes before you pass:

a. Fake high, pass low.

b. Fake low, pass low.

c. Fake low, fake high, pass low.

7. Repeat steps 1–6 using the right foot as your pivot foot.

8. *The reverse pivot*—Using the left foot as your pivot, fake a stride pass to your right. Do a 180-degree reverse pivot on the ball of your left foot into the same position as though you had done a front crossover step to your left. (See Drill F-14.)

9. Repeat steps 3–7 using the reverse pivot.

(a)

(b)

Figure 4-6 (a) Stride Pass,
(b) Crossover Stride Pass, and
(c) Hook Pass

(c)

Skill: The Hook Pass

The hook pass is identical to the stride pass up until the release of the ball. The hook pass is thrown with one hand behind the ball and the arm always fully extended. It is very similar to the stride pass and offers one major advantage and disadvantage.

Advantage: It increases the potential extension on the pass because one arm can reach to a side farther than two.

Disadvantage: You lose some of the control that two hands give you. Once you begin the forward motion on the hook pass you cannot change your mind and pull it back. The stride pass can be faked and pulled back up until the last moment because it is held in two hands.

Drill PR-9

1. Repeat Drills PR-7 and 8, including the regular and crossover steps and the reverse pivot using the hook pass. Do all your faking while the ball is in both hands. (See Figure 4-6c.)

Skill: The Baseball Pass

The baseball pass is used for long passes, especially when your team is looking for the fast break. Because it is a long pass and takes a little longer to throw, it should be thrown only when you have time and the receiver is sufficiently open.

The baseball pass is difficult to throw when you are closely guarded and should not be thrown to a teammate unless he or she is either ahead of the field or is sufficiently distanced from a defensive player so that the pass will not be intercepted. Many smart passers will fake the baseball pass if it is uncertain whether or not the defensive player is in position to make a steal. This forces the defense to react and lets the passer know whether he or she should throw the pass or not.

Another good device for completing the baseball pass, if you have the time, is to fake the pass in the direction opposite the receiver for the purpose of making the defense shift farther away from the intended receiver.

This pass takes considerable strength and coordination. Therefore, most players only learn and practice it with their dominant hand.

Drill PR-10

1. Stand twenty feet from the wall with your left shoulder to the chest-high target with your feet about a shoulder width apart and your right foot as your pivot. Your weight is on the right foot.

Hold the ball two to six inches off the right hip, with your right hand directly behind the ball and your left hand in front. Your fingers are spread comfortably with the hands slightly cupped so the ball is held by the pads of the fingertips and the heel of the hands. The thumb and the index finger of the right hand should form a U or, in other words, the thumb should be pointing slightly up, not horizontal or down.

Your elbows are out to protect the ball, and your head is up. Your knees and waist are slightly bent. You should feel as if you are ready to throw a baseball.

2. With both hands, raise the ball straight up to at least the level of your right ear (Fig. 4-7a). Step forward with the left foot and throw the ball with the right arm (Fig. 4-7b). Do not release the left hand until the right arm starts forward.

3. Snap the thumb of your right hand down and away with the palm turning outward on the release of the ball so it will go straight instead of curving to the left (Fig. 4-7c).

You hold the ball with two hands as long as possible for three reasons:

a. To protect the ball from a defender.

b. To give the ball more support for a longer time.

c. To allow you to change your mind right up to the last split second in case you decide not to throw the pass.

(a)   (b)   (c)

Figure 4-7 (a) Baseball Pass Grip, (b) Baseball Pass, and (c) Baseball Pass Follow-Through

4. Follow through on your baseball pass by completing your step and fully extending your right arm and hand toward the target. Your eyes should never leave the target (Fig. 4-7c). Players with less size and strength will find themselves dipping the ball or extending it farther back just before they begin their forward motion on the pass. This might be necessary for young players, but by dipping and extending the ball farther behind you, the ball becomes more exposed to the defense. It also will take longer to throw the pass.

5. Repeat this twenty times or until you can baseball pass into the chest-high square target ten times consecutively.

6. Repeat steps 1–5 increasing the distance of the passes up to fifty feet.

POINTS OF EMPHASIS

- The ball is held with two hands for as long as possible.
- Be sure you follow through by snapping your thumb down and away on the release of the pass.

Skill: The Overhead Pass

This is an effective pass for perimeter players because it is quick and can easily be thrown over the defense into the post area. Post players use the overhead pass after they pivot because they are usually tall and find that holding the ball up keeps the ball safe, and they can easily shoot or pass quickly from that position. The ball can be held from the forehead to over the head with the arms almost fully extended depending on the player and the situation.

The hands are placed on the sides of the ball slightly toward the back with the fingers comfortably spread and pointing up. The thumbs are well behind the ball and pointing toward the top of the opposite hand (Fig. 4-8a).

The ball is released with a quick snap of the wrists and fingers and a follow-through toward the target with the arms fully extended and a step (Fig. 4-8b). It is important that the ball not be pulled back over the head before the release. This would "telegraph" the pass to an alert defender.

Drill PR-11

1. Make a six-inch-square target on the wall at your chest level.
2. Face the wall from ten feet with the ball held at the level of the

Figure 4-8 (a) Overhead Pass Grip and (b) Overhead Pass Follow-Through

(a)   (b)

forehead. Your hands are on the sides of the ball slightly toward the back with the fingers comfortably spread and pointing up. The thumbs are well behind the ball and pointing toward the top of the opposite hand.

3. Pass the ball with a quick snap of the wrists and fingers. At the same time step forward with the right foot and fully extend both arms toward the target, allowing the palms to turn out naturally.

4. Repeat until you can pass the ball ten times consecutively into the target square.

5. Repeat steps 1–4 with the ball placed just above your head and then above your head with the arms almost fully extended. Practice, incorporating passing fakes in all directions and stepping with the right foot, stepping with the left foot, and without stepping.

POINT OF EMPHASIS

- This is a pass that relies on a quick release. Do not wind up or pull the ball back over your head, or the defense will be able to anticipate and steal the pass.

Skill: The Jump Pass

The jump pass can be especially effective when guarded closely and is usually preceded by a strong pass fake low.

The jump pass is very similar to the overhead pass. It is executed by first faking a pass low, taking a strong two-footed jump straight up, and, after fully extending both arms, making a crisp two-handed overhead pass. The grip and release of the ball for the jump pass is identical to that of the overhead pass. (See Figures 4-9a and 4-9b.)

Drill PR-12

1. Make a six-inch-square target on the wall at your chest level.

2. Face the wall from ten feet with the ball held at the level of your forehead. Use the same grip as in the overhead pass. (See Drill PR-11.)

3. Jump off both feet at the same time (two-foot takeoff) and extend your arms fully over your head. At the top of your jump, without pulling the ball back behind your head, pass the ball with a quick snap of the wrists and fingers. Your hands should follow through toward the target with the arms fully extended and the palms turned outward.

4. Repeat until you can pass the ball ten times consecutively into the square target.

5. Repeat steps 1–4 alternating passing fakes low and to each side before the jump pass.

(a)   (b)

Figure 4-9 (a) Jump Pass Grip and (b) Jump Pass Follow-Through

POINTS OF EMPHASIS

- Be sure that your arms are fully extended over your head before you pass.
- Do not wind up or pull the ball back over your head, or the pass will take too much time to throw.

Important Note Practice this pass to the chest-high target. However, in game situations, the jump pass is often used when under extreme defensive pressure, and, to pass over the pressure, you may have to release the ball early, thereby passing to a higher target.

Skill: Passing Off the Dribble

Guards, especially point or "1" guards, have to develop the ability to pass off the dribble. This, of course, requires excellent dribbling skills but also a combination of sound footwork and passing fundamentals.

The important things to remember when passing off the dribble are:

- Keep your head up on the dribble.
- Keep the dribble under control—the lower the dribble, the easier and quicker the pass will be.
- Protect the ball at all times and periodically use head and shoulder fakes to keep the defense "honest."
- Bend your knees and get as low as possible on your last dribble to get better balance for your stop.
- A smaller last step before your stride stop will add to your body control and balance.
- Use the stride stop with the inside foot (the foot closer to the defensive player) as your pivot.
- Protect the ball on your stop and hold the ball firmly with both hands, elbows out, and a low center of gravity.
- From the stride stop position, you must be ready to pass, square up to the basket or reverse pivot.

Drill PR-13

In this drill we will throw different types of passes to the six-inch targets on the wall. Remember that this means the target is at waist level for all bounce passes and chest level for all other passes.

1. Dribble slowly with your right hand, moving to your right, parallel to the wall ten feet away.

2. Stride stop using your left foot as your pivot and execute each of the following passes ten times throwing the pass to the appropriate target:

a. Square up to the wall in a Triple-Threat Position and throw a:

(1) Chest pass.

(2) Chest bounce pass.

(3) Two-handed push pass.

(4) Two-handed overhead pass.

(5) Two-handed jump pass.

b. Repeat (a) with at least one pass fake before the pass.

c. Do not square up after your stride stop. Your left shoulder should be facing the wall.

Execute a:

(1) Stride bounce pass.

(2) Hook bounce pass.

(3) One-handed push pass with the right hand.

d. Repeat (c) with one high-pass fake before the pass.

e. Repeat (c), fake a stride bounce pass, reverse pivot 180 degrees on the ball of your left foot so that your right shoulder is facing the wall and throw a:

(1) Stride bounce pass.

(2) Hook bounce pass.

(3) One-handed push pass with the left hand.

3. Repeat step 2 dribbling to your left hand using a stride stop with the right foot as your pivot.

4. Repeat steps 1–3 increasing your speed to half and three-quarters speed when you can execute each preceding level smoothly, safely and with eight out of ten accuracy for each pass.

POINTS OF EMPHASIS

- Your head must always be up.
- The ball must always be protected.
- Shorten the length of your steps, lower your dribble, and bend your knees as much as necessary to be in complete control of your body.
- Use head, head-and-shoulder, and passing fakes regularly to keep the defense from being able to anticipate your moves.

ADVANCED PASSING AND RECEIVING SKILLS: RECEIVING THE BAD PASS

The skills involved in reception of a poorly thrown or deflected pass are important simply because they happen often in game situations, and, to be a complete player, you must be able to handle the errant pass as well as the easy one.

The first thing to remember is to *get the ball*. When a pass is thrown off target, you must forget, temporarily, any of your anticipatory thoughts about what you were planning to do with the ball when you received it. You must concentrate completely on securing the ball.

This is the crucial part of being a good "bad" pass catcher: Concentrate first on gaining possession of the ball because an errant pass is harder to catch. Often you will have to fight a defensive player for it. Even with an errant pass, you should always try to use two hands on the catch.

When the ball is thrown low, below your waist, or on a short bounce:

- Bend your knees.
- Turn your hands so that the palms are facing the ball, fingers pointed down and comfortably spread.
- Cup your hands slightly and make them "soft."
- Get your body in front of the pass as much as possible by moving your feet in the direction of the pass.
- See the ball into your hands.
- If the pass is thrown hard or with a great deal of spin, you should block the ball, then grab it, and pull it in to your chest securely. (See Figure 4-10.)

Figure 4-10 Catching the "Bad" Pass

When the pass is thrown too far left or right, high or low, and you can only reach the pass with one hand by jumping to it:

- Spread your fingers comfortably and relax them with the palm facing the ball and slightly cupped.
- Block the ball when it makes contact with your hand, give with the fingers, wrist, and arm so that it softens the momentum or force of the ball. This will make it easier to control or catch.
- Grab the ball as quickly as possible with two hands and pull it into your chest securely.

Drill PR-14

1. From fifteen feet, throw the ball off the wall so that it comes back to you at your feet on the short hop.

2. Practice catching the ball ten times with two hands with the fingers pointed toward the floor, elbows in, and knees bent.

3. Repeat step 2, but:

a. Increase and decrease the distance from the wall.

b. Increase and decrease the speed of the pass so that you have to block some of the passes before you securely tuck the ball into your chest.

4. Repeat steps 1–3 throwing the ball to your left and right so that you have to use the one-handed catching principles.

POINTS OF EMPHASIS

- Errant passes must be viewed as loose balls. This means that you should think only of gaining possession of the ball for your team.
- Always try to get in front of the ball and use two hands when possible.
- The palm should face the ball with the fingers comfortably spread, hands "soft" and slightly cupped.
- See the ball into your hands and give with the fingers, wrist, and arms a little to absorb the shock of the incoming pass.
- Block, don't try to catch, passes that are thrown too hard, wide, low, or high or with too much spin.
- Grab the ball with two hands as soon and quickly as possible and pull the ball securely into your chest with the elbows out and the knees bent.
- Never attempt to dribble a loose ball or errant pass until you have gained full control of the ball.

Skill: The One-Handed Pass

This pass is usually thrown on the move off the dribble. It is one of the leading causes of turnovers and should not be used by the vast majority of players.

The one-handed pass is difficult to control and, once begun, cannot be pulled back. Many professional and some college players make this pass look easy because their hands are so large that they can actually grip the ball in one hand and fake a pass without using the other hand for support. However, most players find the one-handed pass impossible to control. It does, however, have the advantage of being quicker to release, and some superior passers can use it to advantage in carefully considered circumstances:

The pass should be *very* open. A one-handed pass can be easily read by a defender, so be sure that you, the passer, are not closely guarded and the receiver is very open, preferably on the move away from the defense.

Make the pass as quick as possible. Often it is a good idea to give a little head or head-and-shoulder fake in the opposite direction immediately before the one-handed pass.

As with any other pass, be sure that your head is up and your balance excellent and that you throw the pass with authority. A weak one-handed pass is almost certain to fail.

Drill PR-15

1. Begin twenty feet from the wall dribbling with your right hand toward the wall at a 45-degree angle to your right.

2. At a spot fifteen feet from the wall, rotate your right hand to the right or outside of the ball and throw a quickly released bounce pass across your body to the waist-high target to your left on the wall. Practice releasing the ball with first the left and then the right foot forward.

3. Repeat until you can hit the target five times in a row with each foot forward on the release of the pass.

4. Repeat steps 1–3 using a straight pass to the chest-high target.

5. Repeat steps 1–4 dribbling with your left hand and moving toward the wall at a 45-degree angle to your left.

6. Begin twenty feet from the wall dribbling with your right hand at a 45-degree angle to your left.

7. At a spot fifteen feet from the wall, rotate your right hand to the left or inside of the ball and throw a quickly released bounce pass to the waist-high target to your right. Practice releasing the ball with first the left and then the right foot forward.

8. Repeat until you can hit the target five times in a row with each foot forward on the release of the pass.

9. Repeat step 6–8 using a straight pass to the chest-high target.

10. Repeat steps 6–9 dribbling with your left hand and moving toward the wall at a 45-degree angle to your left.

11. Repeat 6 to 10 incorporating head and head-and-shoulder fakes to your left when passing with the right hand and fakes right when passing to your left.

POINTS OF EMPHASIS

- Your head must be up at all times.
- The one-handed pass off the dribble requires great control of the dribble and perfect rhythm and timing.
- Bend your knee a little more just before the pass for extra leverage and control.
- Follow through on your pass and see the ball into the target.

Skill: The One-Handed Behind-the-Back Pass

Everything that was said about the one-handed pass is also true for the one-handed behind-the-back pass. In fact, this is an even more advanced skill that most coaches are reluctant to teach because players have a tendency to use it where a simpler and higher-percentage pass would get the job done. However, the pass, when used properly by a skilled passer, is effective when you have to pass to a teammate who is slightly behind you and not too far away. This commonly occurs on a two-on-one fast break, especially if your teammate is the trailer and in a half-court offense when a teammate comes off a screen behind you. It is very important to understand that the one-handed behind-the-back pass is most appropriate when you are attempting to get the ball to a teammate who is angled behind you and the use of this pass will keep you from having to turn and throw across your body and to the rear.

The pass can be either a straight or bounce pass and usually executed off the dribble. The longer the pass the more difficult it is to control. The one-handed behind-the-back pass should be thrown to a target between six and fifteen feet away to be consistently accurate.

The ball is thrown with one hand and, therefore, cannot be pulled back. Be sure of the pass before you decide to throw it.

Drill PR-16

1. Begin ten feet from the wall dribbling with your right hand parallel to the wall with your left shoulder closest to the wall.

2. When you are one step past the target square and your left foot is forward, pass the ball behind your back straight to the target. As you take your last step with your left foot, the ball should be even with your right hip. Slide your right hand to the outside of the ball and flip the ball behind, and straight across, your back to the target. Your right palm should face the target as the pass is made behind your back, and your fingers should follow through toward the target as you reverse pivot on your right foot. The pass is made with the fingers well spread on the side of the ball with most of the power coming from the snap of the wrist.

3. Repeat until you can hit the target five times in a row.

4. Repeat steps 1–3 using a bounce pass.

5. Repeat steps 1–4 passing with the left hand and reversing the directions for hands and feet.

POINT OF EMPHASIS

- Review the introductory comments and Points of Emphasis in Skill: The One-Handed Pass.

Skill: The Alley-Oop Pass

This pass is only used at the advanced level of very good high school, college, or professional basketball. The pass is thrown high, more often cross-court, when the defender has turned his or her head away from the ball, over the top of the defense, to a teammate cutting to the basket timed so that he or she will receive the pass in the air at the top of a jump. The receiver, who is closing in on the basket, catches the ball and dunks it, or lays it in, all in one motion. This play requires great leaping ability, body balance, and timing.

In terms of the passer, the play requires that the ball reach the receiver well above the rim, at the precise time and spot he or she will be at the top of the jump. Time and experience will help the passer to anticipate this, but the secret of throwing this pass is to pretend it is a shot. This means that you imagine the basket is where you have determined the pass should be received and, with either a one- or two-handed pass, pretend you are "shooting" the ball to that spot. This will produce the proper arc and a soft pass that is easily timed and handled by the receiver.

POINTS OF EMPHASIS

- Pick a spot above the rim where the receiver will be at the top of his or her jump.
- "Shoot" the ball to that spot with a soft, arced pass timing it so that the receiver will receive it at the top of his or her jump.

Skill: Faking and Misdirection Passing

It is important that you develop consistently accurate passing skills. However, it is also necessary that your passing involve a certain amount of deception or the defense will learn to anticipate your passes and either steal or deflect them. You must develop a "poker face" so your eyes and/or expressions do not tip off your next move. Two basic methods of keeping the defense "honest" are:

Faking

Passing fakes
Head fakes
Head and shoulder fakes

Misdirection

Looking in one direction and passing in another
Stepping in one direction and passing in another

Whether you are in the Triple-Threat Position or are dribbling the ball, you should regularly use each method of faking to keep the defense from anticipating your next move. Misdirection passes involve more advanced forms of deception. To use them effectively, you will have to devote much more time to practice than you would with "ordinary" passes. The misdirection pass must be thrown with greater care because it may fool your own teammate. It is also more difficult to throw crisply and accurately. (See Figure 4-11.)

Figure 4-11 Misdirection Pass

DRILLING THE FAKE AND MISDIRECTION PASS

1. Practice your passing skills in each of the drills in this chapter until you have mastered them.
2. Begin incorporating each of the fakes into the drills.
3. After faking has been successfully integrated and mastered for each passing skill, begin experimenting with misdirection passing, first from the Triple-Threat Position and later off the dribble.

WORKOUT, EVALUATION, AND PROGRESS CHARTS

Table 4-1 Passing Workout—15 Minutes

Warmup		
DRILL	*TIME*	*INSTRUCTIONS*
PR-3	1 minute(s)	
PR-4	1 "	
PR-5	1 "	30 seconds with each hand
PR-6	2 "	
PR-7	1 "	30 seconds from each side
PR-8	1 "	" "
PR-9	1 "	" "
PR-10	1 "	
PR-11	1 "	
PR-12	1 "	
PR-13	2 "	1 minute off dribble with each hand
PR-14	1 "	
PR-15	1 "	30 seconds with each hand
Cooldown		

Table 4-2 Passing Workout—30 Minutes

Warmup		
DRILL	*TIME*	*INSTRUCTIONS*
PR-2	1 minute(s)	
PR-3	2 "	
PR-4	2 "	
PR-5	2 "	1 minute with each hand
PR-6	3 "	
PR-7	2 "	1 minute from each side
PR-8	2 "	" "
PR-9	2 "	" "
PR-10	2 "	
PR-11	2 "	
PR-12	2 "	
PR-13	4 "	2 minutes off dribble with each hand
PR-14	2 "	
PR-15	1 "	1 minute with each hand
PR-16	1 "	" "
Cooldown		

Table 4-3 Passing Self-Evaluation and Improvement Test

DRILL	NUMBER OF PASSES	SCORE
PR-3	20	No. in target square
PR-4	20	" "
PR-5	20 (10 with each hand)	" "
PR-6	20	" "
PR-7	20 (10 from each side)	" "
PR-8	20 " "	" "
PR-9	20 " "	" "
PR-10	20	" "
PR-11	20	" "
PR-12	20	" "
PR-13	20 (10 off dribble with each hand)	" "
PR-15	20 (10 with each hand)	" "
PR-16	20 " "	" "

Table 4-4 Personal Passing and Receiving Progress Chart

DATE

Drill																	
PR-3																	
PR-4																	
PR-5																	
PR-6																	
PR-7																	
PR-8																	
PR-9																	
PR-10																	
PR-11																	
PR-12																	
PR-13																	
PR-15																	
PR-16																	

CHAPTER FIVE

SHOOTING

Ultimately, all the fundamentals of basketball lead to the shot. After all, the only way you can score, and win, in a basketball game is to put the ball in the basket. Each field goal, a shot made from the floor during play, is worth 2 points, and each foul shot made is worth 1 point. However, an infinite variety of shots can be taken under an endless number of circumstances.

As a player, you must first learn and master all the shooting skills. Second, you must integrate as many shots as possible into your "game." That means understanding which shots are best for you based on your physical makeup and ability. Third, you must learn the right time to take those shots that make up your "game."

Many coaches believe that when all is said and done, the game of basketball can be reduced to whether or not you can "put the ball in the hoop." This is not to say that all the other fundamentals—footwork, dribbling, passing, and rebounding—are unimportant. It simply means that all these other skills will go for naught if you can't score, because a game is decided in favor of the team that scores the most points.

As a result, shooting has received by far the most attention and is practiced much more than any other fundamental area of basketball. While it is true that shooting is the most complex area and takes the most time to perfect, it is also the most glamorous fundamental and easily the most fun to practice. Unlike the other fundamental areas, shooting has been written about extensively, and every coach seems to have his or her own system of teaching it.

Because shooting is much more than a single skill, we will carefully break it down into three developmental phases. Phase I emphasizes the form and rhythm of the basic shots. *You should not move from phase I to phase II until you have completely mastered every aspect of phase I.* Phase II integrates footwork and dribbling skills with shooting so that you learn to shoot with movement. Phase III requires mastery of both phases I and II because it teaches the one-on-one moves from the guard, forward, and center positions.

PHASE I: SPOT SHOOTING, LAYUPS, HOOK SHOTS, AND JUMP SHOOTING

To begin, a player must concentrate on the form and rhythm of the basic shots in basketball. Phase I is unquestionably the most important aspect of shooting and must be practiced every day, even after you have moved on to phases II and III. Learning good shooting form and rhythm is an important investment in your game. It must be constantly reinforced. Unfortunately, too many young players develop poor shooting habits that result in awkward and fundamentally unsound shooting styles. Improper shooting form is a very difficult thing to correct later in a player's career, so it is crucial that you learn the proper form from the beginning. It is also important to understand that all future success in shooting will be dependent on how well you master phase I.

PHASE II: SHOOTING ON THE MOVE

This phase incorporates shooting with many of the footwork and dribbling skills learned in the preceding chapters, like catching a pass on the run, stopping and shooting, and shooting off the dribble.

PHASE III: ONE-ON-ONE MOVES

This phase teaches the various moves a player can make on a defender from the guard, forward, and center positions.

1. *Guard positions*—moves from the Triple-Threat Position (see Triple-

Threat Postion: Shooting Off the Pass) and off the dribble. Most guard moves are taught from the center of the court from SS # 13, 14, 15, 18, 19, 20, 21, and 22.

2. *Forward positions*—moves from the Triple-Threat Position and off the dribble. Most forward moves are taught from the sides of the court from SS #11, 12, 16, and 17.

3. *Center positions*—moves facing the basket and back to the basket from the low-, medium-, and high-post areas.

It must be emphasized that every player should learn moves from each of the foregoing positions. Many players will play more than one position, and every player will, at least occasionally, find himself or herself in a position where a variety of one-on-one moves will be effective.

THE DIFFERENCE BETWEEN A SHOOTER AND A SCORER

A shooter scores when he or she has the open shot or opportunity, while the scorer cannot only shoot, but can also shoot on the move and create his or her own opportunities to score. This may sound like doubletalk, but it has a profound meaning in the context of this chapter and its developmental system.

If you learn phase I (the form and rhythm of the basic four shots) well, you can develop into a shooter. You will be able to convert a high percentage of your shots as long as you take only those open shots that come with little or no defensive pressure and require a minimum of movement.

Becoming a scorer requires a great deal more work because you must learn phase II, shooting on the move, and phase III, one-on-one moves. The degree to which you master these skills, combined with your natural ability, will determine how good a scorer you will be. Development of phase II requires mastery of phase I, and phase III cannot be mastered without first mastering I and II. The secret, if there is one, is to be blessed with a great deal of natural ability, learn the concepts, and practice hard enough to perfect the skills.

SHOOTING

All players love to shoot, but shooting takes a great deal of practice. First, there are several different kinds of basic shots that have to be learned:

• The spot shot.

- The layup.
- The hook shot.
- The jump shot.

Second, players must integrate many of the previously learned footwork and dribbling skills with their shooting so they can score on the move as well as standing still. Shooting requires more concentration, commitment, dedication, and repetition than any other skill. This is because each shot must be precise, and there are so many different shots that must be learned standing still, moving, and shooting off the dribble. Shooting is precise because, to be successful, you must be able to throw a 30-inch round ball into a 56.5-inch round metal ring, 10 feet off the floor from various distances and angles while opponents do everything within the rules of the game to hamper you. Only the most disciplined and determined players are willing to work hard and long enough to master all the necessary shooting skills.

SHOOTING SPOTS

The game of basketball has evolved to the point where coaches and players know which spots the majority of shots will be taken from in various situations. In addition, players who practice shots from particular spots will develop more confidence in their shooting, especially when they know that those will be the same spots they will be shooting from most often in actual games. For these reasons, we will use Figure 5-1 to indicate the spots from which you will practice your shooting.

A WORD TO THE SHOOTING WISE

Before you begin learning to shoot, read and digest the following advice:

1. Concentrate on perfecting your form. Form is the first key to developing a consistent shot—one that you can rely on time after time to be accurate.
2. Perfect your form by practicing each shot over and over again from spots close to the basket. Good form develops by practicing from short range; it tends to break down as you move away from the basket because of the need to generate more power. This is especially true for young players.
3. Learn to concentrate on every shot you take in practice as though it were a game. From the time you begin each shot until the ball goes in the bas-

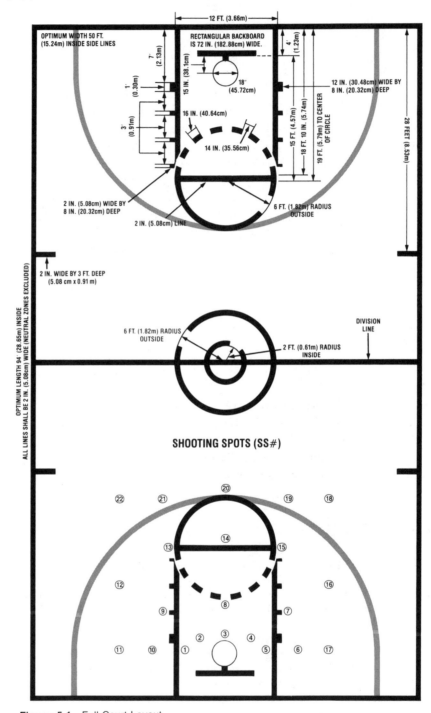

Figure 5-1 Full-Court Layout

ket, use mental visualization to convince yourself totally that the shot is going into the basket. Never practice shooting casually or while thinking about something else. A good shooter always thinks positively.

4. As you develop form, begin thinking about rhythm. Every good shooter learns to feel a rhythm in his or her shot. Rhythm is a sense of timing, like an inner musical tune a good shooter can hear each time he or she shoots.

5. As you develop your shooting game, body balance and proper shot release become more and more important. They are the hardest aspects to maintain as you learn to shoot more quickly, on the move, farther out from the basket, and with greater defensive pressure.

6. Developing quickness and range on your shot will come with practice, physical maturity, and experience. Be patient. Master form and rhythm from shooting spots close to the basket. Increased quickness and range on your shot will come in time. Nothing ruins more young shooters than practicing to shoot from too far out too soon.

7. Use the *Personal Shooting Progress Chart* at the end of this chapter and work as hard as necessary to improve your scores *every day*!

CARDINAL PRINCIPLES OF SHOOTING

We will begin learning about shooting by discussing ten cardinal principles:

- Form.
- Release and follow-through.
- Balance.
- Rhythm.
- Concentration.
- Confidence.
- Relaxation.
- Force.
- Sighting (point of aim).
- Arc.

Form Form is stressed for several reasons. Your shooting will be most consistent when you shoot exactly the same way each time. That's common sense. In addition, there are mechanical principles governing the most efficient and reliable uses of the muscles, joints, and levers of the body. In this chapter the most appropriate of these principles are discussed and applied to shooting. These constitute the rules of good shooting form. The better able you are consistently to repeat the good form principles on your shot, the better chance you have of being a good shooter.

Release and Follow-Through   The release of the shot is really a combination of concentration, form, and balance. The more defensive pressure and the more the shooter is moving, the more important this component impacts on the chances of success. The shooter must release the ball off the fingertips of the shooting hand with a snap of the wrist as the elbow reaches full extension. The fingers of the hand follow through toward the basket, and then the hand relaxes and goes limp.

In game situations with the pressures of an aggressive defense, this requires a great deal of concentration because the shot must be released *without* tensing up. This means you must have the ability to relax even while you are totally concentrating. If the shot is taken on the move, added concentration and agility is needed to balance the body, especially the head and shoulders, on the release of the shot.

Balance   The importance of good balance on your shot cannot be overemphasized. When you first learn to shoot—with the spot shot and foul shot—balance is built into the form. Even the jump shot, layup, and hook shot have most of the balance built into the form. Balance often becomes the most important component in your shot in those situations in which you are on the move and do not have the opportunity to shoot where and when you want to. It is in game situations that you must concentrate on stabilizing yourself just before you release the shot. This all begins with mastering the proper form and release of each shot and developing confidence and the ability to concentrate.

Balance on most of your shots will be perfected by following these guidelines:

1. Your legs should be under you with your feet spread a little less than a shoulder width apart, with the knees and waist bent and the head up.
2. Your center of gravity in preparation for your shot should be as low as possible while you still feel comfortable.
3. Your upper body should be square to the basket with the right side slightly forward and the head motionless and centered.
4. The position of your head is a key to your balance on a shot. Keep your eyes riveted on your sighting point on the rim, and your head centered and steady as you shoot. Even when the jump on your shot is off to a side or you are fouled on your shot, a steady head will keep you as balanced as possible throughout the shot.
5. Release the ball and follow through smoothly on your shot without losing concentration.
6. Land in a balanced position with your feet spread about a shoulder width apart; knees and waist bent; head up, centered, and steady; and weight slightly forward on the balls of both feet. If you land balanced,

there is every probability that you maintained good balance during your shot. In addition, a balanced landing is important because it enables you to follow your shot in case of a miss, to avoid charging into a defensive player and being charged with a foul and/or being injured, and to get back on defense quickly.

7. Concentration: Maintain concentration on your shot from start to finish. Loss of balance begins where concentration leaves off.

Rhythm   Rhythm is an important concept that refers to the timing, smoothness, and synchronization of your movements. Good rhythm is impossible without good balance and body control. On each of your shots, perfect rhythm comes when the ball is released at the top of your jump simultaneous with the full extension of your ankles, knees, waist, and elbow.

Concentration   There are few words that are used as often by coaches as concentration. Yet, its definition and, more important, its application is rarely explained.

Concentration is synonymous with single-mindedness or focus: every fiber of your being is focused on whatever you're supposed to be doing. For example, if you are shooting a foul shot, you are thinking of nothing but making that shot—eyes are riveted on your sight point of the rim, and you are going through the ritual you have developed: relax, bounce the ball three times, take a deep breath, find the familiar seam on the ball for your grip, check your stance, bend your knees, set the ball just below the eyes, picture the ball going through the basket, shoot, and follow through. When you concentrate fully, there is absolutely nothing else on your mind but a picture of what you have to do to complete the task at hand successfully. The great concentrators swear that they never hear the crowd.

Confidence   Coaches are always telling their players to be confident in their shooting: "*Shoot with confidence. You must believe that your shot is going to go in. Never shoot when in doubt.*" But how do you develop confidence? This quality is probably one-fourth natural ability, one-fourth practice, and one-half character.

To be a shooter you must be the kind of person who is not easily discouraged and has a deep belief in yourself in general, not just on the basketball court. Why? Because everyone, even the best shooters, miss and have off days. Confidence is a quality of character that gives you the strength, the inner reserve, and the drive to keep trying until you succeed because you know, deep down, that you will succeed. Superior shooters seem to share certain personality characteristics. Often they are driven to succeed, perfectionists, and good concentrators (at least on the basketball court) and are very goal oriented. If you have some natural ability, are willing to practice hard, and share the same personality traits, you can probably develop into a good, confident shooter.

Relaxation Although relaxation is a part of form, release, and follow-through, it is so important that we must discuss it as a single issue. The ability to relax on the release and follow-through of a shot is difficult because many muscles are contracting and relaxing during the rhythmic, coordinated movements of the shot. Now, at the last possible moment, when the pressure is at its greatest, you have to systematically "let go," releasing the ball softly with a relaxed motion.

This requires enormous concentration and confidence, excellent form, and endless practice. Relaxation is a critical component of good shooting that can easily be taken for granted. When your "game" shot is a little long or short, concentrate on relaxing your hand during the release of the shot.

Force The skill of shooting poses some problems that are not readily apparent. In other sports, the athlete attempts to generate as much power as possible while still maintaining control. For example, in baseball, a hitter swings hard and a pitcher usually throws hard. But in basketball, shooters must learn to control their power; they must coordinate their muscles to shoot (or throw) the ball only a fraction of the distance they are capable of, and they must be sure to throw it "softly."

When shooting a basketball, force is the synchronized and coordinated energy generated from the snap of the fingers and wrist, and the extension of the elbow, waist, knees, and ankles. For shots near the basket, the elbow and wrist supply most of the force, but extension from the other joints is important for rhythm and consistency. Longer shots require added power, generated mostly from the legs by bending the knees more.

Sighting (Point of Aim)—"Eye on the Basket" Coaches are always reminding their players to "keep their eyes on the basket." But what does this mean? And when you look at the basket when taking your shot, what do you look at? The front of the rim, over the front rim, or the back rim?

The skill of shooting a basketball into a basket poses a unique problem in terms of sighting the target. In baseball, a pitcher throws the ball to a target, the catcher's glove. However, the target for a basketball shot is a hole and, therefore, cannot be sighted directly.

For standard shots (we will discuss bank shots later), you must practice shooting experimenting with different sighting points to determine which one works best for you. Because each of us is a little bit different in terms of vision, physical structure, coordination, psychology, and the way we shoot, you will have to experiment to learn which sighting point to concentrate on during your shot. However, be certain that once you select the right spot, you totally concentrate on that fixed point each and every time you shoot. Most players select either the front of the rim or the back of the rim as their sighting point, although the metal rings on the rim and other points have been used successfully by some fine shooters.

Using the front of the rim, shooters have the advantage of being able to pick up their sighting point very quickly as they prepare to shoot. By concentrating on shooting over the front rim, they are more likely to put proper arc on their shot.

Using the back of the rim as the sighting point might offer the advantage of a greater margin of error. If the ball hits short of the sighting point, it can still go in. If the ball is long, especially if it has proper backspin, it can still go in off the back of the rim or the backboard. Advocates of using the back of the rim as the best sighting point also claim that the shot is more likely to go in at the end of games when fatigue sets in because "tired shots" tend to be short.

Most experts agree that the point you select to sight should be the one that gives you the most confidence. Some points to remember about sighting the basket when you shoot are:

1. Select a point on the front of the rim or the back of the rim depending on your personal preference, and always sight the same fixed point for all shots except bank shots.
2. Make your sighting point as small as possible, but one on which you can focus clearly.
3. If you sight the front of the rim, use the mental imagery of "dropping" the ball just over that spot. If you sight the back of the rim, imagine "dropping" the ball just in front of that point.
4. You must concentrate on the sighting point *totally*. It must be held in constant and perfect focus from the start of the shot until the ball goes into the basket. Do not allow your eyes to follow the ball in flight. (See Figure 5-2.)

Arc   The parabolic path the ball travels from the time it leaves your hand until it reaches the basket is called the arc, or arch, or trajectory. If the ball is arched high above the rim so that it can drop almost straight down into the basket, it is called a high arc. If the ball just clears

Figure 5-2 Sighting the Basket

the top of the rim, it is called a low arc or a "flat" shot because the described path or trajectory of the ball is closer to a straight line than a curve. The greater the curve or height of the ball on the shot, the higher the arc. A shooter is interested only in the arc that will give the ball the best chance of going into the basket. There are two major principles to consider in this regard:

1. The higher the arc of the shot, the greater the angle the ball has to the basket, thereby allowing the ball to drop almost straight down into the basket. The high-arched shot "sees" more of the area inside the rim than the "flat" shot because the higher angle gets the ball farther on top of the ring. The "flat" shot, because it "sees" less of the area inside the ring, is more likely to hit the rim and bounce out. (See Figure 5-3.)

   There is obviously a point of diminishing returns when considering how high a shot should be arched. Aside from the increased velocity a higher-arched shot creates, which will be discussed next, there are other practical concerns:
   a. A higher-arched shot requires more strength and energy which becomes a limiting factor in a player's "touch" and range outside of about fifteen feet.
   b. A shooter's sense of distance and ability to shoot straight tends to diminish beyond a certain height on his or her shot.
   c. Shooters often express a positive "feel" and confidence in a particular

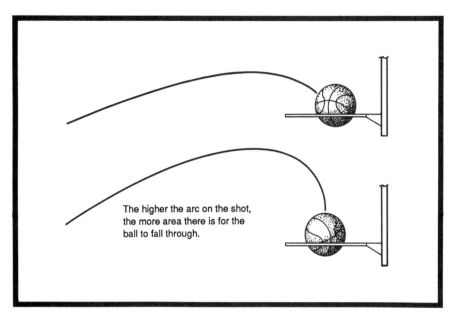

The higher the arc on the shot, the more area there is for the ball to fall through.

Figure 5-3 Shot Arcs

arc on their shots, and if the arc is not too "flat," it is probably the best one for them.

2. The speed or velocity of the ball when it arrives at the basket is the second critical factor. The slower the speed, the "softer" the shot and the greater the chance that it will go into the basket instead of bounding out. The factors involved in the "softness" of a shot are speed of the ball and backspin.

Theoretically, according to physicist Peter Brancazio of Brooklyn College, and the laws of Newtonian mechanics, the ideal trajectory or arc of a shot that would result in the largest effective opening at optimum velocity is between 50 and 55 degrees, as calculated from leaving the shooter's hand. To calculate mathematically the "perfect" arc for a given player, add 45 degrees to half the angle of the incline from the shooter's hand to the front of the rim of the basket.

Practically speaking, each shooter must experiment to find the arc on his or her shot that will result in the lowest possible velocity at the highest possible arc. In other words, arc the ball as much as possible, with proper release and follow-through, as long as the speed at which the ball arrives at the basket is slow enough to result in a "soft" shot.

Some additional points should be considered when discussing arc:

• A shot with a high arc is more difficult for a defender to block.

- A shot with high arc is easier to shoot with proper follow-through.
- A shot with a low arc may be easier to shoot straight at the basket, especially for the young shooter.
- A shot with low arc can be released more quickly.
- The factors involved in a "soft" shot are the velocity at which the ball arrives at the basket and the backspin on the ball. Without proper follow-through on the shot, a "soft" shot will be almost impossible to attain. However, proper follow-through is as or more important than arc on the softness of a shot.

Most good shooters use medium to high arc. The right amount will depend on what feels most natural to you and gives you the most accurate and consistent results. Taller players release the ball closer to the rim so they often appear to shoot a flatter shot. Often, young players are prone to shooting with too little arc because they lack sufficient strength. This is another reason to only practice shooting well within shooting range. Form breaks down to add power when a player shoots outside of his range, and often the shot gets flatter as it is taken farther from the basket. It is important to note that in almost all cases, the aspect of form that breaks down when a shooter shoots beyond his or her range is follow-through.

Here are some hints for developing the proper arc for your shot:

1. Bend your knees on your shot. The farther you shoot, the more your knees should be bent.
2. A shot should have sufficient arc so that the ball can drop straight down into the basket without touching the sides of the rim.
3. On the release of the shot, you should always feel that you are shooting the ball *up* to the basket and not *out* or *at* the basket.
4. Experiment with different arcs, but always within your shooting range, and ask yourself the following questions:

    At what arc do I feel most comfortable and have the most confidence that the ball is going to go in?

    At what arc does the ball drop cleanly into the basket most consistently?

    At what arc is my shot "softest" when it hits the rim? (Be sure you are following through properly).

Skill: The Spot Shot— Arm Position, Grip, Release, and Follow-Through

The following drill will walk you through the proper fundamentals of arm position, grip, release, and follow-through of the spot shot.

Practice this drill often because much of your shooting accuracy will depend on how well you master these points.

Drill S-1

     1. Lie down on the floor on your back. Your left hand is by your left side. (See Figure 5-4.)

     a. *Arm position*: Hold the basketball in your right hand so that you are looking straight up at the back of your hand. Your elbow is bent and directly under the ball so that the forearm, elbow, and upper arm are in a straight line with the right hip and leg. The ball should be five to ten inches above your face directly over the forehead. The ball may be held in the center of the forehead or just to the right of the right eye.

     b. *Grip*: Look at the back of your right hand. Your wrist should be extended backward comfortably and fully without strain. You should see wrinkles across the back of your wrist at the base of your hand.

     Rotate the ball with your fingers until you find a comfortable position and balance the ball with your fingers comfortably spread apart.

     Important note: Look at your fingers on the ball. Your thumb and forefinger should form more than a 45-degree but less than a 90-degree angle. In other words, your thumb and forefinger should form a U, not a backwards L. If you do form a backward L, it means the thumb is spread too wide. This is important because if the thumb is spread too far it causes the ball to rest too heavily on the palm, and your shooting will take on a pushing or shot-putting form.

     A good shot rolls off the fingertips. The ball should be held primarily on the pads of the five fingers but may be supported, especially in the young player with small hands, by the pads and heel of the palm. The ball must not rest on the palm but may brush against it.

     There are three different positions in which the fingers may grip the ball.

Figure 5-4   Drill S-1

You should choose the one you feel most comfortable with. To determine which is the best position for you, let's look at the three options:

(1) *Finger-grip position I*: The forefinger is the midpoint between the thumb and the pinky (Fig. 5-5a).

(2) *Finger-grip position II*: The midpoint between the thumb and pinky is the V formed by the forefinger and middle finger (Fig. 5-5b).

(3) *Finger-grip position III*: The middle finger is the midpoint between the thumb and the pinky. Look at the back of your shooting hand (Fig. 5-5c).

Draw an imaginary line dividing the ball equally into a right and left side while you are holding the ball in your right hand. If the forefinger is right on that imaginary line, you are using finger-grip position I. When you release the ball on your shot, the ball should roll off the forefinger last.

If the imaginary line splits the forefinger and the middle finger as in finger-grip position II, then the ball will roll off the middle and forefingers simultaneously on the release of the shot.

If the middle finger is right on the imaginary line, then you are using finger-grip position III and the ball should roll off the middle finger last on the shot release.

You should take the time to experiment with each finger-grip position to see which feels most secure and comfortable. If your hand is small, however, finger-grip position I may be the least satisfactory because only the thumb is to the left of the midpoint, while three fingers are to the right. Smaller hands might be better advised to start with finger-grip position III because there are two fingers on each side of the midpoint and it is easier to balance the ball this way if your hands are small.

2. Now rotate the ball in your right hand on the pads of your fingertips selecting one of the finger-grip positions. Many of the great shooters like to hold the ball exactly the same way for every shot. They have practiced shooting so much that the ball seems automatically to fall into the same place in their hands as they prepare to shoot.

Figure 5-5 (a) Finger Grip Position I, (b) Finger Grip Position II, and (c) Finger Grip Position III

(a)   (b)   (c)

Feel the ball as you rotate it and experiment with several grips or positions until you find the one most comfortable for you. A common grip is with the pads of one or two fingertips, usually the middle and forefingers, across the seams of the ball. (See Figure 5-6.)

One warning about shooting grip: do not allow the very tip of any finger to fall on a seam where the fingernail might impede your shot by scratching against the seam on the release.

Your hand and fingers on the ball should be relaxed. The ball should be held with the pinky and thumb exerting slight pressure so the ball feels secure in your hand. The other three fingers are relaxed.

Important Note: When you first begin to learn how to shoot, take the extra time to grip the ball exactly the same way each time. For most players, this means the guide hand will be on the natural side of the ball and the shooting hand will be across the seams behind and under the ball.

In a very short period of time, this grip will become automatic; from then on, you will reflexively put the ball in that same position. If you do not learn to grip the ball the same way each time before you shoot, it will be very difficult and time consuming at a later date to change that habit and learn to grip it the same way each time.

3. *Release and follow-through*: "Shoot" the ball straight up two or three feet in the air by extending your arm and snapping your wrist forward.

As you snap your wrist, your elbow should fully extend and "lock out" simultaneously. You should feel the ball roll off your fingertips on the release of the ball.

Your fingers should follow through in the direction of the flight of the ball on the release and then fall forward and down as the wrist completely relaxes.

If you have done this correctly (and it will take practice), the ball will have gone straight up and have backspin (or reverse rotation) on it.

It is a mistake to snap your wrist down on the shot.

Release the ball with the fingers extending toward the target and then relax the wrist and let the hand go limp. If the ball rolls off the fingertip of the forefinger (finger-grip position I) on the release, you should rotate the hand out (to the right) slightly on the follow through.

Figure 5-6 Shooting Grip: Gripping the Ball Across the Seams

If the ball rolls off the fingertips of the middle and forefingers or just the middle finger (finger-grip positions II and III), the hand should follow through straight to the target.

Good shooters always have a relaxed shooting hand and proper follow-through for a soft shot.

Good shooters shoot straight because the elbow is in close to the body directly under the ball and the motion of the shot is in one smooth, continuous movement where the knees and shooting arm fully extend or "lock out" simultaneously with the snap of the wrist.

4. As the ball reaches its full height, bend your elbow back to the original position, spread your fingers, and catch the ball in your shooting hand. Rotate the ball again in your shooting hand until you have found the comfortable grip you have selected. Do not use your left hand at all during this drill.

5. Repeat this ten times, catching the ball after each "shot."

6. Now increase the height of the "shot" to five or six feet.

Is there still backspin on the ball? Practice this drill often and at different heights but be sure the ball goes up straight and there is backspin on the ball. This is one drill you can practice at home laying on your bed without making noise.

POINTS OF EMPHASIS

Check the following points every time you do this drill:

- Elbow in close to the body, directly under the ball, and bent so the upper arm and forearm form about a 90-degree angle. The elbow and forearm are in a straight line with your body.
- The fingers are spread comfortably with the thumb and the forefinger forming a U. The ball rests on the pads of the fingertips and only brushes the palm of the hand.
- Find a comfortable grip on the ball with the pads of your fingertips on the seams, and use the same grip for every shot.
- The ball is placed directly in front of your forehead or just to the right of your right eye so that you are looking at the back of your hand.
- "Shoot" by extending the arm fully and "locking out" at the same time as the wrist snaps. The ball rolls off the fingertips imparting backspin. The hand and fingers extend toward the target and then, as the wrist relaxes, fall limply forward and down. The ball goes straight up with backspin. Be sure your hand does not turn in or out as your wrist snaps.

BACKSPIN

When a shot is released it is important that the ball roll off the fingertips of the shooting hand, imparting backspin to the shot. But the word "backspin" is misleading because you actually do not want the ball to "spin." If the ball is "spinning" backward, it means the shooting hand was snapped down on the shot instead of properly releasing the ball where the hand and fingers follow through, pointing toward the basket and then relaxing and going limp. The ball should "roll" off the fingertips whereby a slower backward "rotation" results. A "spinning" ball will jump off the backboard or rim while a shot taken properly with backward rotation will be "soft" and have a greater chance of going in. In addition to a "soft" shot, backward rotation is desirable because it prevents the ball from floating in the air and indicates a proper release on the shot.

SPOT SHOT

The spot shot is the first phase of learning how to shoot. The spot shot is taken standing still, and facing the basket well within your range as a shooter. We will begin work on your spot shot very close to the basket because practicing close-in shots develops good form.

Depending on your age and upper-body strength, you may hold the ball in one of two ways. If you are strong enough, hold the ball above your eyes at about the forehead level. You should be able to see the back of your shooting hand. If you are a younger shooter and cannot hold the ball that high with enough strength to shoot in good form, lower the ball below your eyes so you can see the basket over the ball. *This will not hurt your form, accuracy, or development in any way*! Your shot will develop with all the proper form, and when you get a little older and stronger, you will simply raise your shot to the higher level.

A word of advice for young shooters: Eventually you will shoot the ball by holding it above your eyes at the forehead level or a little higher. However, it is important that you do *not* pull the ball back over your head when you shoot. You should learn to shoot looking over the ball first, until you are strong enough to hold the ball up over your eye level in a stable position, and shoot smoothly by just extending your arm at the elbow and wrist.

The checkpoint on your shot is the back of your hand. You should be able to see the back of your hand on your shot when you shoot. If you have to pull the ball back over your head where you can no longer see the back of your hand, it means you do not have enough strength yet to shoot properly from that position. Many players bring the ball up high on their shot too early before they have the strength to execute it smoothly.

This leads to such bad habits as leaning back and bringing the ball back over the head for extra power. The result is a jerky release with poor accuracy because the power generated for the shot comes from the shoulders. Great shooters are able to keep their heads and shoulders remarkably still when they shoot, and this is where their great balance and accuracy come from. Power for your shot must come from the extension of three joints only—your knees, elbow, and wrist. (For purists, it is true that the ankles and waist also extend as a natural consequence, but for teaching and learning purposes, concentration on the knees, elbow, and wrist produce the proper shooting rhythm without overburdening the learner with detail.)

Skill: The Spot Shot

Drill S-2

1. Begin at SS #1 facing the basket. Your right foot is forward with the toes of the right foot pointing directly at the basket.

Your knees are bent, your weight is forward on the balls of your feet, and your shoulders are squared so your chest is facing the basket.

Your waist is slightly bent forward, your feet are spread about a shoulder width apart, and you feel balanced. Hold the ball in your right hand with the same grip described in Drill S-1. This might not feel comfortable because you will have to bend your knees more to balance the ball carefully in your right hand.

Important Note: Some very young players may not be able to do this drill because their hands are too small to hold the ball in one hand. In these cases, use the left hand as a guide by placing the fingertips gently on the side of the ball. Be sure you release the left hand *before* each shot.

2. Practice this until you can hold the ball perfectly balanced in your right hand without any movement for five seconds.

3. Shoot the ball directly into the basket with enough arc on the shot so that the ball drops straight down through the basket.

4. Continue shooting from SS #1 until you have made three shots in a row. Remember, you are *not* to use your left hand on the ball at all. This will ensure proper position of your shooting hand behind the ball. (See Figures 5-7a and 5-7b.)

5. Repeat step 4 from SS #2–10.

6. Add your left hand but only as a guide on your shot and repeat steps 4 and 5.

The left hand, or guide hand, is placed on the side of the ball for support only and is removed *before* the ball is released on the shot.

SPOT SHOT SHOOTING CHECKPOINTS

1. Feet spread at least six inches but less than a shoulder width apart with right foot forward and pointing directly toward the basket.
2. Knees are bent comfortably.

(a)

(b)

Figures 5-7a and 5-7b   Drill S-2

3. Waist is bent slightly forward and your weight is on the balls of your feet.

4. The ball rests in your right hand with wrist extended back. The hand is relaxed with most of the grip on the ball coming from the thumb and pinky fingers. The hand is slightly cupped so the ball is on the pads of the fingers between the fingertips and the first joint. The fingers are spread comfortably with the thumb and forefinger forming a U not an L. The fingers are pointing up.

5. The ball is placed above the eyes in front of the forehead or just to the right of the right eye. Some young players who do not have the physical strength to shoot smoothly at this level may begin with the ball below the eyes at the chin or upper chest levels. The forearm is straight or perpendicular to the ground, the elbow is in close to the body and bent. The upper arm and forearm are in line with the right leg.

6. Your head is balanced with your eyes sighted on the rim. The shot is an extension of the body from this position. Mostly it involves the straightening of the knees, the right elbow, and the right wrist, with a little coming from the straightening of the waist and ankles.

It is essential to understand that the rest of the body must be as motionless as possible to gain maximum accuracy. The more stable the head, shoulders, hips, and legs, the more consistently accurate the shot. Short shots involve mostly wrist, with longer shots requiring more and more power from the elbow and knees. This does not mean that you do not extend the elbow and knees on every shot. It simply means on most very short shots you can feel the action of the extending wrist supplying the necessary power for the shot. The extension of the elbow and knees is still critical for your form and rhythm.

7. Your left hand is placed lightly on the left side of the ball. It is there to provide support only.

SHOT RELEASE CHECKPOINTS

1. The shot is an extension of the body levers. As the lowest point of the knee bend is reached in preparation of the shot, the wrists may unlock dropping the ball about two inches. (This is more often true when the ball is initially held below eye level. The higher the ball is held on the initial set of the spot shot, the less chance the shooter will unlock his or her wrists and drop the ball a few inches before she shoots.) Each shot should begin in your legs with extension of your knees.

2. As you release the ball you should feel the toes and balls of your feet push into the floor as you straighten your knees and waist.

3. Your right elbow straightens smoothly and "locks out" as you extend your arm directly to the basket.

4. The knees and elbow "lock out" simultaneously with the snap of the wrist.

5. Your back is straight and relaxed, not arched. Your weight is slightly forward on the balls of your feet so that as you release the ball, you extend slightly forward, toward the basket. Depending on the distance of the shot, you may or may not jump off the floor. Do not allow yourself to extend straight up or go backward on the release of the shot.

6. The ball rolls off the tip of your forefinger or middle finger or both as your wrist snaps your hand toward the basket. Do not snap your shooting hand down. As the ball is released, the fingers point toward the basket, but the wrist relaxes after the release and the hand falls limply down on the follow-through.

7. It is most important on the release to shoot up to, not at, the basket so that you get the proper arc and backspin.

8. The left hand is removed from the ball just *before* the ball is released.

9. Your head, shoulders, hips, and legs should have been balanced and therefore motionless during the shot. By this it is meant that they stayed in perfect line with the body as it extended and did not pull or jerk the body out of balance on the shot.

10. During the whole process of the shot, your eyes should be concentrating on the rim until the ball goes through the basket. Do not let your eyes follow the ball on the shot. (See Figures 5-8a, 5-8b, and 5-8c and Figures 5-9a, 5-9b, and 5-9c.)

(a)

(b)

(c)

Figure 5-8 (a) Spot Shot Stance, (b) Spot Shot Release, and (c) Spot Shot Follow-Through

Figure 5-9 (a) Spot Shot Stance, (b) Spot Shot Release, and (c) Spot Shot Follow-Through

(a)

(b)

(c)

139

Drill S-3

      1. Face the basket at SS #1. Review all the Spot Shooting Position Checkpoints and Shot Release Checkpoints.

      2. Shoot from SS #1 until you have made three spot shots consecutively.

      3. Repeat this from SS #2–15. Remember, you must remain at each spot until you have made three in a row. This might take you quite a bit of time to complete, but concentrate and work on developing consistent form and rhythm.

      4. Repeat steps 1–3 beginning each shot with your right foot behind your left foot and your left foot as the pivot.

      Step forward with your right foot into proper shooting position before each shot.

      This should be a rocking motion where your weight shifts from your right foot to your left foot as you step forward to shoot.

      Be sure you keep your head up. Your feet should be about a shoulder width apart. (See Figures 5-10a, 5-10b, and 5-10c.)

      5. Repeat step 4, but begin with your left foot behind your right foot with the right foot as your pivot.

      This will feel a little more awkward than using the left foot as your pivot and stepping forward with the right.

      In this case, with your right foot as your pivot, you will have to shift your weight from your left foot to your right as you bring your left foot forward.

      Bring your left foot forward only to the point where the toe of the left foot is even with the heel of the right. At this point you shift your weight back slightly onto your left and shoot.

Figures 5-10a, 5-10b, and 5-10c   Drill S-3, Step 4

    (a)   (b)   (c)

This is a more difficult move than using the left foot as your pivot and explains why most righties prefer to use their left foot as their pivot.

POINTS OF EMPHASIS

- Your head is always up, with your eyes sighted on the rim.
- Your knees are bent and your weight is on the balls of your feet.
- You feel balanced at all times.
- Your shot is released in one smooth, continuous rhythm, with the elbow and knees locking out simultaneously.
- The ball rotates backward as it arcs straight toward the basket because you released the ball by rolling it off your fingertips.
- The fingers on your shooting hand point toward the basket on the release of the shot and then fall limply down as the wrist and hand completely relaxes.

Drill S-4

1. Begin at SS #6 facing the basket with your right foot as your pivot and your left foot forward.
2. Simultaneously take one dribble with the right hand as you step forward with the left foot.
3. Catch the ball on your right hip and step forward with your right foot into shooting position and shoot. (The shot should have been on SS #5.) Be sure your head is up, with your eyes sighted on the rim.
4. Shoot from SS #6 until you have made three in a row.
5. Repeat steps 1–4 beginning at SS #7–17.
6. Repeat steps 1–5 using one dribble with the left hand and stepping first with the right foot.

Begin facing the basket with your left foot as your pivot and your right foot slightly forward.

Remember that the second step with the left foot must not come as far forward as the step with the right foot so that you are in good shooting position.

This move is a little more complex for right-handed shooters because, as you step into shooting position with the left foot, you must bring the ball across your body from your left hip to your right hip before you shoot.

Skill: The Bank Shot

There are areas on the court where using the backboard on your shot is a definite advantage. By using the backboard from certain angles and distances, the shooter can use the whole circumference of the rim because the ball drops into the basket from above and has less chance of hitting the rim and bouncing out. The bank shot is especially effective when taken from a 45-degree angle to the basket and within fifteen feet (See Figure 5-11.)

As the angle increases or decreases, the use of the bank shot may become less effective. You should first learn to shoot your bank shots from in close at exactly a 45-degree angle to the basket. After you have mastered the bank shot at that angle from both sides and from three to fifteen feet out, you should experiment banking the ball from angles slightly less and more than 45 degrees to see how wide an angle you can use the bank shot to your advantage.

At some point, as you move toward the base line and the foul line, your accuracy will decrease. You have to practice your bank shot often and from enough different angles to know where you will want to use it in a game situation.

If your backboard has a target square on it, sight your bank shot to carom off the backboard inside the square. The bank shot should use the same arc as your regular shot. It should be shot as softly as possible and aimed twelve to fifteen inches above the rim so that the ball can drop into the basket. The lower the ball hits the backboard (below twelve inches), the more chance the ball will hit a part of the rim and bounce out of the cylinder.

As you move farther from the basket, you must take extra care to bank the ball higher off the backboard. Ideally, a layup should be banked at least twelve inches above the rim, but a fifteen-foot bank shot should carom fifteen inches above the rim to have the best chance of going in.

Figure 5-11 Best Angles for Bank Shots

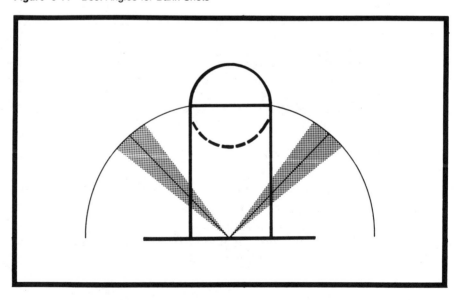

The single biggest mistake or most common error in shooting the bank shot involves the breakdown of basic shooting fundamentals. Players get so confident in their bank shot that they get "lazy" and lose their concentration. The shot is thrown up with too little arc, too hard and with improper follow-through. The bank shot from the proper angle and distance *can* be an easier shot but that is no excuse for a breakdown of concentration and shooting form. Be *disciplined*.

Concentrate on all the proper fundamentals of shooting when you take a bank shot—especially proper arc, release, and follow-through. The softer the shot off the backboard, the more consistently accurate the shot will be.

Drill S-5

    1. Begin at SS #2 and bank the ball into the basket until you have made five in a row.
    2. Repeat Step 1 from SS #4, 9, and 7.

POINTS OF EMPHASIS

- Be sure that you sight each shot at least twelve inches (twelve to fifteen inches) above the rim on the backboard.
- Concentrate on using all the proper fundamentals of good shooting especially arc, release, and follow-through.
- Notice the different feeling you get shooting bank shots from the left side as opposed to the right side of the court. This is because a 45-degree angle from the left side is a step closer to the base line than is a 45-degree angle from the right side, as measured from your right shoulder.

Skill: The Foul Shot

When you are fouled in the act of shooting or fouled when your opponents are over their foul limit, you will get the opportunity to shoot a free throw, or foul shot. This means you will be handed the ball at the foul line, fifteen feet from the basket, and be given ten seconds to shoot the ball into the basket for 1 point for each shot made. This is the only time in the game of basketball where the defense can do nothing to stop you from scoring. Now your only opponent is lack of concentration! Use this opportunity to relax, concentrate, take your time, and score as often as possible. In my opinion, there is no reason for any player to ever shoot less than 80 percent from the free-throw line if he or she practices and concentrates hard enough.

The ability to make a free throw is especially important because close games will often be decided by the team that can make free throws under pressure. Although the free throw or foul shot is not particularly difficult, it must often be shot under a great deal of pressure and when you are tired. For these reasons, you must practice foul shots every day so that you have complete confidence in yourself to make them. (See Figure 5-12.)

The foul shot is identical to the spot shot. You should select the shot that you feel most comfortable with and that is usually your spot shot. Review the spot shot position and shot release checkpoints in addition to the following points:

1. *Relax at the foul line.* Look at the basket, bounce the ball a few times, and roll it around in your hands to get a familiar feel. You should develop a routine at the foul line and use the same one each time. For example, you should bounce the ball the same number of times and take one deep breath. This will help you develop a rhythm and confidence that the shot will go in each time.

2. *Concentrate.* Even when you practice you should concentrate as hard as you can on each foul shot. Clear everything else out of your mind except relaxing and putting the ball into the basket. You must envision the ball going through the basket all the way through your preparation and shot.

3. Your weight should be balanced on the balls of your feet with your right

Figure 5-12 Foul Shot

foot slightly ahead of the left and the feet spread at least six inches apart. Your waist and knees are bent, eyes on the basket, right hand behind the ball, right elbow in and back relaxed not rigid. You should feel balanced and comfortable.

4. After bouncing the ball and getting the familiar grip that you have chosen, the ball must come to rest or "set" for at least one count above your waist before you shoot. This will ensure that your center of gravity is below the ball and the momentum on your foul shot will be toward the basket facilitating a smooth, rhythmic effort.

5. Release the ball by removing the left or guide hand first as you lean straight forward toward the basket. Shoot the ball with the proper arc, *straight* to the basket. Your eyes never leave the basket. Extend the knees and arm together so that the ankles, knees, waist, and arm all fully extend in one fluid motion at the same time.

6. The follow-through should see the elbow "lock out", with the ball rolling off the fingertips, after which the wrist relaxes and the hand hangs down. The eyes are fixed on your sight point on the rim. Do not back off the foul line.

MOST COMMON MISTAKES IN FOUL SHOOTING

1. Shooting too quickly.
2. Taking eyes off the basket.
3. Not following through on the shot. You should finish each foul shot with a locked out elbow and relaxed wrist.
4. Backing off the line on the shot.
5. Poor balance on the line because either the feet are too close together or the body is not balanced. This causes the extension on the shot to be slightly left or right instead of directly toward the basket.
6. Poor concentration and lack of relaxation. This usually means that the player lacks confidence and is feeling the pressure. Hurrying his shot is a way of getting it over with because he feels uncomfortable and unsure of himself. You must be confident that your foul shot is going in. Relax, take your time, and concentrate. Keep envisioning the ball going through the basket, and it will.

HOW TO PRACTICE YOUR FOUL SHOT

1. Practice foul shooting everyday.
2. Practice several times during your regular workouts so that you are comfortable shooting foul shots cold, warmed up, and when you are very tired.

   Always practice at least once after wind sprints so that you get in the habit of making them when you are very tired.
3. Never practice free throws without total concentration. Don't talk to a friend, fool around, or think about something else while you are practicing. Practice free throws with total focus on what you are doing, the same as you will in a game situation. Any other type of practice confuses

your "motor memory" when you are tired and under pressure in a game situation. You want your "motor memory" to have to remember only one thing—the right way to put the ball in the basket.

4. Shoot your foul shots in pairs because you will never shoot more than two in a row in a game unless there are technical fouls involved.

5. Create games to put yourself under pressure: Take two foul shots in a row. If you miss either one of them, you have to sprint to the opposite base line and back to the foul line and shoot two more in a row. Each time you miss, you have to run. See how long it takes you to make ten pairs of free throws.

   a. See how many foul shots you can make before you miss five.
   b. See how many free throws you can make out of one hundred tries.
   c. Repeat (b) and (c) with a radio blaring beside you as a distraction.

   Extra Tip: When you are very tired or feeling great pressure on a foul shot, bend your knees a little extra, relax, concentrate, and follow through.

Drill S-6

1. Take one hundred free throws. If you are fortunate enough to have a friend rebound for you, be sure you step off the line after every other shot. In a game situation, unless there are technical fouls involved, you will never shoot more than two free throws in a row. Therefore, never shoot more than two in a row without stepping off the line and resetting yourself.

Skill: The Layup

The layup is the first shot you will learn on the move. It is the shot often used on the fast break and when the defense fails to guard a player in the half-court offense. The layup is a shot taken as you move toward the basket, usually at about a 45-degree angle, with or without using the dribble. This is because a 45-degree angle is the easiest angle from which to shoot off the backboard. With practice and increased size and strength, the more talented player will be able to make layup shots from a variety of angles.

IMPORTANT NOTES

1. The head must be up at all times.
2. The ball should be on the right side and dribbled with the right hand for the right-handed layup from the right side of the basket. The opposite is true for the left-handed layup.
3. As you approach the basket, your last step with the left foot (for a right-handed layup) should be small enough so that your momentum is up toward the basket. Too large a last step will propel you under the basket and result in poor body control and balance.

4. As the left foot lands on the last step (for the right-handed layup), bend the right knee and drive it straight up toward the basket.

5. The ball is brought high overhead and released softly at the top of your jump with the elbow fully extended.

6. Do not take your eyes off your sighting point on the backboard as you lay the ball into the basket by banking it softly off the backboard twelve inches above the rim.

7. Follow through on your shot the same way as you do with your spot shot.

8. You should land as softly as possible on the balls of both feet or on the ball of the opposite foot you took off on, with your knees bent and your arms and legs comfortably spread for extra balance.

The layup is the first shooting skill learned while on the move. When necessary, it is a good idea to practice all or any part of these drills without the ball to learn more easily the rhythm of the skill. (See Figures 5-13a, 5-13b, 5-13c, 5-13d, and 5-13e.)

Drill S-7

1. Begin at SS #2 facing the basket.

2. Shoot a right-handed spot shot off the backboard and into the basket.

3. Take one small step with your left foot at a 45-degree angle toward the basket. As your left foot lands, bend your right knee and drive it straight up to the basket. As your knee comes up, raise the ball straight up overhead and shoot the ball with your right hand softly off the backboard in the basket.

Do not dribble the ball. Your head should be up during this sequence. Pretend that a rubber band is attached from your right elbow to your right knee. After you step with the left foot, the right elbow pulls the right knee up as you extend toward the basket.

The step with your left foot should not be too long because you want the thrust of that step to take you up high to the basket not under it.

4. Practice steps 1–3 until you make ten in a row, taking one step with the left foot and completing the right-handed layup in one smooth motion.

Remember to release the ball at the top of your jump and follow through on your shot. Do not take your eyes off the backboard until the ball goes through the basket.

5. Back up to SS #9 and practice the layup with three steps until you can make ten in a row with the proper form described.

For this phase of the drill you will have to dribble the ball once with your right hand by pushing the ball in front of your right leg on your first step with the left foot and catching it on the second step when your right foot lands. Practice this at half speed so that your head is up at all times.

Concentrate during this phase of the drill on balance, form, and rhythm so that you can execute the layup smoothly.

6. Back up to the right side line, just below the hash mark, and practice your right-handed layup with several dribbles at different speeds.

a. Keep your head up.

b. Keep your body under control.

c. Use as few dribbles as possible.

Figure 5-13 (a) The Layup Approach, (b) the Layup Approach, (c) the Layup Takeoff, (d) the Layup Shot, and (e) the Layup Follow-Through

d. Make your last step smaller so you drive your body up to the basket.

e. Be sure you keep the ball well protected on the shooting side. The elbow on the nonshooting side should be up and out as you raise the ball on your layup.

f. Follow through on your shot and see the ball go through the hoop.

g. Be sure you land balanced and under control.

Continue this until you have made ten in a row.

Important Note: As you increase your speed and jump higher on your layup, you must concentrate on releasing the ball more softly to compensate for your momentum. Do not release the ball on the way up, or your layup will be either too hard or erratic. At the top of your jump, just before you begin to descend, is the perfect time to release a soft layup.

7. Repeat steps 1–6 beginning from SS #4 and shooting with the left hand and jumping off the right leg.

It will take considerably longer to master this skill with the left or nondominant hand and coordinating jumping off the right leg.

It may be necessary to practice with the left hand twice as much as with the right for awhile. Don't be discouraged if the nondominant hand comes along slowly. This is very common, especially with younger players. Keep practicing, and suddenly, one day, it will be almost as comfortable as shooting with the right hand.

Skill: The Underhanded Layup

The underhanded layup involves many of the same mechanics of the standard layup, except that the ball is brought up from the hip on the shooting side with the shooting hand under the ball and the nonshooting hand on the side of the ball for support and protection. The major advantage of the underhanded layup is that it can be released or delivered against the backboard more softly, especially when the layup is taken at high speed.

The ball is extended up and out to the backboard with the palm of the shooting hand under the ball facing up toward the basket. The fingers are comfortably spread and relaxed.

The ball is shot at the top of your jump with a flip of the wrist and fingers imparting forward spin to the ball as the ball rolls off the tips of the fingers. The nonshooting hand is released just before the shot. (See Figure 5-14.)

Important Note Many advanced players will release the ball on this shot with the right hand on the right side of the ball from the right

Figure 5-14 The Underhanded Layup Release

side (the left hand on the left side from the left side) and impart side spin on the ball off the backboard. This variation can be effective from certain driving angles. However, the side spin is more likely to hit the rim and cause the ball to spin out of the basket.

Drill S-8

1. Repeat Drill S-7 using the underhanded layup shot in place of the one-handed spot shot.

Skill: The Power Layup

This has become a very popular shot, especially for big and strong players. It is most often used when a player receives the ball from a pass or offensive rebound within six feet of the basket. The player collects himself after receiving the ball and does a two-foot jump straight to the basket. The player using the power layup protects the ball by holding the ball firmly in both hands and placing his body between the ball and the defense. The shot is released softly at the top of the jump with both arms fully extended usually laying the ball against the backboard.

The power layup is difficult for the defense to block without fouling the shooter. It cannot be executed at as fast a speed as other layups because it requires a two-foot jump. Attempting the two-foot jump at fast speeds will often result in the player going out of control and missing the shot. When it is executed correctly, the player is more stable as he goes up and more likely to make the layup even if he is fouled on the play.

Because the ball is released so close to the basket, the player may release the ball with both hands or either hand, as long as the shot is released softly at the top of the jump and the ball is well protected at all times.

Drill S-9

1. Begin at SS #2 facing the basket.
2. Take one small step with the left foot at a 45-degree angle toward the basket (Fig. 5-15a.) As your left foot lands, bring your right foot up even with your left and bend your knees to almost a 45-degree angle (Fig. 5-15b).
3. Jump straight up off both feet simultaneously toward where the rim and the backboard meet. Your head is up, both arms are extended toward the backboard, and, at the top of your jump, lay the ball softly off the backboard into the basket with your right hand the same way you learned for the standard layup (Fig. 5-15c).

(a)   (b)   (c)

Figure 5-15 (a) Power Layup Step, (b) Power Layup—Collecting Yourself,
and (c) Power Layup

4. Repeat steps 1–3 until you have made five in a row.

5. Repeat steps 1–4 releasing the ball with both hands.

6. Repeat steps 1–5 beginning from SS #4, stepping first with the right foot and shooting a power layup with the left hand.

7. Repeat steps 1–5 beginning at SS #9 and using one dribble with the right hand to the basket followed by a jump stop and a power layup with the right hand.

8. Repeat step 7 beginning at SS #7 and using one dribble with the left hand followed by a jump stop and a power layup with the left hand.

9. Repeat step 7 beginning at SS #12 and using two dribbles with the right hand.

10. Repeat step 8 beginning from SS #16 and using two dribbles with the left hand.

POINTS OF EMPHASIS

- Your head is up at all times and the ball is well protected by your arms and body.
- Make sure you are not going so fast that you cannot stop; collect yourself and jump straight up to the basket with perfect body control and balance.

Skill: The Hook Shot

There are two basic types of hook shots that are commonly used. The standard hook shot involves bringing the ball up from the hip area with a *straight* arm (elbow locked out) over the head before the ball is flipped into the basket. This is a very difficult shot to block because not only has the shooter placed his or her body between the ball and the defender, but the straight arm adds more distance between the defender and the ball and the elbow of the nonshooting hand is held high for protection.

The second type of hook shot is called the "baby hook." It is used most often by taller players who do not have to worry as much about getting their shots blocked. The "baby hook" is executed the same way as the standard hook except the ball is brought straight up with the elbow *bent* instead of extended (locked out). The ball is brought up with both hands usually right over the ear on the shooting side until the arms can extend straight up over the head before the hook shot.

It is prudent to learn the standard hook shot first because the "baby hook" has a more limited range and application, especially for the smaller player. In addition, the "baby hook" can be easily learned later. For post players, the "baby hook" is developed into the jump hook (see Post Moves).

In the following drills, use the standard hook shot. After you have mastered the standard hook, begin experimenting with the "baby hook" in those drills where the shot is taken close to the basket. One word of advice on the "baby hook": Be sure that your last step before the shot is not too long. You want your momentum to be *up* and not *out* on your shot. (See Figures 5-16a, 5-16b, and 5-16c.)

Drill S-10

1. Begin at SS #2 with your back to the basket. Hold the ball in both hands and look over your left shoulder at the basket. Your feet should be about a shoulder width apart.

Because this shot is often executed in heavy defensive traffic, it is a good idea to practice holding the ball well protected with your knees bent, elbows out, and ball held firmly into the chest area.

Figures 5-16a, 5-16b, and 5-16c   The Hook Shot

(a)   (b)   (c)

2. Take one step with the left foot to SS #1 pointing your left toe toward SS #1 and pointing your left shoulder toward the basket as you step and turn.

Do not take your eyes off the basket. Be sure the ball is well protected.

3. As your hips and shoulders begin to turn toward the basket, bring your straight right arm up over your turned head and shoot the ball with the same snap of the wrist you learned for the spot shot.

Your right foot will come up off the floor as your right arm comes up on the shot. Hold on to the ball with both hands until the ball gets to chest or shoulder height on the shot. Your left elbow is held high for added protection.

Shoot the ball so that it caroms in to the basket off the backboard the same way you learned on the bank shot. Be sure your right hand follows through to the basket in the same manner as your spot shot.

This maneuver is executed without a dribble.

If your hands are big enough and you are sufficiently strong, try this trick to improve your hook shot accuracy: As you turn on your hook shot, point the forefinger on your outstretched left hand to the basket and continue pointing until the ball goes in. Of course, you will not be able to do this in competition, but as a practice drill it will line you up on your pivot so that your hook shot will be more consistently accurate.

4. Repeat steps 1–3 ten times or until you can make five hook shots in a row.

5. Repeat steps 1–4 beginning from SS #4 using the left hand. As in the case with the lefty layup, this will take extra practice, but, with time and effort, you will master it.

6. Repeat steps 1–4 beginning at SS #4 with your back to the basket. Stepping with the left foot first, use the slide step (see Footwork, Sliding Drill F-7) and one dribble to get to SS #1 and execute the hook shot off the backboard. Do not look at the ball during this maneuver. Be sure you step first *before* you take your one dribble.

7. Repeat step 6 beginning from SS #2 using a left-hand dribble, moving to your left to SS #5 for the left-handed hook.

Drill S-11

1. Begin at SS #15 facing the basket. Using your right foot as your pivot, crossover with your left foot, take one right-handed dribble by pushing the ball out in front of you toward SS #8 and drive to the right of the basket. Execute a right-handed hook shot off the backboard when you arrive at SS #1.

2. Repeat step 1 twenty-five times or until you can make five in a row.

3. Repeat steps 1 and 2 beginning from SS #13, starting with the left foot as your pivot, crossing over with the right foot, and using the left-handed dribble for the left-handed hook shot.

4. Repeat steps 1 and 2 beginning at SS #13 and driving straight down the lane for the right-handed hook shot.

Be sure you do not go too far down the lane where you cannot use the backboard. You should shoot from above the block where you have a good angle to the backboard.

5. Repeat steps 1 and 2 beginning at SS #15 and driving straight down the lane for the left-handed hook shot.

POINTS OF EMPHASIS

- Your head is up at all times.
- The ball is well protected with your knees bent, elbows out when necessary, and the ball held firmly in close to the chest area.
- Be sure that your last step before your hook shot is not too long. A long last step before a shot propels the shooter horizontally along the floor like a broad jumper. The last step should be short enough so that the shooter's momentum is up and not out. This means your weight (center of gravity) must get over your feet on your last step for your momentum to be straight up on your shot.

Drill S-12

1. Begin at SS #5 with your back to the basket. Your knees are bent, your elbows are out, your head is up looking over your left shoulder, and the ball is held firmly with both hands in the chest area.

2. Take one step with your left foot toward SS #3 and shoot a hook shot directly into the basket.

3. Repeat this ten times or until you can make five in a row.

4. Repeat steps 1–3 starting from SS #1, stepping with the right foot toward SS #3 and using the left-handed hook shot.

5. Repeat steps 1–3 using one dribble with the right hand, a slide step to SS #3, and a right-handed hook directly into the basket. Remember to step *before* you dribble.

6. Repeat step 5 beginning at SS #1 and using the left-handed hook shot.

Skill: The Reverse Layup

The reverse layup is a driving hook shot that is taken after passing under the basket. From the left side, the reverse layup is executed by dribbling under the basket and laying the ball off the backboard on the right side with the right-handed hook shot. From the right side, the converse is true.

Your head is up and looking at the basket throughout the move. This keeps your body balanced and in line with the basket.

Your last step must be small enough to allow your momentum on the shot to be up and not away from the basket. Be sure the ball is well protected at all times. (See Figures 5-17a and 5-17b.)

Drill S-13

1. Begin at SS #6 facing the basket. Dribbling with the right hand, cross under the basket and lay the ball in off the backboard from the right side.

(a)   (b)

Figures 5-17a and 5-17b   The Reverse Layup

     2. Continue until you have made five in a row.

     3. Repeat steps 1 and 2 dribbling with the *left* hand.

     4. Repeat steps 1–3 from SS #7, 17, and 16.

     5. Repeat steps 1–3 from SS #10, 9, 11, and 12 using the left-handed hook shot laying the ball in from the left of the basket.

Skill: The Jump Shot

    Before we begin discussion of the mechanics of the jump shot, it is important to head off the most common problem young players develop. Because the jump shot is the single most often means of scoring in the high school, college, and professional game, young players cannot wait to start learning how to shoot the jumper. Most problems are the result of learning this shot before you are strong enough to execute it properly and trying to shoot from too far too soon. Before beginning this section, make sure that you stay with your spot shot until you are strong enough to take the jumper. When you do begin to practice the jumper, do so from in close to develop perfect form. Range will come as you get bigger and stronger.

The jumper requires considerable strength in the legs, arms, and wrists. If the young shooter has insufficient strength in these areas, he or she often compensates by adding shoulder movement to the shot. This leads to a career of inconsistency and inaccuracy because shoulder action can push the elbow out or bring the ball over and behind the head before the shot. Be patient with yourself and practice for perfect form. As your body matures and your constant practice pays off, your shot will develop range.

Generally speaking, the jump shot is very similar to the spot shot in terms of form. The advantage of the jumper is that you can shoot it at a higher elevation because of the jump and therefore make it a more difficult shot to defend. The jumper is set up off three different offensive situations:

- Standing still.
- Off the dribble.
- Catching the ball coming off a cut or screen.

JUMP SHOT CHECKPOINTS

Stance

1. Feet are spread comfortably apart—usually less than a shoulder width but not too close together where balance is impeded.
2. The toes of both feet point toward the basket, with the right foot slightly ahead of the left.
3. Knees are bent so that your weight is forward on the balls of your feet and your heels come off the floor.
4. You are in your best balanced position to jump straight up.

Grip and Arm Position

1. Use the same grip as the spot shot.
2. Because you are going to jump before you shoot, the ball is held lower in preparation of this shot. Hold the ball at waist level in line with your right hip with the elbow in.
3. Your waist is bent but your back is straight. Your head is up so you can concentrate on your target, the basket. The ball is now in the "slot."

Shot Action

1. From this position, jump straight up, raising the ball up the center of the body to above your forehead without extending your arms. The ball may be released from the center of your forehead or just above and to the right of your right eye. You must feel your jump shot begin in your legs with the extension of your knees.

Note: Although you jump straight up off both feet, you should be aware that more power is generated from the left leg for the right-handed jump shooter.

2. At this point you should be able to see the basket by looking under the ball and the back of your shooting hand. If you cannot see the basket, the ball is not high enough, and if you cannot see the back of your hand, you have pulled the ball too far back over your head.

3. Your elbow is still in line with your right leg and is bent at about a 90-degree angle. If the angle between your right forearm and upper arm is greater than 90 degrees before you shoot, you have extended the ball too far out, and you will lose power, arc, and accuracy on your shot. Keep the ball in close to you in preparation of your shot. The angle between your forearm and upper arm on the shooting hand must be 90 degrees or less.

4. Your left hand is on the side of the ball but only for protection and support. It must not grip the ball tightly or impede the shot in any way.

Release and Follow-Through

1. The release of the basketball is identical to the spot shot.

2. The power for the shot is generated from the legs, elbow extension, and the snap of the wrist.

3. Your head is up with your eyes focused on your sight point on the basket.

4. Release the ball at the top of your jump by straightening the right elbow and snapping the right wrist simultaneously.
   Note: Many coaches insist that the only proper time to release the ball is at the top of your jump. However, many excellent jump shooters release the ball near the top of their jumps.

5. Do not try to jump as high as possible. Concentrate on going straight up and maintaining good balance all the way through the jump. This is a very important point, especially for young players. If too much energy goes into the jump, there is often not enough strength left to maintain good balance and body control. The net result is that the shooter stiffens on the release of the shot instead of relaxing. The shoulder and back muscles tense where the shooter looks almost as though he or she is leaning backward in the air and the shot is too hard and often with little arc.

6. The follow-through of the hands is exactly the same as in the spot shot, only it is more difficult to accomplish on the jumper because you are in the air. This means you will have to concentrate harder on following through properly, maintaining good balance, and seeing the ball go through the basket.

7. You should maintain your balance and body control after the ball is released so that you land on the balls of both feet, spread about a shoulder width apart, in a stable position either in the same spot as your takeoff or a little forward of that spot. (See Figures 5-18a, 5-18b, 5-18c, 5-18d, and 5-18e.)

(a)   (b)   (c)

(d)   (e)

Figure 5-18   (a) The Jump Shot Stance, (b) the Jump Shot Grip and Arm
Position, (c) the Jump Shot Jump, (d) the Jump Shot
Removal of Guide Hand, and (e) the Jump Shot Release

Drill S-14

  1. Face the basket at SS #1. Review *Jump Shot Checkpoints*.
  2. Shoot jump shots from a standing position until you have made three consecutively.
  Your right foot is slightly forward with your feet spread comfortably apart and knees bent.
  Your head is up, and you never take your eyes off the rim until the ball goes through the basket.
  Jump straight up and release the ball with proper backspin and follow-through.
  Land balanced on the balls of both feet spread comfortably with knees bent. You should land on or slightly forward of the spot you took off from.
  Important Note: Short jump shots develop form because little power is necessary. The secret to hitting the short jumper consistently is to put proper arc on the ball (do not shoot too flat) and exaggerate the follow-through.
  Because the shot is short and needs little power, many shooters make the mistake of pulling their shooting hands back immediately after the release of the ball. This results in a hard shot that often bounces out of the basket. Exaggerate the follow-through on close shots, and the "soft" shot will often bounce in instead of out of the basket.
  3. Repeat steps 1 and 2 from SS #2–15.
  Note: If you are a young player, you should eliminate SS #11–15 from this drill if shooting from those spots causes any breakdown in form.

POINTS OF EMPHASIS

- This is a much more difficult drill than it appears to be. It could take you hours to complete the first time, but you will improve rapidly as you relax, learn to concentrate, and improve your form.
- Take your time and execute each shot, concentrating on form and rhythm.
- Begin each shot well balanced on the balls of your feet.
- Your head is up with your eyes sighted on the rim until the ball goes through the basket.
- As you prepare to jump, your weight should shift slightly onto your left foot as you bend your knees.
- Your right elbow is in with your right hand behind the ball.
- The ball is released with proper backspin at the moment of full extension of the arm.
- The fingers of the right hand follow through directly toward the basket and then fall limply down as the hand relaxes. Remember the shorter the shot, the more you must concentrate on proper arc and exaggerate the follow-through.
- Land on the balls of your feet simultaneously, with your legs comfort-

ably spread apart, and knees bent, on the spot from which you took off or slightly forward. Your head should still be up.

Important Note When you first learn your jumper, practice by jumping straight up and landing slightly forward from where you took off. This is to ensure that you jump off the balls of your feet while leaning forward. Many young players, probably because they start using the jumper in competition too early against older and taller players, develop the habit of jumping backward and fading away on their jump shots.

Aside from the fact that this is a much more difficult shot, it forces the player to straighten and stiffen his or her back, a habit that often continues for all jump shots. This adversely affects the rhythm of the shot. Perfect rhythm requires the simultaneous full extension of all the joints—ankles, knees, waist, and elbow—with the release of the shot. If the back stiffens, the waist straightens prematurely, and the rhythm is never perfect.

Skill: The Jump Shot with One Step

Drill S-15

1. Face the basket standing six inches to one foot farther from the basket than SS #1.

2. Begin each shot with your feet comfortably spread, right foot behind your left, with your left foot as your pivot. Step forward with your right foot into proper shooting position before each shot. Continue until you have made three shots consecutively.

This should be a rocking motion where your weight shifts from your right foot to your left foot to both feet as you step forward to shoot. Be sure you keep your head up.

3. Repeat steps 1 and 2 from SS #2–15.

4. Repeat steps 1–4 using your right foot as your pivot and step forward with your left foot.

This will feel a little more awkward than using the left foot as your pivot and stepping forward with the right.

In this case, with your right foot as your pivot, you will have to move the ball from your left hip to your right hip as you shift your weight from your left foot to your right as you bring your left foot forward.

Bring your left foot forward to the point where the toes of the left foot are even with the heel of the right foot. At this point you will shift your weight back slightly onto your left and shoot. Your head should be up and your feet comfortably spread apart.

Now you know why most right-handers prefer to use their left foot as their pivot. It takes a great deal of practice to master the standing jumper off a right- as well as a left-foot pivot.

SHOOTING **161**

Skill: The Jump Shot with One Dribble

Drill S-16

1. Face the basket standing one to two feet farther from the basket than SS #1.

2. Simultaneously take one right-handed dribble and one step with your left foot directly forward into SS #1 and shoot your jump shot. Continue this until you have made three consecutively. Be sure your head is up and your eyes remain sighted on the rim.

Your dribble should be waist high just to the right and in front of the right foot. The dribble should be a hard bounce so that it aids your momentum upward.

Be sure that your step is small enough so that your momentum is straight up. You should land in a balanced position in either the same spot you took off from or slightly forward.

3. Repeat steps 1 and 2 from SS #2–15.

4. Repeat steps 1–3 using one dribble with your left hand and one step forward with your right foot.

You will have to swing the ball across your body from your left hip to your right as you bring your left foot up into shooting position.

In situations where you know you are going to shoot, you can make this move quicker and smoother by bringing the ball up the center of your body to shoot instead of from your left hip to your right hip and up. However, if you are not sure that the shot is open, you are better off swinging the ball across your body onto your right hip where it will be better protected. You can also either drive to the basket or pass to a teammate more easily. Practice both movements so you can use the appropriate move in game situations.

Skill: The Jump Shot with the Turn

Drill S-17

1. Begin one step from SS #6 with your back to the base line and your left shoulder pointing toward the basket. Hold the ball on your right hip.

2. Simultaneously take one dribble with your right hand and one step with your left foot onto SS #6. Review the points made in Drill S-16, step 2.

a. Point the toes of your left foot toward the basket as your left foot lands.

b. Step forward with the right foot on the dribble and, all in one motion, swing your right leg around into shooting position catching the ball on your right hip. Be sure your right foot swings around so that it is forward of the left, in good shooting position.

c. Whenever you shoot off a lateral move, it is important to step at an angle slightly toward the basket. A completely lateral move or a step angling away from the basket will cause your momentum to pull you away from the basket making the shot very difficult. Whenever possible, the last step before you shoot should be at least slightly toward the basket.

d. Take your jump shot and repeat the move until you have made three consecutively.

3. Repeat steps 1 and 2 stepping into SS #7–10 and in descending order #17–11.

4. Repeat steps 1–3 stepping into SS #10–6 in descending order and #11–17. Step with your right foot and dribble with your left hand and pivot on the ball of your right foot.

Review the points made in Drill S-16, step 4.

POINTS OF EMPHASIS

- The last four drills take you from a standing jump shot through the jump shot off one dribble forward and lateral using either foot as your pivot. It could take you hours to complete just these drills!
- Take your time and execute each shot and move with perfect form and rhythm.
- Your head is up with your eyes sighted on the rim until the ball goes through the basket.
- Maintain a low center of gravity with good balance and body control throughout the drills. Any time you feel your balance waver, bend your knees and be sure you are well balanced on the balls of your feet that are comfortably spread apart.
- Get the ball into the "slot" on your right hip as quickly as possible.
- As you prepare to jump on your jump shot, your weight should shift slightly onto your left foot as you bend your knees.
- Your right elbow is in line with your right hand behind the ball.
- The ball is released with proper backspin, full extension of the arm, and proper follow-through.
- Land on the balls of your feet simultaneously, with your legs comfortably spread apart and knees bent, on the spot from which you took off of or slightly forward.

COMMON JUMP SHOOTING FAULTS

Problem: Inconsistency. *Solution*: Inconsistency is usually the result of a breakdown of form and concentration. Most frequent areas of form breakdown are:

1. Failing to keep the shooting elbow in line with the right leg and the right hand under the ball. In preparation of their shot, many players incorrectly rotate the ball in their hands so that, as the shooting hand rotates behind the ball, the elbow rotates out. Always slide your shooting hand behind the ball keeping the elbow in tight.
2. Jerking the head and/or shoulders on the shot. A good shot involves no motion from the head or shoulder. The elbow extension and the wrist

snap should provide all the power from the upper body. Shoulder action will result in an inaccurate and inconsistent shot as it often signals that the shooter is either off balance or is shooting out of his or her range and is trying to generate extra power by using his or her shoulder. Remember two things regarding shooting range:

a. Always practice shooting within your range. Practicing long shots often results in developing bad habits such as jerking your head and/or shoulder or pulling the ball back over your head on shots. Short shots develop proper form and accuracy.

b. The power for longer shots should be generated by the legs. The upper body, except for the elbow extension and wrist snap, should remain as motionless as possible. Learn to bend your knees more on longer shots and push off the floor harder as your knees straighten. This will supply extra power while maintaining as much form and accuracy as possible. Begin each shot in your legs.

Problem: Length of Shot. *Solution*: As long as your shot is consistently on line to the basket, the length of the shot can usually be adjusted with little problem. If your shot tends to hit the front rim:

1. You may be leaning back on the release.
2. You may be shooting the ball off your palm instead of your fingertips. This might result in a "shot-putting" motion.
3. You may not be following through.
4. You may be tired and not bending your knees enough.

If your shot is regularly bouncing off the back rim:

1. Your shot may be too "flat."
2. You may be extending too quickly on your shot and getting too much arm into the shot. This may cause you to "throw" the ball instead of shoot it.
3. You may not be following through.

In any case, you may have lost concentration or be either shooting out of your range or shooting too quickly.

Problem: Shot Is Off Line. *Solution*: A good shooter shoots straight. It is relatively simple to make adjustments for a shot that is a little long or short, and every player learns those adjustments by doing such things as bending his or her knees a little more or adding arc to the shot. However, shooting off line is much more serious and if your shot is not consistently on line, you will never be a good shooter. While the distance of a shot can often be corrected with an adjustment, the line of a shot may be the result of a serious flaw in form.

1. Feet must be comfortably spread apart, with the weight on the balls of the feet leaning slightly forward. The right foot has to be slightly forward so the shooting arm (right) is lined up to the basket. If the right foot is even or behind the left, the shooter has to rotate his or her shoulders left to right on the shot.

2. If the feet are too close together or too spread, the jump might be at an angle causing an off-line shot. An on-line shot requires good balance. Once you lose balance on your shot, you must compensate with movement from some area such as your head or shoulders and this can cause the shot to go off-line. When shooting off the move or the dribble, be sure your feet are securely under you before you take off on the shot.

3. Hand and elbow must be behind and under the ball, respectively. If the hand is not behind the ball, either the ball cannot be released properly off the fingertips or the elbow must rotate out to get the hand behind the ball. Either way, both the elbow and hand must be in proper position for your shot to be consistently straight.

4. Release the left or guide hand *before* the release of the shot. This is a particular problem for young players who lack strength and the player who does not get his or her right hand directly behind the ball on the shot. This results in an inconsistent two-handed shot where the right hand is generating most of the power.

5. Be sure the shooting hand and fingers follow through straight to the basket. If the wrist turns in or out, the ball will frequently be off line.

6. *Concentration*: You must discipline yourself to concentrate totally on each shot. That means that your eyes are focused on your sight point on the rim throughout the shot, you follow through properly, and you land in a balanced position.

Problem: Touch—The Ball Seems to Always Bounce Out. *Solution*: A "soft" shot is the result of proper release and follow-through and sufficient arc on the shot.

1. Not finishing the shot is what coaches call it, and it is a particular problem, even for normally good shooters, when a player shoots under pressure. Many players think that it does not matter what they do after the ball has left their hand on a shot. Nothing could be farther from the truth. It is very possible that the follow-through is the *most* important part of the shot! Finish every shot with a "locked out" (fully extended) right elbow, palm and fingers relaxed and pointing toward the floor and your eyes on the basket.

2. Rhythm on a shot is the synchronization of the full extension of the ankles, knees, waist, and elbow. The release of the shot should coincide with all these joints fully extending at the same time. If the knees, waist, or any other joint reaches full extension before the others, the shooting rhythm will be jerky instead of smooth. In addition, the shot must be released simultaneously with the full extension of these joints.

3. The ball must be released off the fingertips with proper backspin. Do

not snap the hand down on the release of the shot. Allow the ball to roll off the fingertips, point the fingers toward the basket, and relax, allowing the fingers and hand to go limp.

4. *Proper arc*: Although each player will select the arc that he finds best for his shot, players who have poor "touch" often shoot with too little arc. It is interesting to note the relationship between arc and the position of the elbow. Many players who shoot too "flat" have their elbows out. This is because it is difficult to shoot "up" with the elbow out. When the hand is behind the ball and the elbow is under the hand and in line with the right hip, the natural extension of the arm on the shot tends to bring the elbow and hand up naturally, creating proper arc.

Problem: Shooting Slumps. *Solution*: Many players are streak shooters—when they are hot, they can't miss, but when they are cold, they can't hit. The two reasons for this phenomenon—the ability to sustain confidence and concentration—usually relate to the personality of the shooter.

1. Concentrate on taking good shots—shots you have practiced and know you can make.
2. Be sure that your feet are under you before you shoot and you are well balanced.
3. Your eyes must be fixed on your sight point on the rim.
4. Extend all your joints rhythmically and release the ball off the fingertips and follow through.
5. Do not stiffen or tense your hand, arm, back, and leg muscles on the shot. To relax on a shot means that you can smoothly synchronize the extension of your body on the shot without stiffening any area. This takes concentration—especially under pressure.
6. Land balanced.
7. *Confidence*: From the moment you have decided to shoot until the ball goes through the basket, visualize the shot going into the basket.

Skill: Shooting Off the Pass

The following drills use some terminology that need defining:

The Triple-Threat Position   Whenever you receive the ball facing the basket in the offensive zone, you should immediately get into the Triple-Threat Position. This is the best possible position for you to shoot, pass, or drive to the basket:

1. Your feet are squared to the basket in shooting position, with the right foot slightly ahead of the left, about a shoulder width apart.

(a)   (b)

Figures 5-19a and 5-19b Triple Threat Position

2. Your knees and waist are bent, your head is up, and the ball is in the "slot," right over your right hip in close to your body.
3. Your right hand is behind the ball in shooting position with the left hand on the side of the ball for support and protection. (See Figures 5-19a and 5-19b.)

Spinning the Ball Out To begin many of the drills, it will be necessary for you to simulate a game situation by spinning the ball to a specific spot, going after it, and, after one bounce, catching it in the air with both hands and landing with a two-foot jump stop. You should spin the ball out by first holding the ball with two hands between your knees with your arms extended. Underhanded, flip the ball out in front of you with backspin to a height of at least ten feet to the prescribed spot. (See Figures 5-20a and 5-20b.)

Shooting Off the Pass The ability to shoot quickly and accurately after catching the ball is a very important skill to master. In a half-court offense, this often means catching a pass moving toward the passer. Whether you catch the ball coming off a screen from a teammate or not, you must be able to:

1. Catch and protect the ball.
2. Pivot into the Triple-Threat Position. Get your shoooting hand behind the ball.
3. Get off a quick and accurate shot.

(a)   (b)

Figures 5-20a and 5-20b Spinning the Ball Out

The secret to getting off a quick and accurate shot is good preparation (anticipation) and body control.

Drill S-18

1. Begin at the base line facing the court and spin the ball out to SS #6. Catch the ball in the air after one bounce and do a jump stop.

2. Using your left foot as your pivot, front pivot one quarter turn into the Triple-Threat Position and shoot a jump shot.

Your head is up, your center of gravity is low, your body control is good, and the ball is well protected.

This is a good move for a right-handed shooter because, on the pivot, the right foot moves into perfect shooting position just ahead of the left foot facing the basket.

3. Repeat steps 1 and 2 spinning the ball from:
   a. SS #6 to 7
      #7 to 8
      #8 to 9
      #9 to 10
   b. Base line to SS #17
          #17 to 16
          #16 to 15
          #15 to 14
          #14 to 13
          #13 to 12
          #12 to 11

4. Repeat steps 1–3 using the right foot as your pivot. This will involve a quarter turn reverse pivot pulling your left leg back into the Triple-Threat Position.

Be sure that your right foot is slightly ahead of the left after you pivot into your Triple-Threat Position.

5. Begin at the base line. Spin the ball to SS #10. Catch the ball in the air after one bounce and jump stop.

6. Repeat steps 2 and 4 front pivoting on the right foot and reverse pivoting on the left foot.

a. Catch the ball on your left hip.

b. With your elbows out, swing the ball to your right hip as you pivot into your Triple-Threat Position.

This is a more difficult and awkward move for a right-handed player because you have to shift the ball across your body into shooting position. If a defensive player is close to you, you must protect the ball with your elbows out as you swing the ball across your body.

7. Repeat step 6 spinning the ball from:

a. SS #10 to 9

#9 to 8

#8 to 7

#7 to 6

b. Base line to #11

#11 to 12

#12 to 13

#13 to 14

#14 to 15

#15 to 16

#16 to 17

8. Repeat steps 1–3 using a stride stop with the left foot as your pivot and front pivoting into your Triple-Threat Position.

On the stride stop, catch the ball on your right hip in shooting position and point your left foot toward the basket on your landing so that you can pivot and shoot all in one motion.

9. Repeat steps 5–7 using a stride stop with the right foot as your pivot and front pivoting into your Triple-Threat Position.

POINTS OF EMPHASIS

- Begin practicing these moves slowly so that you can do them with your head up, with the ball well protected, without creating a walking violation, smoothly and in perfect balance and control of your body. Speed will come with practice.
- Repeat all or parts of this drill using chairs or other objects to simulate shooting off a screen. Some players practice by placing brooms in chairs or ladders to teach them how to shoot over screens and defenders.
- On your stride and jump stops be sure your knees are well bent and you get your legs under you.
- When you catch the ball doing a stride stop, land with the pivot foot pointing toward the basket so that you can pivot and shoot all in one quick, smooth motion.

Skill: Shooting Off the Dribble

Shooting off the dribble is one of the most exciting and enjoyable parts of the game of basketball. The skills involved are a smooth, rhythmic combination of footwork, dribbling, and shooting, combined with a sense of timing and judgment.

Shooting off the dribble commonly occurs in two situations:

1. When a teammate sets a screen for you.
2. When you are in the "transition" game.

After your team gains possession of the ball from a rebound, violation, steal, or made basket, the ball can be advanced up the court, with a combination of passing and dribbling, very quickly in an attempt to gain a team advantage and an easy basket. This aggressive style of trying to move the ball into scoring position as quickly as possible is called "fast-break" basketball, and the "transition game" is where the team that gains possession of the ball tries to attack their opponent before it can successfully switch from offense to defense. If the attacking team is successful in the transition game, it might find itself attacking with a two on one, three on two, or some such team advantage.

Even a three on three or four on four can be an advantage for some teams because fewer players mean more open space for highly talented and skilled players to maneuver. It is in the "open court," where there is plenty of space to maneuver and achieve team advantages, that the ability to make moves and shoot off the dribble are most effective.

All the sound fundamentals of footwork, dribbling, and shooting apply to making good offensive moves off the dribble. However, because these basic skills must be integrated and executed at various speeds, often while changing speeds and direction, many of the fundamentals must be further refined.

FUNDAMENTALS OF MOVES OFF THE DRIBBLE

1. Your head must always be up.
2. Use the appropriate dribble: high for speed when unguarded and low for protection when guarded.
3. Good offensive moves are a combination of solid skills, judgment, deception, timing, and changes of pace and direction.
4. You must always be under control, especially when you make a move off the dribble. Be sure that you are under control and not decreasing your speed during your move. This makes your move easy to anticipate and difficult to control. Get your speed down where you are under complete

control before you make a move, and your moves will be quicker and more deceptive and powerful. This is the single most common error that young players make when attempting to make an offensive move off the dribble. *Do not make your move while decelerating.* Slow down and be sure you are under complete control *before* you make your move.

5. The best way to stay under control before you make a move off the dribble is to bend your knees and cut your steps before you make the move. You will find that the effectiveness of a move is not based on the speed at which the move is made but the *change* of speed and direction. This means that the best moves are those that change speed and direction the most. Slowing down and accelerating on the move is better for your control and more difficult to defend.

6. Offensive moves off the dribble are intended to get you past your defensive opponent. However, this does not mean that you will always be able to go to the basket for a layup. You must be prepared, after beating your defensive opponent, to make a variety of moves, and this means you must be under control. You are under control if you are capable of making a jump stop at any time after you have made your move.

7. Often, a player gets into trouble after he or she makes a good move off the dribble because his or her center of gravity gets too high. Anytime you jump off balance or allow your upper body to get too far in front of your legs, you are in danger of losing control. Be conscious of keeping your feet under you on all your moves and jumps. When you go to the basket for a layup or power move, make the last step small enough so your momentum is up and not out. This also holds true for the last step of any move—make the last step short enough so that your forward momentum is not so great that you cannot stop and collect yourself.

Drill S-19

1. Begin facing the basket at SS #21.

2. Dribble slowly with your right hand to SS #9 and stride stop with your left foot back as your pivot. Your last step must be smaller to improve balance and control.

3. Bend your knees and lower your dribble on your last step or two before your stop so that you can stride stop into a compact position with your feet no more than a shoulder width apart. Your head is up and the ball is well protected. Your shooting hand should slide behind the ball after the last dribble.

4. Square yourself to the basket by front pivoting into the Triple-Threat Position and shoot. You should practice taking both your spot and jump shot.

5. Continue until you have made three shots in a row.

6. Repeat steps 1–5, except on the stride stop point the toes of your left foot toward the basket on the last step of the stop. This will smooth out the move on the pivot.

7. Repeat steps 1–6 dribbling from SS #19 to 7 and using the left-handed dribble and the right foot as your pivot on the stride stop.

Remember: When you square off into the Triple-Threat Position from the left side with your right foot as your pivot, the left foot must be pulled back to about the heel of the right foot so that you are in proper shooting position. You can smooth this move out by angling slightly left on your last step with your left foot so your right foot will be forward after the pivot.

You will also have to swing the ball from your left hip across your body and up into shooting position. Be sure the ball is well protected.

8. Repeat steps 1–7 using jump stops.

9. Repeat step 8, but on your jump stop, twist your body in the air so that you land with the toes of both feet facing the basket, right foot slightly forward, in the Triple-Threat Position.

You can do this by turning the inside foot in on the last step before you jump stop or you can do the turn completely in the air.

Body control is a must in these maneuvers, and you must not jump too high, move too fast, or stride too long where you are not in complete control of your body.

10. Dribble with the right hand from SS #20 to 14 with the right hand and execute a jump stop into your Triple-Threat Position and shoot.

11. Continue until you have made three in a row.

12. Repeat steps 10 and 11 dribbling with the left hand.

13. Repeat steps 11 and 12 with stride stops using both the right and left foot as your pivot.

14. Repeat steps 10–13 dribbling from SS #20 to 13 with the right hand and from SS #20 to 15 with the left hand.

POINTS OF EMPHASIS

- The shot off the dribble requires excellent dribbling skills. You should not have to look at the ball during these moves. Your head should be up.
- Bend your knees and make your last step before stopping smaller to improve your body control.
- The stops and shots off the dribble to your left require more attention to footwork and protection of the ball.
- Be sure that your right foot is ahead of your left in shooting position after your pivot, or you will be off balance on your shot and your shot may be off line.
- Get your shooting hand behind the ball as the ball comes up on the final dribble.
- Be sure you protect the ball as you bring it across your body after your stop. If you know on the stop that you are going to shoot, bring the ball about halfway across your body and straight up into shooting position. If you are not sure whether you will pass, fake, dribble, or shoot, swing the ball across from your left hip to your right hip into Triple-Threat Position.

WORKOUT, EVALUATION, AND PROGRESS CHARTS

Table 5-1 Shooting Workout—30 Minutes

Warmup

DRILL	SKILL	INSTRUCTIONS
S-3	Spot shot	Make two in a row from SS #1–17.
S-5	Spot shot, bank	Make two in a row from SS #2, 9, 12, 4, 7, 16.
S-6	Foul shot	Make fifty.
S-7/8	Layup	Using the layup of your choice, make ten in a row from each side using the appropriate hand.
S-10/12	Hook shot	Make two in a row from SS #1, 2, 3, 8, 9, 10 with the right hand and SS #5, 4, 3, 6, 7, 8 with left hand.
S-14	Jump shot	Make two in a row from SS #1–17.
S-18	Jump shot off pass with turn	Make two in a row from SS #6 –10, 17–11 pivoting on left foot, SS #10 – 6, 11–17 pivoting on right.
S-5	Jump shot, bank	Make two in a row from 2, 9, 12, 4, 7, 16.
S-19	Jump shot off dribble	Make two in a row dribbling from SS #21 to 9, 19 to 7, 20 to 13, 20 to 14, 20 to 15. Do once with stride stops and once with jump stops.
S-6	Foul shot	Make fifty.

Cooldown

Table 5-2 Shooting Workout—60 to 120 Minutes

Warmup

DRILL	SKILL	INSTRUCTIONS
S-3	Spot shot	Make three in a row from SS #1–17.
S-4	Spot shot with one dribble	Make three in a row from SS #6 –17.
S-5	Spot shot, bank	Make three in a row from SS #2, 9, 12, 14, 7, 16.
S-6	Foul shot	Make fifty.
S-7	Layup	Make ten in a row from each side using appropriate hand.
S-8	Underhanded layup	Make five in a row from each side using appropriate hand.
S-9	Power layup	Make five in a row from each side.
S-10/12	Hook shot	Make three in a row from SS #1, 2, 3, 8, 9, 10 with right hand and SS #5, 4, 3, 6, 7, 8 with left hand.
S-11/13	Hook shot	Make three in a row driving from SS #15 to 1, 6 to 2 using right hand and SS #13 to 5, 10 to 4 using left hand.
S-14	Jump shot	Make three in a row from SS #1–17.
S-15	Jump shot with one step	" " "
S-16	Jump shot with one dribble	" " "

Table 5-2 (*Continued*)

Warmup

DRILL	SKILL	INSTRUCTIONS
S-17	Jump shot with turn	Make three in a row from SS #6 –10, 17–11 pivoting on left foot and 10 – 6, 11–17 pivoting on right foot.
S-18	Jump shot off pass with turn	" " "
S-5	Jump shot, bank	Make three in a row from SS #2, 9, 12, 4, 7, 16.
S-19	Jump shot off dribble	Make three in a row dribbling from SS #21 to 9, 19 to 7, 20 to 13, 20 to 14, 20 to 15. Do once with stride stops and once with jump stops.
S-6	Foul shot	Make fifty.
Cooldown		

Table 5-3   Shooting Self-Evaluation and Improvement Test

DRILL	SKILL	INSTRUCTIONS	SCORE
S-3	Spot shot	Take three shots from SS #1–17.	No. of shots made
S-4	Spot shot with one dribble	Take three shots from SS #6 –17.	" "
S-5	Spot shot, bank	Take three shots from SS #2, 9, 12, 4, 7, 16.	" "
S-6	Foul shot	Take one hundred shots.	" "
S-7	Layup	Take ten shots from each side using appropriate hand.	" "
S-9	Power layup	Take five shots from each side.	" "
S-10/12	Hook shot	Take three shots from SS #1, 2, 3, 8, 9, 10 with right hand, SS #5, 4, 3, 6, 7, 8 with left hand.	" "
S-11/13	Hook shot	Take three shots driving from SS #15 to 1, 6 to 2 using right hand and SS #13 to 5, 10 to 4 using left hand.	" "
S-14	Jump shot	Take three shots from SS #1–17.	" "
S-15	Jump shot with one step	" "	" "
S-16	Jump shot with one dribble	" "	" "
S-17	Jump shot with turn	Take three shots from SS #6 – 10, 17–11, pivoting on left foot, SS #10 – 6, 11–17 pivoting on right.	" "
S-18	Jump shot off pass with turn	" "	" "
S-5	Jump shot bank	Take three shots from SS #2, 9, 12, 4, 7, 16.	" "
S-19	Jump shot off dribble	Take three shots dribbling from SS #21 to 9, 19 to 7, 20 to 13, 20 to 14, 20 to 15. Do once with stride stops and once with jump stops.	" "

Table 5-4 Personal Shooting Progress Chart

Drill	DATE							
S-3								
S-4								
S-5								
S-6								
S-7								
S-8								
S-9								
S-10/12								
S-11/13								
S-14								
S-15								
S-16								
S-17								
S-18								
S-5								
S-19								

ONE-ON-ONE
MOVES

One-on-one moves incorporate many of the individual fundamental skills we have learned in footwork, dribbling, and shooting. In a half-court offense, where five defensive players are defending against five offensive players, these skills are essential. One-on-one moves are the skills needed when you receive the ball within twenty-five feet of the basket.

From this position you must assess the defense and decide what you are going to do: shoot, pass, or dribble. Because you have three options, the basic position you assume while facing the basket after receiving the ball on a pass is called the Triple-Threat Position. Posting Position refers to when you receive the ball closer, from next to the basket to ten or fifteen feet out, with your back to the basket. Different one-on-one moves are required for the Post Position.

You will learn all the one-on-one skills by breaking down the moves from the Triple-Threat Position (where you will face the basket and shoot, pass, or dribble) and the posting moves (including low-, middle-, and high-post options). In this chapter you will learn many options from the one-on-one position, both triple-threat and posting moves. However, it is important that you understand that no player perfects or uses them all.

As you practice these skills and develop your "game," you will select those moves that are most effective for you, depending upon your size, strength, quickness, deceptiveness, and temperament. Practice them all at first, and, in time, those most appropriate for you will develop and find themselves into your "game." Although you do not have to master every move, it is important that you develop enough of a variety of good moves so that you cannot be defensed easily. This means that you must develop at least one good move to shoot, drive right, and drive left from each position. This way, the defense must play you "honestly," and you will have the best chance of scoring.

LEARNING THE MOVES

The following section is going to take you through various one-on-one moves. These moves are not difficult if you take the time to learn them slowly and thoroughly. First, read through each move before you begin practice; then, walk through the move several times *without* the basketball until you feel the rhythm of the move. Even when you begin practicing with the ball, begin slowly and only increase the tempo of the move when it can be done smoothly and without losing your body control and balance.

Remember: These moves must be mastered so that you can repeat them flawlessly as a conditioned reflex in game situations. They must be practiced over and over until you can do them without thinking. This can only be accomplished by first learning them properly and then practicing them tirelessly.

Each player will develop favorite moves and even individual variations that make his or her moves special and particularly difficult to defense. It is important for you to learn each move and practice them because it will make you a better player. However, in time you will select only those moves you do best and put them into your "game."

You do not need to possess every move in your repertoire to be a complete basketball player. From the Triple-Threat Position within shooting range of the basket, each player must be able to shoot, drive left, or drive right, depending on what the defense gives you. The more *effective* moves you develop, the harder you will be to stop. But remember: You must be able to shoot from the outside, or the defense will sag off on you for the drive, and you must be able to go either right or left, or the defense will overplay you to your strong side.

In this chapter you will learn and practice all the moves and learn to use either foot as your pivot. But be aware that later, you will decide the moves that are most effective for you and rarely use the others.

As for using either foot as your pivot on your moves, most players favor the use of one foot—usually right-handers like to use the left foot as their pivot and lefties prefer the right foot. This is because it is easier to shoot: You will have more balance and body control jumping and pushing off the nondominant foot. However, in game situations, you will be a more versatile player if you can effectively use either foot as your pivot.

Skill: The Triple-Threat Position

When you receive the ball, usually on a pass from a teammate between ten and twenty-five feet from the basket, you must assess the defense and decide what you are going to do: shoot, pass, or dribble. To be a constant threat, you must develop a variety of "moves" that will enable you to score when the opportunity presents itself. But before you can make a move, you must learn how to catch the ball, protect the ball, and square yourself to the basket so that you will be in the best possible position to shoot, pass or dribble. Hence this is called the Triple-Threat Position.

Important Note   It should be pointed out that the single most important concept regarding receiving a pass in good position to score is your movement *without* the ball. This means that you must learn how and when to take your defensive opponent *away* from the ball and cut back to receive the pass. This is commonly achieved by timing your cuts off screens or simply dropping your opponent—taking a step or two away from the ball and cutting back to receive the pass. In our drills, we will simulate game conditions by "spinning" the ball to spots and coming to meet the ball from various directions.

Drill 000-1

1. Begin with your back to the basket at SS #4. Place your two hands on the sides of the basketball and extend your arms down in front of you so the ball is just below waist level.
2. Flip the ball underhanded, with backspin, at least ten feet in the air, and try to have it land on SS #16. From this point on we will call this "spinning the ball out." Run to the ball, and, after it bounces once, catch it in the air, with both hands, landing on SS #16 with a two-foot jump stop and your back still to the basket (Fig. 6-1a):
    Your feet are parallel and about a shoulder width apart.
    Your knees and waist are bent but your back is straight.
    Your elbows are out.

(a)   (b)   (c)

Figure 6-1   (a) Catching The Ball "Strong," (b) the Quick Look, and (c)
180 Degree Forward Pivot on Left Foot into the Triple Threat
Position

You are holding the ball firmly in both hands.

Your head is up.

Since you landed on both feet simultaneously, you are allowed to use either foot as a pivot.

3. Without turning your head more than an eighth of a turn, take a quick peek over your left shoulder (Fig. 6-1b). In general, it is usually better to look over the shoulder toward the open court or away from the nearest sideline or base line. This will give you the most information about where the defense is and where a teammate is most likely to be open.

4. Front pivot 180 degrees on the ball of your left foot to your left and square your shoulders to the basket (Fig. 6-1c).

Your feet are about a shoulder width apart with your right foot slightly in front of your left. The toes of both feet point to the basket.

Your knees and waist are bent, and your weight is evenly distributed on the balls of your feet.

You are holding the ball firmly in shooting position—elbows in, right hand behind the ball, and left hand on the side—just above your right hip and in line with your right leg in close to your body.

This is called the *Triple-Threat Position*, and when the ball is held in shooting position just above the right hip, we say the ball is *in the slot*. From the *Triple-Threat Position*, you are able to put maximum pressure on your defender because you are in the best possible position to shoot, pass, or dribble, depending on which option would most easily get your team a basket.

It is from the Triple-Threat Position that we will learn one-on-one, facing the basket moves from about ten to twenty-five feet out, that are absolutely necessary for all guards and forwards.

5. Repeat step 4 spinning the ball out from SS #9 to 12 and reversing the directions for hands and feet. This means you will front pivot 180 degrees on the ball of your right foot to your right and square your shoulders to the basket.

Skill: The Reverse Pivot Into
the Triple-Threat Position

The front pivot described in the last drill is the most common method of establishing yourself in the Triple-Threat Position when you receive the ball with your back to the basket. However, there is a second and very effective reverse pilot maneuver that has become popular, especially with forwards and centers receiving the ball from six to fifteen feet from the basket.

The reverse pivot move is identical to the front pivot move up to the point of the pivot. After you peek over your shoulder, you pivot into the Triple-Threat Position by reverse pivoting. This means you will swing your leg around behind you toward the defender and into the Triple-Threat Position.

The tighter your defender is playing you (that is, the closer he is to your back at the start of the move), the more difficult it will be to execute the reverse pivot without either charging into him or exposing the ball where he might be able to knock it out of your hands.

The reverse pivot into the Triple-Threat Position can always be used after receiving the ball when your defender is more than six feet behind you. Many players claim that the reverse pivot is more effective than the front pivot because it can be made quicker and allows you to pick up the basket sooner. It also prepares you to either shoot or make a move before the defender has time to react.

The most effective reverse pivot move into the Triple-Threat Position is to spin in the same direction as you look over your shoulder. In this way, you never lose sight of the basket, and the move can be executed quickly and smoothly with excellent balance.

Drill 000-1A

1. Repeat Drill 000-1, except in step 4, do a reverse pivot on the ball of your right foot instead of a front pivot on the ball of your left foot.

Be sure that the ball is well protected as you pivot. Hold the ball firmly with your head up, knees bent, and elbows out.

If you are very tall, you should also practice this move with the ball held up high over your head for those occasions when you are being guarded by a smaller player.

For added protection, you should also practice this reverse pivot maneuver when you use your left foot as your pivot, by swinging the ball around while holding the ball very low by bending your knees and waist. This method is effective when your defender is your size or taller and is playing you tight.

POINTS OF EMPHASIS

- Be sure you peek over your shoulder to locate where your defender is before you reverse pivot.
- Be careful not to charge into your defender on the reverse pivot. If your defender is very tight on your back when you receive the ball, consider going around him or her with a quick or long drop step or using the front pivot.
- The reverse pivot into the Triple-Threat Position requires protecting the basketball. Practice pivoting with the ball high over your head, at waist level, and low, at about knee level.

Important Note   The following drills feature one-on-one moves and series of one-on-one moves using front pivots. This is done because the front pivot into the Triple-Threat Position is the safest and most commonly used maneuver. However, after you have mastered the front pivot for each move, you should experiment using the reverse pivot in the place of the front pivot.

Skill: The Jab Step

The first move you will learn off the Triple-Threat Position is the jab step. The jab step is a forceful step with your nonpivot foot toward your defender for the purpose of keeping your defensive opponent from attacking you and keeping the ball in your possession. There are three different ways to jab step: directly at your defender, at an angle approximately 45 degrees to the right of your defender, and at an angle approximately 45 degrees to the left of your defender. If the defensive player does not respect your jab step and back off you, simply drive right by him or her to the basket. But remember these important points regarding the jab step if you want it to be successful:

1. You must maintain a low, well-balanced body position with your head up and the ball well protected at all times.
2. The jab step must be long enough to force the defender to give you room, but not so long that your balance is impaired.
3. Your step must be short enough so that you can continue on to the basket using the dribble if that option is open or withdraw the step quickly back into the Triple-Threat Position. (See Figures 6-2a and 6-2b.)

Drill 000-2

1. Spin the ball out to SS #16, jump stop, peek over your left shoulder, and front pivot on the ball of your left foot into the Triple-Threat Position.

(a)   (b)

Figure 6-2 (a) Triple Threat Position and (b) Jab Step

 2. Forcefully jab step with the right foot forward one to two feet according to your size, shifting your weight forward onto the ball of your right foot as you step. Be sure you keep your knees bent, the ball well protected and in tight to your body, and do not step too far, which may cause you to lose your balance.

 3. Shift your weight back onto your left foot and pull the right foot back into the Triple-Threat Position. Your right foot should be slightly ahead of the left with your feet about a shoulder width apart, shoulders square to the basket, head up, and the ball is on your right hip in shooting position.

 4. Repeat steps 2 and 3 five times concentrating on forceful jab steps with good balance and low body position as you shift your weight forward and back.

 Did your left foot—your pivot—move? It shouldn't.

 Were you capable of shooting or driving to the basket at any time during the drill? If not, your balance and body position need more work.

 Did you feel any sway from your hips, shoulders, or head as you jab stepped? If so, balance and body position is again the problem.

 5. Repeat steps 1–4 using the jab step at an angle to your right and then again crossing over at an angle to your left.

 When you jab step left, be sure the ball is well protected, in close to your body as you shift the ball to your left hip.

 6. Repeat steps 1–5 spinning the ball out to SS #12, front pivoting on the ball of the right foot to your right and jab stepping with the left foot.

 JAB STEP CHECKPOINTS:

 1. Check your feet. Are they wide enough apart?
 2. Are your knees bent enough?
 3. Is your butt low enough? Bend at the waist but keep your back relatively straight.
 4. Your head is up and balanced, not jerking from side to side.
 5. Practice the jab step slowly, over and over again until you feel the rhythm. Once you do, you know that your balance is improving.

6. The jab step does not have to be executed rapidly to be effective. Its purpose is to push the defensive player off you so that you will have room to either shoot or pass. If the defender fails to back up on your jab step, drive around him or her on the dribble.

Skill: The Ball Fake and the Head Fake

The ball fake, also called the shot or pump fake, and the head fake are two of the most important and effective moves off the Triple-Threat Position. As a general rule, the head fake is used when your defender is less than three feet from you and the ball fake is preferable when he is more than three feet away. The reasons should be obvious: If your defender is close to you, the head fake will freeze him for a split second and, because he is so close, allow you to make a move before he can recover. However, if you use a ball fake when the defender is so close, he might be able to slap the ball out of your hands. The head fake is particularly useful when you have the ball close to the basket either posting up or from an offensive rebound.

You should employ the ball fake when your defender is more than three feet away because this forces him or her to react. If he or she goes for the ball fake and comes at you, you can easily go by him or her. If he or she does not close in on you after a ball fake, you can shoot over him or her.

The head fake is executed by jerking your head straight back and raising your chin (Fig. 6-3a).

The ball fake is executed by bringing the ball all the way up to your eye level or higher, exactly the same way you would if you were going to shoot either your spot shot or jump shot. This is your chance to be an actor. The more your ball fake looks like your regular shot, the more effective it will be (Fig. 6-3b).

Timing and balance are the keys to good fakes:

Timing Time your fakes so that the defense has to react and then either shoot or drive. This means that you must develop a sense of when a fake will put pressure on the defense.

Balance Be sure your feet are comfortably spread, knees are bent, elbows are in close to your body, and head is up when you fake. If not, your fakes may be unconvincing, and you will be more likely to commit a walking violation.

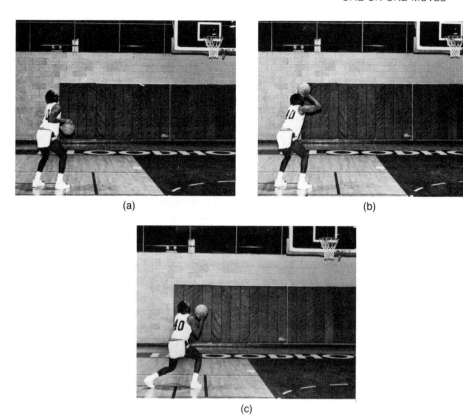

(a) (b)

(c)

Figure 6-3 (a) Head Fake, (b) Ball (Shot) Fake, and (c) Head and Shoulder Fake

---

Drill 000-3

      1. Spin the ball out to SS #16, jump stop, peek over your left shoulder, and front pivot on the ball of your left foot into the Triple-Threat Position.

      2. Head fake, making sure your feet do not move and the ball is well protected.

      3. Ball fake, identical to your spot shot or jump shot up to the release or jump. Convince yourself that you are going to take the shot and at the last moment don't jump and release the ball.

      This is not a quick move. Use the same timing and motion as your shot and give the defense time to react.

      4. Repeat steps 1–3 ten times.

      5. Repeat 1 and execute each of the following sequences using your left foot as your pivot:

      a. Head fake, shot.

      b. Ball fake, shot.

      c. Jab step, head fake, shot.

d. Jab step, ball fake, shot.

e. Jab step, head fake, jab step, head fake, shot.

f. Jab step, ball fake, jab step, ball fake, shot.

6. Repeat step 5 five times.

7. Repeat steps 5–6 spinning the ball out to SS #12, front pivoting on your right foot and reversing the directions for your hands and feet.

Notice that when you jab with the left foot, you must bring it back behind your right foot before you shoot. This is another reason most right-handers prefer to use the left foot as their pivot on one-on-one moves.

POINTS OF EMPHASIS

- Repeat these sequences over and over as slowly as necessary until you feel in perfect balance and you can go from one movement to the other smoothly and with rhythm.
- Be sure that you pull your jab step back into the Triple-Threat Position before your ball fake.
- Be sure you are well balanced on your fakes: feet between nine inches and a shoulder width apart, knees bent, elbows close to your body, head up, and the ball well protected.
- The most common error on the ball fake is that players tend to do it too quickly, not giving the defender sufficient time to react to it. Ball fake at the same speed as your shot and give the defense time to take the fake before you make your next move.

Skill: The Head-and-Shoulder Fake

The head-and-shoulder fake is especially effective when done immediately upon receiving a pass on the perimeter. This move will usually freeze the defense momentarily, giving you a little extra time to either shoot or set up. The head-and-shoulder fake is executed by raising your shoulders and chin at the same time you bend your knees and lean forward on your front foot in the Triple-Threat Position. The ball may be raised to eye level if the defense is at a safe distance (Fig. 6-3c).

Drill 000-4

1. Spin the ball out to SS #16, jump stop, peek over your left shoulder, and front pivot on the ball of your left foot into the Triple-Threat Position.

2. Execute a head-and-shoulder fake by stepping forward on a 45-degree angle to your right while simultaneously bending your knees and jerking your head and shoulders back. This will cause a lurching movement.

You may not have to step forward on this move if your feet are sufficiently spread apart in the Triple-Threat Position. The move is possible with or without a step.

This is a quick move, and you have to be able to change direction easily by shifting your weight from one foot to the other and back to be able to make another move. If you cannot do this, it means you are shifting your weight too much on the fake. Correct this by bending your knees a little more and not lurching so far on the fake. The head and shoulders do not have to move more than a couple of inches.

3. Repeat steps 1 and 2 five times, experimenting with no step and different-size steps on the fake. Concentrate on maintaining good balance and body control so that the fake is quick and deceptive. Be sure you do not commit a walking violation by moving your pivot foot.

4. Repeat steps 1–3 spinning the ball out to SS #12, front pivoting on your right foot, and using the right foot as your pivot.

Skill: Straight Move

The straight move is a quick step from the Triple-Threat Position with your nonpivot foot. After you have set your defensive opponent up with jab steps and/or ball fakes, you may be able to drive straight to the basket. (See Figures 6-4a, 6-4b, and 6-4c.)

Figure 6-4 (a) Triple Threat Position and (b) and (c) Straight Move

(a)

(b)

(c)

Drill 000-5

1. Spin the ball out to SS #16, jump stop, peek over your left shoulder, and front pivot on your left foot into the Triple-Threat Position.

2. Jab step with your right foot on a 45-degree angle to your right and withdraw back onto the Triple-Threat Position.

Be sure your head is up, your knees are bent, and the ball is well protected. The ball and your elbows are in tight to your body on your right hip.

Do not pull your right foot farther back than necessary after your jab step. You should jab step and pull back into the Triple-Threat Position, with the right foot slightly forward of the left.

From this position you will be best able to shoot or drive to the basket. Many players get into the poor habit of pulling the right foot back behind the left where they are in poor position to shoot or drive.

Lower your body position by bending your knees and, with a long, quick first step with the right foot, drive to the basket using one dribble. Execute a right-handed layup off the backboard from the right side of the basket.

To be "explosive" on this move, there are two secrets: After you jab step, shift your weight back onto the ball of the left foot and lower your body position by bending your knees a little extra just before you "explode" to the basket. Then, with the right hand, "push" the ball out in front and just to the right of the right foot on your dribble so that the ball and your right foot land simultaneously on your first step.

Only the first step is "explosive." Be sure that you get yourself under complete control after that first step and make your last step small enough so that you can jump up to the basket with your head up.

This move can be dangerous because the ball is not well protected from the defense. Be sure you hold the ball strong and in tight on your right hip with your elbows in. The move must be made quickly and decisively so the ball is not exposed to the defense any longer than necessary. Repeat ten times.

4. Repeat steps 1–3 using the head fake, the head-and-shoulder fake, and the ball fake. Remember to give the defense time to react to your fakes before you "explode" to the basket with your straight move.

5. Repeat steps 1–4 spinning the ball out to SS #12, using the right foot as your pivot, and reversing all the directions for your hands and feet. You must be extra careful swinging the ball across your body from right to left.

POINTS OF EMPHASIS

- Your head is up and the ball is well protected at all times.
- The straight move is quick and "explosive." After your jab step or fake, shift your weight back onto your left foot and lower your center of gravity by bending your knees a little extra.

Skill: Crossover Move

The crossover move is a *must* for every player. While the crossover is not as quick or as "explosive" as the straight move, it is often the move of choice because it offers excellent protection of the ball from the defense and is a very powerful move where a player can more easily keep his or her body under control. Not all players are quick enough to use the straight move very often; however, every player can find many opportunities to use the crossover move successfully. (See Figures 6-5a, 6-5b, and 6-5c.)

Drill 000-6

     1. Spin the ball out to SS #16, jump stop, peek over your left shoulder, and front pivot on your left foot into the Triple-Threat Position.

     2. Jab step with your right foot on a 45-degree angle to your right and withdraw back into the Triple-Threat Position, rocking your weight back onto the ball of your left foot.

     Keep your head up and bend your knees a little more. With your right foot, step across and in front of your left foot at a 45-degree angle to your left, swinging the ball from your right hip to your left and dropping your right arm and shoulder as you step. Lay the ball out with your left hand and use one or two dribbles executing a left-handed layup off the backboard from the left side of the basket.

     The crossover step should be quick and long enough to get by the defender.

Figure 6-5 (a) Triple Threat Position and (b) and (c) Crossover Move

(a)

(b)

(c)

The ball is shifted quickly from your right hip, across and in tight to the body, to your left hip as you pivot on the ball of your left foot.

As the ball is shifting to your left hip, drop your right arm and shoulder and take a low quick step with the right foot at a 45-degree angle to your left by stepping across your body. This can best be accomplished by bending your knees a little more and keeping your weight forward on the balls of your feet.

At this point, your arm and shoulder should be closed, protecting the ball from your defensive opponent. The first dribble, with your left hand, should land simultaneously with the right foot on the crossover step. The ball should bounce just to the left and in front of the right foot.

Practice this move over and over, but begin slowly until you have the form down perfectly.

The most common error made by players using the crossover move is to drag or take a little step with the pivot foot before the crossover step. To avoid this, be sure you shift your weight back onto your pivot foot before you crossover, do not try to take too long a crossover step, and keep your head up at all times.

3. Repeat ten times.

4. Repeat steps 1–3 using the head fake, the head-and-shoulder fake, and the ball fake in place of the jab step. Remember to give the defense time to react to your fakes before your crossover move.

5. Repeat steps 1–4 taking one dribble with the left hand and executing a jump stop at SS #6 into the Triple-Threat Position. Finish the drill with a jump shot from that spot.

6. Repeat steps 1–5 spinning the ball out to SS #12, using the right foot as your pivot and reversing all directions for your hands and feet. When you repeat step 4, you will jump stop at SS #10.

POINTS OF EMPHASIS

- Keep your head up throughout the move.
- The ball must be well protected at all times.
- The jab step preceding the crossover move must be convincing enough to either freeze the defender for a split second or cause him or her to take a step or shift his or her weight in the direction of the jab step.
- Be sure you shift your weight back onto your pivot foot before your crossover step. The lower your center of gravity, knees bent, and butt low to the ground, the easier and quicker you can shift your weight.
- The crossover step must be quick and long enough to step past the defender and yet not so long that you lose any balance or body control. Getting low on the crossover step by keeping your weight forward and bending your knees is very important.
- Be sure that the arm and shoulder are dropped as you cross over. Push your first dribble in front and to the outside of the foot that crossed over (away from the defense). This keeps your momentum forward and allows you to pass your defender as quickly as possible. If you are in the open court, you may be able safely to push the ball out several feet; however, in more congested areas, you will have to be more conservative and keep that first dribble closer.

- You must be prepared to either drive to the basket or jump stop off this move. This means that your balance and body control must be excellent and your head up. In game situations, you will have to be prepared to pull up with a jump stop to shoot or pass and avoid charging into a defender.

Skill: Hesitation Move

The hesitation move has become very popular with players who have a quick first step. It is usually set up with a jab step and is really a straight move with a deceptive hesitation.

Drill 000-7

    1. Spin the ball out to SS #16, jump stop, peek over your left shoulder, and front pivot on your left foot into the Triple-Threat Position.

    2. Take a jab step with your right foot at a 45-degree angle to your right and withdraw back into the Triple-Threat Position.

    3. Take a second, but smaller, jab step with your right foot at a 45-degree angle to your right, but just before your right foot touches the floor, "explode" to the basket by extending that right foot into a long step by your defender. This move is especially effective after your defensive opponent has seen your jab step a few times and is beginning to time it.

    The ball is well protected on your right hip. Your head is up, your knees are bent, and your butt is low.

    Hold your weight back on the left foot as you jab step on the hesitation move so that you can "explode" off it. If you shift your weight forward too soon, the move will be weak or you may commit a violation shuffling your feet to gain balance.

    The ball is bounced on the first dribble forward and to the right of the right foot simultaneously with the first step the same as in the straight move.

    Important Note: There is a common variation to the hesitation move that you should try. On the short jab step, try putting the right foot down softly on the toes only, but be sure that you keep your weight back on the left foot. From this position you hesitate and "explode" to the basket by extending the step with the right foot.

    4. Repeat ten times.

    5. Repeat steps 1–4 spinning the ball out to SS #12, using the right foot as your pivot and reversing the directions for your hands and feet.

POINTS OF EMPHASIS

- Your head is up and the ball is well protected at all times.
- Your knees are bent, your butt is low, and you maintain good balance and body control.

Skill: Rocker Step

The rocker step is a basic move off the Triple-Threat Position that can set up a shot, pass, or any one of the one-on-one moves. (See Figures 6-6a, 6-6b, and 6-6c.)

Drill 000-8

1. Spin the ball out to SS #16, jump stop, peek over your left shoulder, and front pivot on your left foot into the Triple-Threat Position.

2. Jab step with your right foot and withdraw the right foot back *behind* the left foot so the toes of the right foot are farther from the basket than the heel of the left foot.

Your feet are comfortably spread apart.

Your weight has shifted onto the right foot in a rocker motion.

Your head is up and the ball is well protected.

Figure 6-6   (a) Triple Threat Position, (b) Jab Step, and (c) Rocker Step

(a)   (b)

(c)

Important Note: If you are right handed, you will not be able to shoot from this position. However, the move does open up good passing angles, and, if your defensive opponent comes too close, you should be able to "explode" by him with a straight or crossover move. When you feel the defensive opponent close in on you, drop low by bending your knees, protect the ball on your right hip, keep your head up, and make your straight or crossover move.

3. Jab step again with the right foot shifting your weight in the rocker motion first to your left foot and then to your right foot as it lands on the jab step forward.

4. Repeat steps 1–3 ten times, practicing jab steps straight ahead and at a 45-degree angle to your right.

Concentrate on shifting your weight in the rocker motion forward onto your right foot on the jab step, back onto your left as you withdraw the jab step and step back, and onto the right foot behind the left as the right foot lands.

5. Repeat steps 1–4 spinning the ball out to SS #12, using the right foot as your pivot, and reversing all directions for your hands and feet.

Important Note: If you are right handed, the rocker step using the right foot as your pivot will put you in perfect position to shoot either your spot shot or jumper.

6. Repeat step 5, and after two rocker steps, take your spot shot or jumper.

ONE-ON-ONE SERIES

To be effective as a one-on-one player, you must develop not only good moves but several series of moves that make it impossible for the defense to anticipate what you are going to do with the ball. Notice that each of the series involves shooting, driving left, and driving right off the Triple-Threat Position incorporating various fakes. Each series is designed to force the defense to give you at least one move by having to respect your ability to shoot and drive in either direction. When practicing these series observe the following:

1. Practice each series *slowly* until you can execute each move smoothly and without committing a walking violation. If you are having difficulty mastering a move, practice it without the ball for awhile until you get the rhythm.
2. Practice each move five times.
3. Be sure your head is up, the ball is well protected, and you maintain good balance throughout.
4. When a dribble is called for, you should be able to lay the ball out and use only one dribble to get to the basket for a layup or to a spot for your jump shot. However, if you are a young player, you may use two dribbles on the drive to the basket.

5. All layups should be taken either from the right or the left of the rim and layed off the backboard with a strong, high jump up to the basket. Be sure you use the right-handed layup from the right side and the left-handed layup from the left.

6. You should vary the number of jab steps in these series to keep your moves unpredictable.

Series I

1. Spin the ball out to SS #16, front pivot left on the left foot into the Triple-Threat Position:
   a. Shot.
   b. Jab step, shot.
   c. Jab step, straight move right, layup to the right of basket.
   d. Jab step, crossover move (step with right foot across to your left), layup to the left of the basket.
   e. Jab step, hesitation move, layup to the right of the basket.
   f. Jab step, straight move one dribble to SS #8, jump stop, jump shot.
   g. Jab step, crossover move, one dribble to SS #6, jump stop, jump shot.
2. Repeat step 1 front pivoting right on the right foot into the Triple-Threat Position and reversing the directions for the hands and feet. Now you will be using your right foot as your pivot and jab stepping with your left.
3. Repeat steps 1 and 2 at SS #17, 12, 11, and 20.

POINTS OF EMPHASIS

- Your head is up.
- The ball is well protected at all times.
- You have good balance and body control.
- Your jab steps are forceful, and your first step on the straight and crossover moves are quick.

Series II

1. Spin the ball out to SS #16, front pivot on the left foot into the Triple-Threat Position:
   a. Jab step, ball fake, straight move right, layup.
   b. Jab step, ball fake, shot.
   c. Jab step, ball fake, crossover move, layup.
   d. Jab step, ball fake, straight move with one dribble to SS #8, jump stop, jump shot.
   e. Jab step, ball fake, crossover move with one dribble to SS #6, jump stop, jump shot.
2. Repeat step 1 front pivoting right on the right foot into the Triple-Threat Position and reversing the directions for the hands and feet.
3. Repeat steps 1 and 2 at SS #17, 15, 14, 13, 12, and 11.

Series III

      1. Spin the ball out to SS #16, front pivot on the left foot into the Triple-Threat Position:
      a. Head fake, straight move, layup.
      b. Head fake, shot.
      c. Head fake, crossover move, layup.
      d. Head fake, straight move with one dribble to SS #8, jump stop, jump shot.
      e. Head fake, crossover move with one dribble to SS #6, jump stop, jump shot.
      2. Repeat step 1 replacing head fakes with ball fakes.
      3. Repeat step 1 replacing head fakes with head-and-shoulder fakes.
      4. Repeat steps 1–3 front pivoting right on the right foot into the Triple-Threat Position and reversing the directions for hands and feet.
      5. Repeat steps 1–4 at SS #17, 15, 14, 13, 12, and 11.

POINTS OF EMPHASIS

- Make your head fakes, ball fakes, and head-and-shoulder fakes convincing.
- You should learn to use all three types of fakes because each is useful depending on the situation. If the defender is close to you, the head fake is best. The ball fake and head-and-shoulder fakes force the defender to either move closer to you or let you shoot. Mix them up so that the defender cannot anticipate your next move.
- The most common problem players have with these fakes is committing a walking violation. Be sure that you do not move your pivot foot on these fakes.

Series IV

      1. Spin the ball out to SS #16, front pivot left on your left foot into the Triple-Threat Position:
      a. Shot.
      b. Rocker step, half step forward with the right foot into the Triple-Threat Position, shot.
      c. Rocker step, straight move to SS #8, jump stop, shot.
      d. Rocker step, crossover move to SS #6, jump stop, shot.
      Note: The position of the right foot after you jab step and bring the right foot back behind the left on the rocker step. This opens up space between you and the defender that improves your passing angles, but, if you are right-handed, it is a poor position for a one-on-one move.
      Because your left foot is forward, you will not be able to shoot easily. Also, a quick move to the basket will be difficult because you must bring the right foot forward past your left before you can drive in any direction. However, if the defender does close in on you, the straight move angling right or the crossover move angling left is a possibility.

2. Repeat step 1 from SS #17, 15, 14, 13, 12, and 11.

Note: When you use the right foot as your pivot on the rocker stop, you are in the Triple-Threat Position after your jab step. Now you can use all of your one-on-one moves.

3. Spin the ball out to SS #16, front pivot right on your right foot into the Triple-Threat Position:

a. Shot.

b. Rocker step, shot.

c. Rocker step, straight move left, layup to the left of the basket.

d. Rocker step, crossover move right, layup to the right of the basket.

e. Rocker step, hesitation move, layup to the left of the basket.

f. Rocker step, straight move to SS #6, jump stop, jump shot.

g. Rocker step, crossover move to SS #8, jump stop, jump shot.

h. Rocker step, ball fake, shot.

i. Rocker step, ball fake, straight move left, layup.

j. Rocker step, ball fake, crossover move right, layup.

k. Rocker step, ball fake, hesitation move left, layup.

l. Rocker step, ball fake, straight move to SS #6, jump stop, jump shot.

m. Rocker step, ball fake, crossover move to SS #8, jump stop, jump shot.

n. Repeat, replacing ball fakes with head fakes.

o. Repeat replacing ball fakes with head-and-shoulder fakes.

4. Repeat step 3 from SS #17, 15, 14, 13, 12, and 11.

ONE-ON-ONE MOVES AGAINST PRESSURE DEFENSE

There will be times when you receive the ball under pressure. Your defensive opponent may be so close to you that any normal series of one-on-one moves will be impossible. Your first concern will be to protect the ball and maintain a strong, balanced position. From this position you could pass the ball to a teammate and cut to the basket for a return pass (give and go) and a layup. While this is one excellent option you will use, there will be times when you will have to beat your opponent one-on-one in this situation.

You must always be prepared for pressure. Whenever possible, come strong toward the passer to meet the ball and receive the pass.

After receiving the ball you might have to bend your knees a little more. This lower-body position provides a lower center of gravity, which increases your balance. You will be able to "explode" to the basket better from this position.

Protect the ball by holding it tighter in close to your body with your elbows out and your head up.

From this position, whether your back is to the basket or you are in the Triple-Threat Position, you will be in excellent position to beat your opponent.

Drill 000-9

For the following situations you might want to use a chair or other object in the position of the defender. This will help you "feel" the situation and create more accurate angles for your moves.

Situation A: You have just received a pass on SS #12 with your back to the basket. You did a jump stop so you can use either foot as your pivot. Your defensive opponent is right behind you, so that you cannot pivot into a Triple-Threat Position.

1. Spin the ball out to SS #12 and jump stop.

a. Peek over your right shoulder.

b. Turn your hips, trunk, and shoulder a couple of inches to the right, just enough to show your defender a small piece of the ball.

c. As you show the ball, be sure the ball is well protected and shift your weight onto your right foot.

d. Take a 45-degree drop step with the left foot (see Footwork Drill F-15), by swinging your left leg to your left.

e. As you take that long, first step with your left leg, swing the ball from your right side, with both hands, to your left and lay your first, and only dribble out in front and to the right of your left foot as it lands.

f. You should be able to go to the right side of the basket for a layup with only one dribble.

g. Be sure your head is up and the ball is well protected.

h. The move must be quick and decisive.

2. Repeat step 1 spinning the ball out to SS #16, peeking over your left shoulder and drop stepping to your right.

3. Repeat steps 1 and 2 five times each from SS #11, 20, and 17.

Situation B: You have received the ball on SS #16 and are facing the basket in the Triple-Threat Position with your left foot as your pivot. Your defender is one to two feet in front of you flicking his hands at the ball and giving you a great deal of pressure.

1. Spin the ball out to SS #16 and front pivot on your left foot into the Triple-Threat Position.

a. Bend your knees and hold the ball strong and low, swinging it from side to side.

b. Your elbows are out and your head is up.

2. "Explode" by your defender when the ball is on your right side, using a straight move with one dribble and a layup. Repeat twice.

3. Repeat step 2 with a crossover move when the ball is on your left side.

4. Repeat step 1 and freeze your defender with a quick head fake followed by an explosive straight move.

5. Repeat step 4 with a crossover move.

6. Repeat steps 1–5 from SS #12 using your right foot as your pivot and reversing directions for hands and feet.

Situation C: The same as Situation B, but your defender is very quick and strong and you feel unable to beat him with any of the foregoing moves.

1. Spin the ball out to SS #16 and front pivot on your left foot into the Triple-Threat Position.

a. Bend your knees and hold the ball strong and low, swinging it from side to side. Your elbows are out and your head is up.

2. Do a quick 300-degree reverse pivot on the ball of your left foot.

a. Swing your right leg around behind you.

b. Take a long step with your right foot and swing your right elbow out and around the defender.

c. Keep the ball well protected on your right hip.

d. Lay the ball out on your first and only dribble in front and to the left of the right foot as it lands.

e. You should be able to drive to the basket for a left-handed layup from the left side with only one dribble.

3. Repeat steps 1 and 2 five times from SS #12–15 using both the left- and right-foot pivots.

POINTS OF EMPHASIS

- To be a successful basketball player, you must be able to execute under defensive pressure. You should pay particular attention to the following points:

1. Your head must be up.
2. You must take extra care to protect the ball at all times. This means holding the ball strong, in close to your body, with your elbows out and your knees bent.
3. You must make your moves quickly and decisively from a low center of gravity. The lower your center of gravity, the more stable and explosive you will be.

APPLYING ONE-ON-ONE MOVES— READING THE DEFENSE

The mechanics of one-on-one moves takes a great deal of time to master. However, learning how to read the defense so that you know which move to make and when to make it also takes a great deal of time and experience. When you receive the ball in position to make a one-on-one move, you must learn to evaluate the situation in terms of:

Time left in the game.

Score of the game.

The individual qualities of your defender (i.e., size, strength, quickness, extension, agility, and experience).

Your defender's position guarding you.

The relative position of other defensive players.

Time and Score   The time left in a game and the score are important. For example, you might not make a one-on-one move to the basket if your team is leading by 8 points with one minute left in the game unless you are positive you can get an uncontested layup. A one-on-one move that you might pass up in the above situation might be a good choice if your team is down 8 points with one minute remaining.

Qualities of Your Defender   You must know who you are playing against. If the player guarding you is taller and stronger than you, it will probably be wise for you to keep him or her away from the basket to create space where you can use your quickness and agility to maneuver around him or her. Taking a larger player inside and posting up on him or her will usually be to his or her advantage. By the same reasoning, if you are being guarded by a smaller, quicker player, it might be more prudent for you to post him or her up. You must learn to be honest and realistic about yourself and evaluate what you can effectively do against each defender. The higher the level of competition you play against, the more selective you should be. In other words, use only your best moves.

Defender's Position   Whenever you receive the ball in shooting range, you must immediately evaluate what opportunities are possible. If your defender is far enough that he cannot stop you from getting off a good shot—shoot. If he is too close to you—explode by him. If he is at a distance where you cannot get off a good shot or explode by him, you must use the series of one-on-one moves you have learned. The first thing you should do is look at your defender's stance:

1. Is he well balanced with his knees bent? If not, give him a head fake, get low, and drive past him.
2. Is he flat-footed or are his legs too wide apart or too close together? If so, a strong jab step one way and a drive the other way will usually be effective.
3. Attack the front leg of your defender (Figs. 6-7a, 6-7b, and 6-7c and Figs. 6-8a, 6-8b, and 6-8c). If your defender has his right leg forward, use the moves of your choice, but drive left (to the defender's right) over his top leg. This is the most difficult adjustment for a defender to make. If you attack the front leg of the defender, you can often either beat him to that side or get him to back off so that you will have an easy shot. As for the relative position of other defensive players: You must always "see the court." Whenever you receive the ball, your head must be up and looking toward the basket you are shooting for. This view will give you all the information you need to protect the ball and make the right move.
4. If no one is between you and the basket, drive in for a layup.
5. If your defensive opponent is far enough away, you may choose to shoot.
6. If a second defensive player double teams you, pass to an open teammate.

(a)

(b)

(c)

Figure 6-7 (a) Attacking the Front Leg of the Defender and (b) and (c) Straight Move

Figure 6-8 (a) Attacking the Front Leg of the Defender and (b) and (c) Crossover Move

(a)

(b)

(c)

7. If you can drive past your defender, you must still see the other defensive players. If another defender steps into your driving lane, you must be able to stop and either shoot or pass off to a teammate.

Skill: One-on-One Moves Off the Dribble

One-on-one moves off the dribble are ideal in the open court in a fast-break situation. They combine footwork, dribbling, and shooting skills and require timing and judgment.

For the following drills, place chairs on the court on the spots where you will make your moves from. This will simulate a defender and give you a better idea of the proper driving angles.

Do this drill at half speed until you have mastered the mechanics.

Drill 000-10 (Figure 6-9)

1. Begin, facing the basket, at point A at midcourt, ten feet in from the sideline.
2. Dribble with your right hand at half speed toward the base line staying parallel with the sideline.

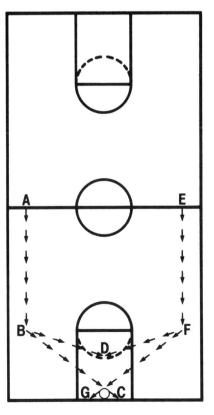

Figure 6-9 Drill 000-10 and Drill 000-12

3. Do a front crossover dribble to your left fifteen feet from the basket (foul line extended) at point B and drive to the basket laying the ball up off the backboard on the left side of the basket at point C with your left hand. You should have been able to do this maneuver with one left-handed dribble after your crossover dribble. Repeat three times.

4. Repeat steps 1 and 2, but after your crossover moves, take one dribble to SS #8, execute a jump stop, and hit your jumper.

5. Repeat steps 1–4 from the other side starting at point E and reversing the directions for hands and feet.

6. Repeat steps 1–5 at three quarters speed but be sure you keep yourself under complete control.

7. Repeat steps 1–6 using each of the crossover moves:

a. Between the legs.

b. Spin move.

c. Behind the back.

POINTS OF EMPHASIS

- Was your head up during the entire sequence?
- Was the ball well protected?
- Did you bend your knees and cut your steps before your move?
- Did you accelerate on, not before, the crossover? Be sure you are not decelerating on the move.
- Did you need more than one additional dribble after the crossover?
- Was your last step to the basket small enough so that your momentum was up to the basket rather than toward the base line?

Drill 000-11 (Figure 6-10)

1. Begin, facing the basket, at point A at midcourt, twenty feet in from the sideline.

2. Dribble to SS #13, point B, and slow to a stop, keeping your dribble alive.

3. Make a head and shoulder fake to the left and drive to your right to the basket, point C, laying the ball in with a right-handed layup. Repeat twice.

Practice this with a straight move, stepping first after the head-and-shoulder fake with the right foot—and a crossover step—stepping first with the left foot. The crossover step will protect the ball better and be more powerful, but the straight move is quicker.

Your head is up, the ball is well protected and you are under control. You should cut your steps, lower your dribble, and bend your knees as you approach the defense.

After your head-and-shoulder fake, you should "explode" to the basket by getting low and accelerating on the first step.

You should use one right-handed dribble to the basket after your head and shoulder fake.

Review the questions asked in Drill 000-10, Points of Emphasis.

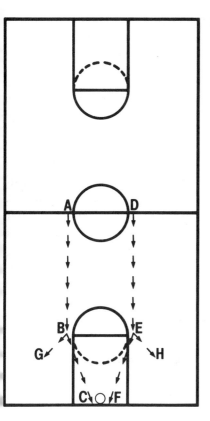

Figure 6-10 Drill 000-11 and Drill 000-12

4. Repeat steps 1–4 from the other side starting at point D and reversing directions for hands and feet.

5. Repeat steps 1–4 using the stutter step and hesitation move.

Your feet should become parallel to the base line on these moves just before you "explode" to the basket. This makes it difficult for the defender to read which way you will go—left or right.

Be careful of your spacing. Keep your dribble low and protected and do not get too close to the defender where he or she can slap the ball away from you on your dribble.

6. Repeat steps 1–5, but after your move, take one dribble to either SS #12, "G," or SS #16, "H," depending on which side you are working, execute stride and jump stops, and hit your jump shot.

POINTS OF EMPHASIS

- Moves off the dribble require excellent dribbling and footwork fundamentals. Practice these moves over and over again until you can execute them flawlessly without looking at the ball, with the ball well protected at all times, and with your body under complete control.
- Begin experimenting with different dribbling speeds and changes of pace. The secret to the effectiveness of these moves is the *change* of pace

and direction rather than the speed of the moves. Slow down as much as necessary *before* you make your move and accelerate ("explode") on the move. This will give you control and the ability to create maximum *change* of speed and direction.

- You will not always be able to drive to the basket or shoot off a move off the dribble. However, if you are under control as described in these drills you will be prepared to avoid a charge, stop, or pass to an open teammate in better position to score.

Important Note Many coaches insist that you always dribble with the outside hand—right hand on the right side of the court and left hand on the left side of the court—so the ball is protected from the defense. However, if you are sure that there is no chance of a defensive player getting a hand on the ball, you may want to dribble with the inside hand because it is your better hand and/or it sets up a better angle for a strong crossover move to the base line which might be the best move in the situation.

Drill 000-12

1. Repeat Drills 000-10 and 000-11 using the inside hand on the dribble.

POINT OF EMPHASIS

- You must only use this move when you are absolutely certain that no defender is close enough to swipe the ball away from you on the dribble.

Important Note Guards, especially "point" guards, must have the ability to dribble up the center of the court and make a variety of moves off the dribble when they get to a spot from twenty-one to fifteen feet of the basket. This ability is important for the fast break as well as for setting up and running the half-court offense.

There is more likelihood of defensive pressure in the center of the court than on the sides.

Because pressure is more likely and possible from all sides, your first concern must be to protect the ball. You will be less often able to reach full speed on your dribble, and you will have to pass the ball more often and earlier than when you advanced the ball on the dribble up one of the sides of the court.

To develop into a "point" guard, you will have to perfect your skills so that you can advance the ball up the center of the court on the dribble from any position as quickly and safely as possible. From a standing and a moving dribble you must be able to beat defenders on the dribble, drive to the basket, shoot and pass off the dribble, and stop at any time for the purpose of passing, shooting, or setting up and running the half-court offense.

With the exception of certain situations off the fast break, many moves off the dribble in the center of the court cannot be taken to the basket because of defensive congestion. It is imperative that every move that is made from the center is made with enough control that you are able to stop if and when it is necessary, and either shoot or pass off to a teammate.

Drill 000-13

1. Begin at the center circle at midcourt facing the basket. Dribble with the right hand to SS #14 jump stop, and shoot a jump shot. Continue until you have made three in a row.

2. Repeat step 1 using the left-hand dribble.

3. Dribble with the right hand from the center circle to one step above SS #14. Head-and-shoulder fake right, front crossover dribble left to SS #15, jump stop, and hit the jumper. Make three in a row.

4. Repeat step 3 using the left-handed dribble, head-and-shoulder faking left, and the front crossover right to SS #13.

5. Repeat steps 3–4 with stride stops.

6. Dribble with the right hand to one step above SS #14, head-and-shoulder fake left, and, using one right-handed dribble accelerate to the basket for a right-handed layup. Repeat twice.

7. Repeat step 6 substituting hesitation moves and stutter steps for the head-and-shoulder fakes.

8. Repeat steps 6 and 7 using the front crossover dribble and proceeding to the basket with one left-handed dribble and a left-handed layup.

9. Repeat steps 6–8 using the left-handed dribble and reversing the directions for hands and feet.

10. Repeat steps 6–9 but jump stop at SS #9 or 7, depending on the side you make the move, and hit your jump shot.

11. Repeat step 10 with stride stops.

12. Repeat step 1–11 making your moves from SS #20. However, after you make your crossover and straight moves, angle your step more sharply to the basket so that you either jump stop or stride stop at SS #13 or 15.

It is important that you practice the above moves from one step above the foul line and SS #20 because the moves are made at different angles and involve different footwork depending on the spot from which they are made. The two spots selected in this drill are the most commonly used in game situations.

POINTS OF EMPHASIS

- Your first priority is to protect the ball.
- You must be prepared and able to change speed or direction, pass or stop, at any time.

Drill 000-14

This drill expands one-on-one moves off the dribble into the full court situation.

1. Begin facing the backboard at a spot midway between SS #14 and 15.

2. Throw the ball off the backboard, meet the ball as it comes off the board, and catch it in the air landing on both feet simultaneously. Peek over your left shoulder and front pivot out on the ball of your left foot toward the left sideline as described in laying the ball out drill. (See Dribbling Drill D-10)

3. Lay the ball out with the right hand and accelerate to full speed as quickly as possible until you are over the midcourt line. After crossing midcourt, slow down and execute Drill 000-13.

4. Repeat steps 1–3 beginning at a spot midway between SS #14 and 13, reversing the directions for hands and feet and executing Drills 000-10, 11, and 12.

5. Repeat steps 1–4 dribbling up the center of the court and executing Drill 000-13.

POINTS OF EMPHASIS

- Lay the ball out in the backcourt and accelerate to full speed as quickly as possible until you are over midcourt.

- Slow down so that you are in complete control in preparation for a one-on-one move off the dribble. Remember, the effectiveness of a move is based on the *change* in speed and direction not the speed of the move. Many otherwise highly skilled players never learn how to slow down to set up a move off the dribble so they can accelerate off the move. Instead, they try to make the move while decelerating and lose control.

- Practice all the moves off different paces to learn what moves go best with each pace.

Drill 000-15

1. Repeat Drill 000-12, dribbling with the inside hand instead of the outside hand. This means that you will dribble with the left hand on the right side of the court and the right hand on the left side of the court.

2. Review points made in Drill 000-12 and 14.

Summary Every time you receive the ball in a basketball game you have a decision to make: Do I shoot, pass, or dribble? If the right decision is to shoot or drive to the basket, you will have to develop a series of one-on-one moves. One-on-one moves incorporate many of the individual fundamental skills you have learned in footwork, dribbling, and shooting. In this chapter you have learned to put these skills together so that you are always a threat to "beat" your defensive opponent for a basket from the Triple-Threat Position, posting up, off the dribble, or moving without the ball.

WORKOUT, EVALUATION, AND PROGRESS CHARTS

Table 6-1   One-on-One Moves Workout—30 Minutes

Warmup

DRILL	INSTRUCTIONS
One-on-One Series I	Do each move until you score—use SS #16, 12, 20.
One-on-One Series II	" " " #17, 15, 14, 13, 11.
One-on-One Series III	" " " "
One-on-One Series IV	" " " #16, 12, 20.

If you have trouble doing one or more of these moves in a series, go back to the original drill for that move and study and practice it individually.

000-9	Situations A, B, C: Do each move until you score.
000-10	Do each move until you score.
000-11	" "
000-12	" "
000-13	" "
000-14	" "
000-15	" "
Cooldown	

Table 6-2   One-on-One Moves Workout—60 Minutes

Warmup

DRILL	INSTRUCTIONS
One-on-One Series I	Do each move until you score twice. Use SS #16, 12, 20.
One-on-One Series II	" " " #17, 15, 14, 13,11.
One-on-One Series III	" " " "
One-on-One Series IV	" " " #16, 12, 20.

If you have trouble doing one or more of these moves in a series, go back to the original drill for that move and study and practice it individually.

000-9	Situations A, B, C: Do each move until you score twice.
000-10	Do each move until you score twice.
000-11	" "
000-12	" "
000-13	" "
000-14	" "
000-15	" "
Cooldown	

Table 6-3 One-on-One Self-Evaluation and Improvement Test

DRILL	INSTRUCTIONS	SCORE
One-on-One Series I	Do each move once.	No. of shots made
One-on-One Series II	" "	" "
One-on-One Series III	" "	" "
One-on-One Series IV	" "	" "
000-9	Do each move twice (situations A, B, C).	
000-10	" "	" "
000-11	" "	" "
000-12	" "	" "
000-13	" "	" "
000-14	" "	" "
000-15	" "	" "

Table 6-4 Personal One-on-One Progress Chart

	DATE							
Drill								
Series I								
Series II								
Series III								
Series IV								
000-9								
000-10								
000-11								
000-12								
000-13								
000-14								
000-15								

CHAPTER SEVEN

POST MOVES

Every player on a basketball team should have some post moves. Obviously, bigger and stronger players will utilize them more often, but guards should be able to take advantage of scoring situations where they find themselves in the post against a smaller defender. This happens in the case of guards more often than one might expect and adds a dimension to a guard's offensive game.

This section deals with one-on-one moves after you have received the ball relatively close to the basket. Most of the time, because of defensive pressure, you will receive the ball with your back to the basket. Therefore, we will begin each drill from that position. Posting areas, usually defined as within fifteen to seventeen feet of the basket, are generally the most contested spots on the basketball court. They are the "war zones" each team must try to control to have the best chance of winning.

These are the areas where the best shots are taken, where most rebounds will come and most fouls will occur. Therefore, you should expect most defenses to contest or defend these areas vigorously. Because the post area is so well defended, you will have to learn more and work harder just to get the ball in these positions. You must learn to fake one way and go another before you have the ball just to get into position to receive a pass in the post. You will have to use all the footwork skills you have learned just to get free for a pass in the post. Reverse pivots, changes of direction, and balance skills will be invaluable. Good footwork can turn an otherwise slow individual into a relatively quick inside player.

Because the post is well defended, it is important that you come on "strong" to the ball or meet the pass at every opportunity. In addition, when you come to the ball, you must learn to make yourself as big as possible by spreading your legs wide and keeping your arms and elbows up and out. Your palms should be facing away from you.

After receiving a pass in the post, you should try to remain "big." You should be well balanced on the balls of your feet, your feet are spread wider than your shoulders, your knees and waist are bent, your elbows out, and your head is up. You must hold the ball strong and be ready to pivot or step in any direction. Whenever possible, catch the ball with both feet landing at the same time and your knees well bent. Well-bent knees will allow you to "explode," and the two-foot landing allows you to pivot off either foot.

BIG MAN MOVES

The single most important aspect of learning to play in the low post, from block to block, is mental. The low-post area is like a war zone. You work like hell to get position so that you can receive a pass in the low hole and, when you get it, it's power all the way to the square on the backboard for 2 or 3 points. But you have to feel it.

You must be totally aggressive when you receive the ball in this position: Catch the ball strong with both hands, elbows out and knees bent. Collect yourself by bringing all your weight into the center of your body, and get as low as possible with the ball well protected. Take a quick peek at the basket and power your body, through your hips, chest, and shoulders, to the basket. Hold on to the ball for as long as possible with both hands and take it to the box on the backboard for your 2 or 3. You must have the attitude that you will not be denied.

The single most important aspect of the low-post game is attitude. A player must want the ball close to the basket where he or she can overpower the defender by taking the ball to the basket. The low-post player must be able to generate power through the legs, hips, chest, and shoulders as he or she takes the ball strongly to the basket. In basketball, the area in front of the basket from block to block is the most contested and protected area by the defense. In a sense, it is the "war zone" that your opponent will protect most vigorously.

When you receive the ball in this area, from an offensive rebound or a pass from a teammate, you must expect the defense to give you maximum pressure. This is no time for weakness or indecisiveness. The low-post player must have the proper attitude and skills to take the ball up strong or he or she will be unsuccessful a high percentage of the time. If you want to develop into a good low-post player, regardless of your size, you must think, feel, and act strong when you are in the low post. In fact, many players lift weights as much for the confidence and feeling of power it gives them as the real gains they make in upper-body strength.

Important Note   There is considerable debate among basketball experts concerning whether or not a tall player should bring the ball down after receiving the ball off a rebound or a pass inside. Many coaches teach the tall player to never bring the ball down where smaller players can steal it. These coaches teach the tall player to shoot the ball or pass it to a teammate without ever bringing the ball down. Other coaches teach the tall player how and when to bring the ball down.

The purpose of this book is to present all the individual fundamentals of the game. In the case of the unusually tall player, it is a good idea to practice how to shoot and pass without bringing the ball down. However, few players will be able to continue this system as they develop and move up to stronger and taller opposition. Therefore, it is probably a good idea for them also to learn how to bring the ball down under certain circumstances and protect the ball before they outlet pass or shoot.

Post moves can be roughly divided into three categories: low-post, midpost, and high-post moves.

Low-post moves involve those options available when you receive the ball within two or three feet of the basket with your back to the basket. Because you are so close to the basket and your defensive opponent is probably very close, there is usually not enough room to turn and face the basket without risking a charging or offensive foul. Some players will be able to turn and face the basket from the low-post for either "powering" the ball up or jump shots because of their size, strength, quickness, or deceptiveness. However, for teaching purposes, it is best to learn a set of moves where the defensive congestion dictates that back to the basket moves are practiced. You should be prepared to shoot almost every time you receive the ball in the low post.

Low-post area is where the offensive player, after receiving the ball, cannot turn and face the hoop. He must use back-to-the-basket options or moves. The midpost is the area where both back-to-the-basket and facing moves are possible. It will not be unusual for you to receive the ball in a game twice in the same spot, three feet from the basket, for example, and because of the defensive alignment, it will be the low post one time and the midpost the other. Midpost moves are from three to about twelve feet from the basket where you receive the ball with your back-to-the-basket and can either turn and face the basket or make a back-to-the-basket move depending on the situation. From the midpost area you can expect to shoot about 50 percent of the time and pass the other 50 percent of the time.

The high post is usually defined from about twelve to seventeen feet from in front of the basket where you receive the ball with your back to the basket, and, unless very closely guarded, you would turn and face the basket. In most cases, back-to-the-basket moves from the high-post position are not considered as high a percentage option as facing-the-basket options. From the high post, you should only shoot when you are open and can hit the 12- to 17-foot jumper. Passing skills, including good fakes, become more important as you receive the ball farther from the basket. Of particular importance is the ability to fake high and bounce pass into the low post. (See Figure 7-1.)

THE POST AND THE DRIBBLE

Before we begin, it is important to discuss the concept of the dribble from post positions. The single, biggest mistake players make in post play is dribbling immediately after receiving the ball in the post. Because of this serious error, many coaches do not allow their post players to dribble at all from the low post, because it is so congested with defenders that the

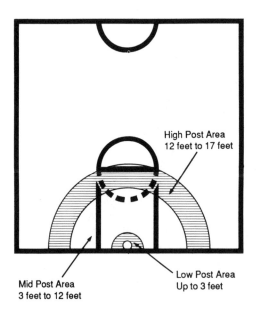

High Post Area
12 feet to 17 feet

Mid Post Area
3 feet to 12 feet

Low Post Area
Up to 3 feet

Figure 7-1 Areas of High, Mid, and Low Posts

chance of a turnover is great. Other coaches allow one, well-controlled dribble but *only* if necessary to improve position for a shot or a pass. It is, therefore, important that you practice all the low-post options, wherever possible, with and without a dribble so you are prepared to play for any coach in any situation. If you do use one dribble in conjunction with a post move, you must see where you are moving to, improve your position, and be sure to step *before* you dribble.

One other important point: Some players have a great feel for how and when to use a dribble from the low-post position and others do not. You should practice all the options, and, as you develop your game, eliminate those options that are not successful for you. As we pointed out earlier in the One-on-One Moves chapter, you will learn and practice a large number of moves, but you should select those options that make you most effective. You only need one great move each way and one shot from each position to keep the defense "honest." So don't be upset if you don't master every move. Learn and practice them all the best you can, and in time you will incorporate those most appropriate for you into your "game."

POST BODY POSITION

The post, especially the low post or "hole," is the most vigorously defended area on the basketball court. You must work hard to receive the ball in this position, protect the ball well after receiving it, and develop decisive moves for the purpose of scoring.

You will begin each drill by spinning the ball out, underhanded with both hands, from under the basket to the one designated spot. You will come to the ball strong and, after one bounce, catch the ball in the air, with both hands, with a jump stop. You will land solidly on both feet with your back to the basket.

POST BODY POSITION CHECKPOINTS (Figs. 7-2a and 7-2b)

1. Your back is to the basket.
2. You are balanced on the balls of both feet.
3. Your feet are spread at least and probably a little more than a shoulder width apart.
4. Your knees and waist are bent, your butt is low.
5. Your elbows are out.
6. The ball is held firmly, close to the body at chest level.
7. Your head is up.

(a)   (b)

Figures 7-2a and 7-2b   Post Body Position

THE QUICK LOOK (Figs. 7-3a and 7-3b)

After you have established yourself in the post with the ball in well-protected position, you are ready to make a move. Without turning your head more than an eighth of a turn, you will take a quick peek over your shoulder toward the open side of the court. This means that you will turn away from the nearest sideline or base line. If you receive the ball on one side of the three-second lane, you will look into the lane over your shoulder turning your head away from the base line toward the foul line. The quick look or peek over the shoulder from the low post is very important. Even though you know where the basket is from the lines on the floor, often you will not know where your defensive opponent is after you receive the pass. In this congested area, the quick look will do three things for you:

1. Pick up the sight of the basket. It is difficult to make a good move without sighting the basket.
2. See the position of the defense.
3. See the position of your teammates.

(a)   (b)

Figures 7-3a and 7-3b The Quick Look

With the information provided from your look, you will be able to make the right offensive decision. For example:

- If there is no defender near you, shoot or take the ball to the basket.
- If the defender guarding you is making contact with you on one side, lean into him or her slightly, and make a move in the opposite direction.
- If a teammate is wide open going to the basket, pass.
- If the defense double teams you, pass to the open teammate.
- If the defender guarding you is small, either shoot over or overpower him or her.
- If the defender guarding you is big, either beat him or her with quickness or pass the ball out.

Occasionally, you will feel a defender on your back when you receive the ball in the low post. In this situation you may be able to make a quick move without looking, but the quick peek is a necessary habit to get into. The quick look allows you to see what move is open, a possible double team situation, or a free teammate in a better position to score than you. Players who get into the habit of making a move without looking are subject to charging fouls, off-balance shots, and blind passes.

THE BABY HOOK

The baby hook is an adaptation of the regular hook shot. In executing the baby hook, the shooting arm and ball are brought straight up the shooting side from the hip instead of in an extended position. Many players prefer the quicker baby hook from the congested low-post position because the ball is better protected and less likely to be blocked from behind.

Do not extend your shooting arm out. Bring the ball straight up the shooting side with both hands from your hip to full extension directly over the ear. Use the nonshooting arm for protection from the defense but release that hand just before you flip the ball over your head into the basket.

Drill P-1

1. Spin the ball out to SS #5. Check your Post Body Position carefully.

2. Take a quick look over your left shoulder.

3. Take one step with your left foot toward SS #4 and execute a baby hook shot. Make three in a row.

Point the toes of your left foot in the direction of your step. Turn your head and look at the basket as you step.

Drive your right knee up as you turn your shoulders and raise the ball straight up with both hands from your right hip to above your right ear with your arms fully extended.

When your left shoulder is pointing toward the basket with your right arm fully extended, release the protecting left hand from the ball and flip the ball off the fingertips of the outstretched right hand into the basket.

Your right hand must follow through to the basket the same way as in your spot shot.

4. Repeat steps 1–3 beginning on SS #4, 3, 2, and 1.

5. Repeat steps 1–3 from SS #1–5, using the left-handed baby hook and reversing directions for hands and feet.

POINTS OF EMPHASIS

- The ball must be well protected.
- The shot must be executed quickly—unless you are very tall—and with full extension of the shooting arm.
- The ball should roll off the fingertips on the release so the shot is soft with backspin.
- Follow-through properly by extending the shooting hand to the basket the same way as on your other shots.
- Do not turn your shoulders square to the basket on the release because i

will make your shot easy to block. Keep your body between the defender and the ball until after the release of the shot. From this position you will be able to turn quickly and go for an offensive rebound.

THE JUMP HOOK

The jump hook has become a popular shot especially for big players. It developed as a variation of the baby hook for use in the low-post area, even though some very big college and pro players employ it farther out.

The jump hook is effective because:

1. It provides good protection of the ball.
2. It is a difficult shot to block.
3. It can be a high percentage shot from the low-post position where it may be difficult to face the basket. (See Figure 7-4.)

Drill P-2

1. Spin the ball out the SS #5. Check your Post Body Position.
2. Take a quick look over your left shoulder.

Figure 7-4 The Jump Hook

3. Using your left foot as your pivot, take one step with your right foot and pivot one quarter turn to your left so that if you drew a straight line from the toes of your right foot to the toes of your left foot and extended it, the line would go to the basket.

The ball is on your right hip. Your head is turned facing the basket. You are in otherwise Post Body Position.

4. Jump off of both feet and raise the ball straight up over your right ear fully extending both arms over your head.

Your left elbow should be bent to protect the ball. At the top of your jump, flip the ball with the right hand into the basket, releasing the left hand just before the shot is released. Make three in a row.

5. Repeat steps 1–4 on SS #4, 3, 2, and 1.

6. Repeat steps 1–4 from SS #1–5, using the left-handed jump hook and reversing directions for hands and feet.

THE DROP STEP

You learned the drop step without the basketball in Footwork Drill F-15. As a low-post move, the drop step is somewhat controversial in that some coaches teach it with one dribble while others insist that it be executed without a dribble. Depending on whether you receive the ball on a one-foot or two-foot landing, the interpretation of the officials, and how smoothly you execute the move, it is sometimes called a walk by referees when the one dribble is not used. This text will employ one dribble with the drop step. However, you and your coach can decide whether to use the dribble or not on the drop step.

Drill P-3

1. Spin the ball out to SS #1. Catch the ball in the air after one bounce with a jump stop and check your Post Body Position (Fig. 7-5a).

2. Take a quick look over your right shoulder. With your head turned an eighth to the right, bend your knees and shift your weight onto your right foot (Fig. 7-5b).

Using your right foot as your pivot, reverse pivot by stepping back with your left foot at about a 45-degree angle toward the basket (Fig. 7-5c).

As the left foot touches the floor, shift your weight back onto your left foot and dribble once *with the left hand* so that the ball bounces just inside and in front of the left foot as it lands.

Shift your weight back onto your left foot and bring the right leg around as you pivot on the ball of your left foot "gathering" or "collecting" yourself as you square yourself to the basket in Power Layup Position (Fig. 7-5d).

'Gather" or "collect" yourself by bending your knees and waist as you

Figure 7-5 The Drop Step (a) Post Body Position, (b) Quick Look, (c) Drop Step, (d) Collecting Yourself, and (e) Power Layup

pull your arms and legs into a well-balanced Power Layup Position. At this point you are facing the basket at a 45-degree angle right between the backboard and the rim.

Important Note: The drop step is selected based on the information you get when you take the quick look over your shoulder to the open side of the court. If you can feel or see your defender on your right side, it means the drop step to your left is open.

It is important to bend your knees and shift your weight onto your right foot as you take your quick look over your shoulder so that your drop step with the left foot is quick and balanced. Equally important is that you use your one dribble, if you decide to use a dribble, properly. You must swing the ball around to your left as you step with your left foot and bounce it just inside and in front of your left foot so that your defender cannot reach in and hit the ball. Remember he or she is on your right side when you make this move. Be sure you step first *before* you bounce the ball.

Bounce the ball inside your left foot to protect against the possibility of "weakside help." This is where another defender comes from behind to help. By taking your one dribble inside and just in front of your left foot, neither defensive player should be able to get to the ball without fouling you.

3. Execute a power layup (review Skill: Power Layup, Drill S-9, Fig. 7-5e). Make five in a row.

a. You are balanced on the balls of both feet.

b. Your feet are spread no wider than a shoulder width.

c. Your knees and waist are bent, but your back is straight.

d. Your elbows are out.

e. You are holding the ball very firmly in both hands, close to your body just above the waist.

f. Your head is up.

g. "Power" the ball up by jumping ("exploding") up to the basket off your strongest two-foot jump, holding the ball firmly in both hands for as long as possible.

h. Jump straight up to the basket, but turn your body a little to the right with the left elbow out to screen off the defense and provide better protection of the ball.

i. Lay the ball off the backboard as softly as possible at the very top of your jump with both arms fully extended. The longer you hold on to the ball

(1) The softer the shot will be.

(2) The more chance you will be fouled.

(3) The more difficult it will be for the defense to time and block your shot.

4. Repeat steps 1–3 from SS #5, drop stepping with the right foot and reversing the directions for hands and feet.

POINTS OF EMPHASIS

- The drop step and power layup are invaluable moves in the low-post area. You will not be effective in the "hole" without perfecting them. Practice this drill everyday even after you have mastered it.

- Committing a walking violation by shuffling your feet is the single biggest problem on the power move. Establish your pivot foot and concentrate on not moving it. This will become increasingly important later in this chapter when you incorporate various fakes and other moves into your power game.

- Your head must be up, your knees bent with your center of gravity low, and the ball well protected at all times in the low-post area. Remember, this is the most contested area on the basketball court, and it is no place for the timid.

- Power basketball is as mental as it is physical. You must think and feel strong when you get the ball in the low-post area where a power move is called for.

- Be as quick as possible on your power moves, but do not hurry them. The drop step and power layup will get you many 2- and 3-point plays if you execute the moves properly and are willing to take the "hit." After you swing your leg around on the drop step, you must "gather" or "collect" yourself before you power the ball up.

Skill: The Quick Step

This is a simple move, similar to the drop step, that can be very effective when used in the right situation. On the quick step you use quickness and go to the basket off one foot with a layup or hook instead of a power move. This move is executed without a dribble.

Drill P-4

1. Spin the ball out to SS #1. Check your Post Body Position (Fig. 7-6a).
2. Take a quick look over your right shoulder and shift your weight onto your right foot (Fig. 7-6b).
3. Bend your knees and take a quick step with your left foot to the basket executing a right-handed layup (Figs. 7-6c and 7-6d). Make three in a row.
4. Repeat steps 1–3 with right-handed baby hooks.
5. Repeat steps 1–3, but after you look over your right shoulder, do not shift your weight onto your right foot. Instead take one step with the right foot toward SS #2 and execute a baby hook directly into the basket.
6. Repeat steps 1–5 from SS #5, reversing directions for hands and feet.

(a)

(b)

(c)

(d)

Figure 7-6 The Quick Step (a) Post Body Position, (b) Quick Look, (c) Quick Step, and (d) Layup

POINTS OF EMPHASIS

- Your head is up.
- Your body is balanced with a low center of gravity.
- The ball is held firmly in both hands and well protected at all times.

Skill: The Spin-Out

The spin-out move involves a quick shoulder fake and show of the ball to the inside followed by a 100-degree front pivot toward the base line for a jump shot. In very close to the basket, some players have modified this move to a 90-degree front pivot and a jump hook.

Drill P-5

1. Spin the ball out to SS #1. Check your Post Body Position (Fig. 7-7a).
2. Take a look over your right shoulder.
   a. Show your defensive player a little of the ball by swinging your hips and shoulders around in the same direction as your look. This must be done quickly with both hands holding the ball firmly in close to your body (Fig. 7-7b).
   b. Shift your weight onto your left foot and front pivot 180 degrees to your left into jump-shooting position and take your jumper (Figs. 7-7c and 7-7d). Make three in a row.
3. Repeat steps 1 and 2 but front pivot 90 degrees so that your left shoulder is pointing toward the basket and execute a jump hook.
4. Repeat steps 1–3 from SS #5, reversing directions for hands and feet.

POINTS OF EMPHASIS

- The show-ball fake must be made quickly with the ball held firmly in close to the body.
- Be sure that your knees are bent and you shift your weight onto the pivot foot before you spin out. Otherwise, you may shuffle your feet and be called for a walking violation.

Skill: The Spin-In or -Out

The spin-in or -out move is a 180-degree front pivot into the Triple-Threat Position. This move can be executed with or without the show-ball fake. When the spin takes you toward the base line on either side, it is called a spin-out. When your spin takes you into the three-second lane or toward the center of the court, it is called a spin-in move.

Drill P-6

1. Spin the ball out to SS #9. Check your Post Body Position.
2. Take a look over your right shoulder and front pivot on the ball of your

(a)

(b)

(c)

Figure 7-7 The Spin Out (a) Post Body Position, (b) Quick Look with Showing the Ball, (c) Spin Out 180 Degree Front Pivot on Left Foot into Triple Threat Position, and (d) Jump Shot

(d)

left foot 180 degrees into the Triple-Threat Position. Shoot your jump shot. Make three in a row.

3. Repeat steps 1 and 2, front pivoting on your right foot into Triple-Threat Position.

4. Repeat steps 1–3 from SS #7 and reversing the directions for hands and feet.

Skill: The Spin-In or -Out Move with One Dribble

This move adds one step with the nonpivot foot and one dribble with the opposite hand of the stepping foot to move away from the defender. After the additional step and the dribble, you pivot the same as in the spin-in or -out move.

Drill P-7

1. Spin the ball out to SS #9. Check your Post Body Position.

2. Take a look over your right shoulder.

a. Shift your weight onto your right foot and take one step with your left foot pointing your toes toward the base line.

b. As your left foot lands, take one right-handed dribble, bouncing the ball to the right of the left foot.

c. All in one motion, front pivot into the Triple-Threat Position and shoot your jump shot. Make three in a row.

3. Repeat steps 1 and 2 front pivoting on your right foot into the lane and reversing the directions for your hands and feet.

4. Repeat steps 1–3 from SS #7, reversing the directions for hands and feet.

THE POST SERIES

To be effective as a post player, you must develop not only good individual moves but also be able to:

Recognize what move is appropriate in a given situation or "read" the defense.

Execute several series of moves that make it impossible for the defense to anticipate what move you are going to make.

It is for these reasons that each series begins in a well-balanced position, with the ball well protected followed by a quick look over your shoulder. This will enable you to "read" the defense and select the proper move. Each series involves moves right and left with various fakes so that your defender is forced to play you "honestly."

Practice each series *slowly* until you can execute each move smoothly and without committing a walking violation. If you are having difficulty mastering a move, practice it without the ball for awhile until you get the rhythm.

Occasionally do these drills placing a chair or other such item behind your spots so that you get a better idea of the angles of the steps on your moves.

Be sure your head is up, the ball is well protected, and you maintain good balance throughout. Remember the post area is a "war zone," the most contested area on the court, and you must do everything in this area decisively with confidence and power.

Never use a dribble unless it is absolutely necessary and that dribble will enable you to get to a new position. Under no circumstances should you use more than one dribble or a dribble without moving.

All layups from the right or left of the rim should be taken up strong and played off the backboard with the appropriate hand.

Low-Post Series

In the low-post, you will not have much room to operate. This is called the "hole," the most contested area on the court, and only moves that can be executed smoothly, decisively, and with power are used.

Series I

       1. Spin the ball out to SS #1. Check Post Body Position. Take a quick look over your right shoulder.
       a. Drop step left.
       b. Quick step right with baby hook.
       2. Repeat step 1 from SS #5, reversing the directions for hands and feet.

Series II

       1. Spin the ball out to SS #1. Check Post Body Position. Take a quick look over your right shoulder.
       a. Quick step left with layup or baby hook.
       b. Quick step right with baby hook.
       c. Show-ball fake right, spin-out left with jump shot.
       d. Show-ball fake right, spin-out left with jump hook.
       2. Repeat step 1 from SS #5, reversing the directions for hands and feet.

POINTS OF EMPHASIS

- The low-post area is the most contested area on the basketball court. If you are truly in the low post, you will probably not be able to turn around because a defender will be very close, if not touching you. Unless you are very tall or very strong, you will have to make a back to the basket move or spin out, away from the basket and center of the court. That is why the low-post moves favor steps and/or turns *out* instead of in.
- Many coaches teach very tall players to pivot or spin into a facing the basket position with the ball held high over the head. This can be effective, but only when the player has the height and the arm extension where the ball will not be batted out of his hands. For most players, it is advisable to pivot with the ball held close into the trunk of the body with the elbows out, knees bent, and a low center of gravity.
- Never use a dribble from the low-post position unless it is absolutely necessary.
- After you have mastered the low-post series, practice them from SS #2, 3 and 4.

Midpost Series

The midpost is from three to twelve feet from the basket, and, depending on your size, ability and skill level, and the defense, you will use both back-to-the-basket and facing-the-basket moves.

When you receive the ball in the midpost, you are farther from the basket than when you received the ball in the low post. This will give you more time and room to maneuver; therefore, more moves are possible. For the midpost series you will add the following:

1. The Triple-Threat Position—review.
2. The 180-degree reverse pivot—review.
3. The jab step—review.
4. The ball fake and the head fake—review.
5. The spin-in or -out—review.
6. The spin-in or -out with one dribble—review.

Midpost Series I

1. Spin the ball out to SS #9. Check your Post Body Position. Look over your right shoulder.
   a. Drop step left.
   b. Quick step right with baby hook.
   c. Quick step left with layup or baby hook.
   d. Drop step right.
2. Spin the ball out to SS #7; repeat step 1, reversing the directions for hands and feet.

Midpost Series II

1. Spin the ball out to SS #9. Check your Post Body Position. Look over your right shoulder.
   a. Spin-out left, jumper.
   b. Spin-in right, jumper.
   c. Spin-out left with show-ball fake, jumper.
   d. Spin-out left with one dribble, jumper.
   e. Spin-in right with one dribble, jumper.
   f. Repeat all these steps but front pivot 90 degrees and execute a jump hook.
2. Spin the ball out to SS #7; repeat step 1, reversing the directions for hands and feet.

Midpost Series III

1. Spin the ball out to SS #9. Check your Post Body Position. Look over your right shoulder.
   a. Spin-out left into Triple-Threat Position.
   (1) Jumper.
   (2) Head or ball fake, jumper.
   Important Note: The head fake is used when your defensive player is within three feet of you. The head fake will freeze him or her and you will be able to either shoot or make a move. The ball fake is not used in this situation for fear that the defender might bat it out of your hands. If the defender is more than three feet away, you can shoot or use the ball fake.

b. Head or ball fake, straight move to the basket with one dribble, jump stop, power layup.

c. Head or ball fake, crossover move to the basket with one dribble, jump stop, power layup.

d. Spin-in right and repeat the balance of step 1a.

2. Spin the ball out to SS #7; repeat step 1 reversing the directions for hands and feet.

Midpost Series IV

1. Spin the ball out to SS #9. Check your Post Body Position. Look over your right shoulder.

Reverse pivot 180 degrees on the ball of your right foot by swinging your left foot behind you into the Triple-Threat Position.

Important Note: This is an advanced move because it requires better balance and it exposes the ball to the defense. You should practice this move but only use it when you see the defender more than three feet away from you when you look over your shoulder with your back to the basket. The advantage of this move is that it is quicker and puts more pressure on the defense. Be sure that you hold the ball firmly in close to your body on this move.

2. Repeat all the options in Midpost Series III.

Reverse pivot 180 degrees on the ball of your left foot, and repeat step 1, reversing the directions for hands and feet.

3. Spin the ball out to SS #7; repeat steps 1 and 2, reversing the directions for hands and feet.

POINTS OF EMPHASIS

- The closer you are to the basket in the midpost, the more likely you will be closely guarded and have to use either back-to-the-basket moves or spin-out and shoot. As you get farther from the basket, you will have more opportunity of turning and facing.

- All the moves that go to the basket in the midpost series use a jump stop and a power layup or jump hook rather than a layup or dunk. This is because the area is usually congested and the two-foot jump stop offers the most control where you will be less likely to pick up an offensive foul. After you have mastered the jump stop series from the midpost, you will easily be able to recognize the opportunities where you can go straight to the basket and use a one-foot takeoff.

- After you have mastered each of these series, practice them from SS #6, 8, and 10.

- Most moves from the midpost require no dribble. However, when a dribble is called for, it should never be more than once and for a purpose—to take you to a new position.

- Very often you will have to fake after your dribble, especially if you are close to the basket or have lost sight of your defender on your move.

• If you lose some balance or are not sure of your defender's position, use a strong fake to collect yourself.

Skill: The Wheel Move

The wheel move is used when you receive the ball at the high post with your back to the basket and your defender is right behind you.

Drill P-8

    1. From SS #1, spin the ball out to SS #15. Check Post Body Position (Fig. 7-8a). Take a quick look over your left shoulder (Fig. 7-8b). For this drill we pretend the defender is very close to you.
    2. Bend your knees shifting your weight onto your right foot. Take a long

Figure 7-8 The Wheel Move (a) Post Body Position, (b) Quick Look, (c) Long, Quick Sealing Step, (d) Laying the Ball Out, (e) One Dribble, and (f) Layup

(a)   (b)   (c)

(d)   (e)   (f)

drop step with your left foot out and around your defender toward the basket, "sealing" the defender (Fig. 7-8c).

As your left foot touches the floor on the drop step, turn your hips and shoulders to the left, push the ball down for your one dribble with the right hand in front of and to the right of the left foot, and "explode" to the basket (Figs. 7-8d, 7-8e, and 7-8f).

This move is based on quickness, so be sure your head is up and your center of gravity is low.

When you take your look at the basket before you make the move, you should be able to recognize whether you will be able to go all the way to the basket or have to pull up for a shot or pass. Make three in a row.

3. Repeat steps 1 and 2 drop stepping with the right foot and reversing the directions for your hands and feet.

4. Repeat steps 1–3 spinning the ball out from SS #5 to SS #13 and reversing the directions for hands and feet.

POINTS OF EMPHASIS

- Recognizing your defender on your back.
- A good, quick drop step from a low center of gravity, "sealing" the defender.

High-Post Series

The high-post area ranges from ten to seventeen feet from the basket depending on the level of play. The distance from the basket in the high post makes most back-to-the-basket moves low percentage opportunities and unnecessary. Other than the wheel move, used when your defender comes right up on your back in the high post, you will learn to square up and use one-on-one moves from the Triple-Threat Position. In addition, the high post is an important position from which to pass. When you receive the ball in the low post, you should always look to "take it to the hoop" as your first option, but, as you receive the ball farther from the basket, you must consider other options such as passing to a teammate in better position to score.

High-Post Series I

1. Spin the ball out to SS #15. Check your Post Body Position. Look over your left shoulder.
   a. Wheel move left.
   b. Wheel move right.
2. Repeat step 1 spinning the ball out to SS #13.

High-Post Series II

1. Spin the ball out to SS #15. Check your Post Body Position.
a. Look over your left shoulder.
b. Spin out right into Triple-Threat Position.
(1) Jump shot.
(2) Head or ball fake, jumper.
Important Note: From the midpost, you will use the head fake most of the time because your defender will probably be within three feet of you. At the high post, you will find your defender playing farther off you more often increasing your opportunity to use the ball fake.
c. Head or ball fake, straight move to the basket.
d. Head or ball fake, crossover move to the basket.
e. Head or ball fake, crossover move toward SS #6, jump stop, jumper.
f. Spin-in left and repeat step 1 reversing directions for hand and feet.
2. Repeat step 1 spinning the ball out to SS #13.

High-Post Series III

1. Spin the ball out to SS #15. Check your Post Body Position.
a. Look over your left shoulder.
b. Spin out right into Triple-Threat Position.
(1) Jump shot.
(2) Jab step, jumper.
(3) Jab step, straight move to the basket.
(4) Jab step, crossover move to the basket.
(5) Jab step, straight move toward SS #9, jump stop, jumper.
(6) Jab step, crossover move toward SS #6, jump stop, jumper.
(7) Spin in left and repeat step 1 reversing directions for hands and feet.
2. Repeat step 1 spinning the ball out to SS #13.

High-Post Series IV

Repeat High-Post Series II and III using the reverse pivot into the triple threat position. See *Midpost Series IV.*

POINTS OF EMPHASIS

- After you have mastered each of these series, practice them from SS #12, 14, and 16.
- You must never use more than one dribble for any move from the high post and that one dribble must be for a purpose—to take you to a new position.
- Use a fake after your dribble when in doubt of your defender's position or to collect yourself.

WORKOUT, EVALUATION, AND PROGRESS CHARTS

Table 7-1 Post Moves Workout—30 Minutes

Warmup

DRILL	INSTRUCTIONS
Low-Post Series I	Do each move two times.
Low-Post Series II	" "
Midpost Series I	Do each move one time.
Midpost Series II	" "
Midpost Series III	" "
Midpost Series IV	" "
High-Post Series I	Do each move two times.
High-Post Series II	" "
High-Post Series III	" "
High-Post Series IV	" "

      If you have trouble doing one or more of these moves in a series, go back to the original drill for that move and study and practice it individually.

Cooldown

Table 7-2 Post Moves Workout—60 Minutes

Warmup

DRILL	INSTRUCTIONS
Low-Post Series I	Do each move three times.
Low-Post Series II	" "
Midpost Series I	" "
Midpost Series II	" "
Midpost Series III	" "
Midpost Series IV	" "
High-Post Series I	" "
High-Post Series II	" "
High-Post Series III	" "
High-Post Series IV	" "

      If you have trouble doing one or more of these moves in a series, go back to the original drill for that move and study and practice it individually.

Cooldown

Table 7-3 Post Moves Self-Evaluation and Improvement Test

DRILL	INSTRUCTIONS		SCORE	
Low-Post Series I	Do each move three times.		No. of shots made	
Low-Post Series II	"	"	"	"
Midpost Series I	"	"	"	"
Midpost Series II	"	"	"	"
Midpost Series III	"	"	"	"
Midpost Series IV	"	"	"	"
High-Post Series I	"	"	"	"
High-Post Series II	"	"	"	"
High-Post Series III	"	"	"	"
High-Post Series IV	"	"	"	"

Table 7-4 Personal Post Moves Progress Chart

Drill	DATE								
Low-Post Series I									
Low-Post Series II									
Midpost Series I									
Midpost Series II									
Midpost Series III									
Midpost Series IV									
High-Post Series I									
High-Post Series II									
High-Post Series III									
High-Post Series IV									

ADVANCED SCORING: "THE MISSING LINK"

This chapter is meant only for experienced players who have fully developed physically and mastered the preceding fundamentals. This "Advanced Scoring" chapter offers a series of concepts and drills that will make you a more effective scorer in game situations.

The drills here are *not* meant to encourage off-balance shooting, but rather to improve your ability to score when your balance is impeded on your shot in the course of a game. The better your shot preparation and selection is, the less you will need off-balance shooting skills. However, every player can benefit from this chapter after he or she understands that each shot should be taken with the intent of being in perfect balance. These concepts come into play in game situations, when, despite your best efforts to shoot with perfect form, defensive pressure, fouls, and less than perfect execution and timing on offense may result in or dictate a shot where your balance is impeded.

"THE MISSING LINK"

This chapter is subtitled "The Missing Link" because the concept was developed from listening to players ask over and over again: "How come I never miss in practice but I can't hit in a game?" "Is it because I get nervous?" "Do I lack confidence and experience?"

Too many otherwise successful competitors asked these questions for the answer to be so simple. While confidence and experience are certainly important factors, there is one other variable that many coaches fail to take into account. Most teaching sequences stress the spot shot, jumper, layup, and hook shots followed by instruction and drill in one-on-one moves. The "missing link" is that shooting under defensive pressure and while the body is in motion requires some special skills development in the area of kinesiology, or understanding your body in motion.

Most of the standard shots have built-in balance and stability—the form of the shot balances you and lines you up properly to the basket for an ideal release and follow-through. But in a game situation, shots often do not come so wide open and pressure free. You may be moving or fouled on your shot and not have the time to set yourself perfectly as you do in practice. All good scorers have the ability to balance themselves just before they release their shot, regardless of how quickly or in what direction they are moving. In other words, "game players" have developed the ability to take their movements into account when they shoot and compensate accordingly. An example of this is shooting the ball with less force and more arc and releasing it more softly when moving quickly toward the basket.

It is this "kinesthetic" sense or ability to control your body while in motion so that you can release your shot properly that will convert your "practice shot" into a consistently accurate "game shot." In the following drills you will learn how to balance and stabilize yourself while in motion to release your shot properly and compensate for your momentum.

Shooting on the Move

This phase of shooting incorporates many of the skills you have been working on in preceding drills. The secret to shooting on the move is form, body control, and concentration. You learned that a shot involves only the extension of the legs and the arm at the elbow and wrist. As you learn to shoot on the move, remember that, even though you may be floating through space at various angles, your ability to maintain your balance and keep your head, shoulders, trunk, and hips steady will determine how accurate and consistent you will be. Watch the great shooters on the move, and the one thing they all have in common is that after they shake the defensive player and prepare to shoot, regardless of their position in the air, each has the uncanny ability to steady his or her head and shoulders on the release of his or her shot.

Other helpful hints for shooting on the move include:

1. Keeping your eyes on the basket, as this will always give you a point of reference. Once you drop your head, it is difficult to pick up the basket in your vision and shoot at the same time.

2. Trying to maintain good body balance at all times. The more off balance you are, the more difficult it is to shoot accurately and consistently. Good balance on the basketball court is maintained by always having your knees and waist at least slightly bent, running at a speed that is not so fast that you cannot change direction, keeping your head up at all times, and making sure that the last step before a shot is not too long that it throws you out of balance when you shoot. A short last step before you shoot is beneficial because it helps direct your momentum upward.

3. Do not worry about having your shot blocked. Concentrate on maintaining as good balance and shooting form as possible. Thinking about the possibility of having your shot blocked will distract you and often cause you to hurry or change your shot resulting in a breakdown of both form and balance.

The shot on the move can be broken down into five functional aspects:

1. *Preparation.* One thing that separates a "scorer" from other players is his or her preparedness to shoot. While on the move, with or without the ball, the scorer always has an eye on the basket and is ready to shoot if and when the opportunity presents itself. In other words, the scorer is always anticipating the play will end in his or her shot. There is no hesitation because the player is prepared. This is an attitude that is essential because, when you are on the move, there is often no time to *decide* to shoot. You must be ready to shoot so in the split second when that opportunity presents itself, you will be able to take proper advantage. The scorer moves with purpose because he or she is always *anticipating* the shot.

2. *Takeoff.* Your shot on the move is often taken after a change of direction and/or change of pace. Whether the shot comes off the dribble or not, there is a tendency to jump laterally instead of vertically on the shot, which makes balance and body control difficult to maintain. Concentrate on collecting yourself, getting your hand behind the ball quickly, and jumping as straight up as possible with your feet under your body, head up, and eyes on the rim. You will attain best balance and body control possible by taking a small last step before your shot.

3. *Shot release.* All the principles of good form are important—body lined up to the basket, elbow in, hand behind the ball, wrist snap and elbow locking out simultaneously on the release, and the ball rolling off the fingertips. However, because you are on the move, *keeping your head and shoulders* steady on the release of the shot will require extra energy and concentration.

4. *Follow-through.* As you have learned, the follow-through is extremely important for the success of every shot. However, when you are on the

move, there is a tendency to cut the follow-through short to gain balance for the landing or protect yourself from anticipated contact. Even if it means you will have to take a fall or a hit, you must concentrate and use all your self-discipline *not* to cut the follow-through short. You must not be afraid to fall. Finish your shot with your fingers pointing toward the basket on the release, let the hand relax and go limp after the release, hold the head and shoulders steady, and keep your eyes riveted on your sighting point on the rim until the ball goes through the basket.

5. *Landing.* Whenever possible, the landing should be slightly forward, toward the basket, from the spot where the shot was released. You should try to land balanced with your head up and feet spread about a shoulder width apart as you land simultaneously on the balls of both feet. You may spread your arms out for extra balance if necessary. Good balance and body control on the landing is important because:

   a. It usually means the player was well balanced on the release of his or her shot.

   b. It enables the shooter to follow the shot or get into proper position more quickly.

   c. The shooter is less likely to charge into a defensive player and be injured or called for a foul.

It is important for you to understand that the following drills are *not* shots that you will try in a game! They are *exercises* that will teach and prepare you to get better balance on your shots in game situations. Practice these drills to develop the kinesthetic sense of your body in motion.

Drill AS-1

Do Rebounding Drill R-7, Two-Handed and One-Handed Taps.

As a scorer, you will not always be in perfect balance on your shot. After a hard move, with or without the ball, or when you are fouled, you must have the ability to stabilize yourself and shoot accurately. Most of the time when you are thrown off balance, you will have to stabilize yourself and learn to shoot accurately off of one foot.

Drill AS-2

1. Face the basket one step toward the base line from SS #1.

2. Take one side step with your left foot onto SS #1, and balance yourself on the ball of only your left foot.

As your weight shifts onto the ball of your left foot, bend your left knee and use your upper-body strength to hold your head and shoulder steady as you prepare to release your shot.

3. Release your shot with your head and shoulders steady and balanced. Your body should continue to fade to your left after you shoot.

Concentrate on perfect stabilization of your head and shoulders on the release of the shot.

Your eyes are on your sighting point on the rim until after the ball goes through the basket.

Follow-through with your shooting hand so that the fingers point toward the basket and then hang down limply.

Land in as balanced a position as possible. Make three in a row.

4. Repeat steps 1–3 stepping onto SS #2–10 and shooting off the left leg.

5. Repeat steps 1–4 stepping onto SS #1–10 from the left side and shooting off the right leg.

6. Repeat steps 1–4 stepping forward on SS #1–10 and shooting off of the left leg.

In addition to the points made in step 3, you will have to compensate for forward movement by releasing the ball with a higher arc and as softly as possible with a good follow-through.

7. Repeat step 6 stepping forward on SS #1–10 and shooting off of the right leg.

8. Repeat steps 6 and 7 taking one step backwards onto each shooting spot.

In addition to the points made in step 3, you will have to bend the knee of the leg on the floor more for power on your shot as you fade away from the basket. The upper-body strength goes into holding the head and shoulders steady on the shot.

9. Repeat steps 2–4 using one dribble with your left hand.

10. Repeat step 5 using one dribble with your right hand.

11. Repeat step 6–8 using one dribble with your left hand.

12. Repeat step 6–8 using one dribble with your right hand.

POINTS OF EMPHASIS

- Do not let your upper body swing too far out from over your hips and legs, or you will be too off balance to shoot accurately. Try as best as possible to get your legs under you before you shoot.
- Steady your head and shoulders just before you release the shot.
- Concentrate on keeping your eyes riveted on your sighting point on the rim all the way through the shot until it goes through the basket.
- Compensate for movement:
  When moving sideways and even more when going backward, bend your knees more to generate power for your shot.
  When moving forward, release the ball with a higher arc and as soft a release as possible with good follow-through.
- Bend your knees for more power, especially when going backward, and use your upper-body strength to steady your head and shoulders. Do not try to generate shooting power from the upper body because that energy must be used for stability of the head and shoulders.

- Make your last step as small as possible for good balance and upward thrust. If possible, angle slightly toward the basket on lateral steps so you will need less energy from your legs to shoot and less upper-body strength to stabilize yourself.
- Line up your shooting hand and elbow to the basket before you shoot. There should be a last moment hesitation before your shot where your head and shoulders become maximally stabilized and you relax. *Do not hurry your shot.*
- Be sure that your eyes do not leave the rim and your shooting hand follows through to the basket.
- Land balanced after your shot. Bend your knees and land on the balls of both feet simultaneously with your head up. Spread your arms for balance and body control.
- All the foregoing takes enormous energy and concentration, but you must learn to *relax* at the last moment on the release of your shot. That's the final key—everything goes for naught if you can't ultimately relax on the release of the shot.

Skill: Fadeaway Turn-Around Jumper and Up-and-Under Move

This advanced move has developed into a series that can be used most effectively at the midpost position, although some players are clever enough to use it in the low post. After receiving the ball with your back to the basket, you will spin either out or in. From this position, you take a fadeaway jumper or fake a jumper and go up and under.

Be sure that you do not shuffle your feet or move your pivot foot during the move. Your head must be up and the ball well protected at all times.

Learn to shoot after contact on this move by waiting a count or two after your fake. By waiting for the contact after a fake, you will be able to keep your balance and shoot accurately.

Drill AS-3

1. Spin the ball out to SS #9. Catch the ball in the air with a jump stop with your back to the basket. Take a quick peek over your right shoulder.

2. Spin out with a forward pivot on your left foot and shoot a fadeaway jumper. Make three in a row.

If your defender is very close to you, it is very effective to fake spinning out one way with a head-and-shoulder fake and/or the show-ball fake and spinning out the other way.

3. Repeat steps 1 and 2 with head and/or ball fakes before your shot.

4. Repeat steps 1–3, but after the head or ball fake, crossover step with your right foot and go "under" for a jump shot. Practice this up-and-under move

where you wait a count or two after the fake so that if contact is made, it will not throw you off balance and you will have a good chance for a 3-point play.

      a. Be sure that your pivot foot is anchored so that you are not called for a walk.

      b. The crossover step must be made by bending the knees and waist so that you are low and compact as you step across.

      c. Be sure that you do not take too long a crossover step where you will lose your balance and body control.

      d. The ball must be well protected and your head must be up at all times.

      e. Do not hurry your shot.

      5. Repeat steps 1–4 spinning out to your right.

      6. Repeat 1–5 from SS #10, 7, and 6.

POINTS OF EMPHASIS

- If your defender is within three feet of you, use a head fake. A ball or shot fake should only be used if your defender is more than three feet away.
- Keep your balance throughout by not spreading your feet too wide or taking too long a step and keeping your head up and knees bent. Do not hurry your shot.
- On the up-and-under move, practice shooting off your front foot leaning forward and to either side. Even though you are leaning, practice so that you have maximum balance and body control and, most important, that your head and shoulders are still on the release of the shot.

Skill: Following Your Shot

A scorer will almost always follow his or her shot and commonly pick up an extra two to five baskets a game in this manner. Learning to follow one's shot is more of an attitude than a skill because once you get into the habit of following your shot, you will learn to anticipate which way the ball is most likely to rebound. After all, you took the shot so who would know better where it is most likely to rebound?

If you shot it a little long or short, the ball will come back straight. If you shot it a little right go for the rebound off the rim to the right and so on. One word of caution: While it is an excellent habit to follow your shot, do not hurry your shot causing it to miss so that you can get the rebound. Take your time and concentrate on making your initial shot.

Drill AS-4

      1. Repeat AS-3, but after each shot follow it, and, whether the initial shot goes in or not, grab the ball and score with a power layup or jump shot.

POINTS OF EMPHASIS
- Do not lose your balance on your shot.
- Grab every rebound with two hands and take it back up strong with good balance.

Skill: One-on-One Moves Off the Dribble

The use of a variety of fakes and feints off the dribble will keep your defender in doubt as to when and what move you will make and when you will shoot. By constantly using different fakes and feints, your defender will find it difficult to set up for the purpose of jumping to block your shot, taking a charge, or going for a steal. The constant use of little fakes is very effective for keeping the defender defensive in his or her actions. This allows you to move him or her around and set him or her up for whatever move you wish to make.

Drill AS-5

1. Begin dribbling with your right hand, back to the base line, from a spot three feet in from the right sideline at the foul line extended toward SS #15.

The ball is well protected with a low dribble, and your head is up. Use a variety of fakes as you dribble: head, shoulder, fake spin move, and stops and starts.

2. When you get to SS #15, give one strong fake to freeze your defender, front pivot on your left foot, and take your jump shot. Make three in a row.

3. Repeat steps 1 and 2 but use a hesitation and head-and-shoulder fake at SS #15 as though you are going to shoot followed by one quick, long step with the left leg and drive to the basket and score.

Be sure you stay low and under control on your move. After you hesitate and fake, be sure that you wait for your defender to take the fake before you explode to the basket. You must use only one dribble after your last fake before going to the basket. Step with your left leg.

Practice driving to the basket with power and pulling up off of this move. Your head must be up so that you can react to additional defensive players helping out. You must be prepared to stop and either shoot or hit an open teammate at any time.

4. Repeat 3 but use a spin move pivoting off your right foot to the basket after the head-and-shoulder fake.

Your head must be up, and you must be sure that there are no defensive players behind you when you spin. This means you will have to look over your *left* shoulder as you are dribbling toward SS #15 to make sure that the area behind you is open.

5. Repeat steps 1–4 dribbling from the opposite side of the court with the left hand toward SS #13 and reversing directions for hands and feet.

POINTS OF EMPHASIS

- You must constantly mix up your fakes and the intensity of those fakes.
- Use both weak and sharp (or hard) fakes. It is particularly effective when you use a weak fake before a sharp fake and then make your move or take your shot.
- Do not make your move too quickly after a good fake. Give your opponent time to react to the fake.
- Avoid using too many ball fakes when your defender is close to you. Use head and body fakes.
- Your faking will keep your defender off balance, but once you have set him up, make your move or shoot. Do not over fake.

Skill: Shooting Off a Screen with Quick Release

Review Skill: Shooting Off The Pass and Drill S-18.

Every perimeter player can improve his scoring capabilities by working on getting his shot off as quickly as possible when coming off a screen. *There is a big difference between hurrying your shot and a quick release.* If you hurry your shot, it will be less accurate, but the following tips can help you to develop a quick shot without sacrificing any accuracy:

Preparation: As you are moving on offense without the ball, always be thinking and looking for opportunities to score. You must see screens as they are setting up and time your movements so that you arrive at the right spot at the right time for your shot. The great scorer never hesitates when a good shot is there because he has already taken that shot in his mind by having seen the opportunity as it was forming. That is preparation.

Cut the size of your steps and bend your knees as you approach lyour shooting spot behind the screen. This will lower your center of gravity and improve your balance allowing you to jump straight up and under control while you shoot.

The proper distance behind a screen you select to shoot from depends on several factors. If you are tall and/or jump very well, you will be able to shoot from one to two feet behind. However, if the screener is very tall and you are either short or not a good jumper, you will need more room.

This is all part of preparation. As you become more experienced it will become automatic to come off a screen at the proper distance behind it depending on these factors. But you must see the screen as it is setting up and time your moves so that you are in the right place at the right time.

Use the screen as a line of sight to the basket. As you come off the screen, use it to line up your body and your shooting arm to the basket.

The quicker you learn to release your shot accurately, the more effective your fakes will be. If your defender knows that you can shoot well and quickly off a screen, you have set up a move where you come off a screen, catch and fake a shot, and drive to the basket. Your quick release will have forced your defender to commit himself more quickly.

Pivot on the ball of your inside foot as you catch the ball with both hands so that you can catch, pivot, and jump all in one motion. It further helps if you will plant that inside or pivot foot with the toe pointing to the basket on your last step. This will make the pivot and square up to the basket smoother.

Your head must be up at all times. As you approach the spot behind the screen, you use split or peripheral vision to, first, watch the ball coming into your hands and, second, keep yourself properly lined up to the basket for your shot. Get your shooting hand behind the ball as quickly as possible. If you lose sight of the basket, it will be very difficult to pick it up again as you are going up for your shot.

In addition, by keeping a view of the basket out of the corner of your eye, you will see any change in the defense or any forming screens. For example, if your defender jumps out in front of you behind the screen, you can simply do a change of direction to the basket for an easy layup.

Drill AS-6

1. Set up a chair with a broom or mop sticking up from its back on SS #16. With your back to the base line, stand about midway between the SS #7 and the near side line, and spin the ball to a spot behind the screen.

2. Catch the ball on one bounce and, all in one motion, pivot and shoot your jumper (Figs. 8-1a, 8-1b, 8-1c, and 8-1d). Make three in a row.

Was your head up at all times seeing both the ball and the basket? Did you use the screen to sight the basket?

Did you bend your knees and cut your steps as you approached the ball?

Did you point your left toe toward the basket on your last step to facilitate your pivot and line you up to the basket?

Were you able to catch, pivot, and shoot all in one motion?

3. Repeat steps 1 and 2 at SS #15, 14, 13, 12, 11, and 17.

4. Repeat steps 1–3 spinning the ball out from the opposite side of the spot so that you must pivot off of your right foot for the shot.

Important Note: To perfect this skill, you will have to practice this drill coming off screens from almost every possible angle. Learn the angles that allow you to shoot most quickly and accurately and in game situations, try to set yourself up for those opportunities.

5. Repeat steps 1–4, but after you catch the ball, fake the shot, do one crossover dribble, and hit your jumper.

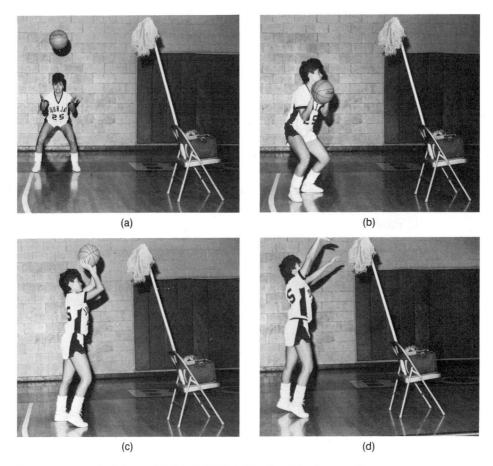

Figures 8-1a, 8-1b, 8-1c, and 8-1d Drill AS-6, Shooting Off a Screen with Quick Release

POINTS OF EMPHASIS

- Practice the foregoing techniques concentrating on accuracy first. If your shot is not straight (on line), work on your footwork, balance, and keeping your head up. Slow your movements down until you gain accuracy.
- Once you are consistently shooting straight, you can pick up your tempo. As the tempo increases, be sure that you do not release the shot too quickly.

Concentrate on releasing the ball with your head and shoulder steady. The ball must roll off the fingertips, and the arm must fully extend toward the basket with the wrist falling limply down on the follow-through. The quicker the shot and the more off balanced you are, the more you will have to fight for a steady head and shoulders and smooth release and follow-through on the jump and release of the shot.

Skill: Shooting Off a Screen on the Dribble

Review Skill: Shooting Off The Dribble and Drill S-19.

Many of the points made in *shooting off a screen with quick release* apply to shooting off the screen on the dribble. Your head must be up at all times and cutting your steps and bending your knees so that you can stop, pivot, and shoot all in one motion is also important. And, of course, you must learn your best angles and the proper distance behind the screen for your shot. In addition, the following points should help you on this move:

1. Use a variety of fakes, including fakes to shoot or change direction as you approach the screen so your defender cannot beat you to the screen.
2. About six to ten feet before the screen, fake a shot or change of direction and accelerate for one or two steps toward the screen. Depending on your strength and experience you may have to slow down before you stop, pivot, and shoot.
3. Collecting or gathering yourself with the ball off the dribble is more difficult than without the ball. Be sure the ball is well protected and your dribble is under control. Practice getting your shooting hand behind the ball quickly.
4. To get extra lift on your jump, bounce the ball hard on the last dribble before you jump. You should begin your jump as the ball is coming up because it is quicker and it aids in your upward momentum.

The position of the last bounce must be in line with your inside foot so that you jump straight up. If the last dribble is too far in front or behind you, it will throw you off balance on the jump. This maneuver takes a great deal of practice because the jump and the positions of the ball and your body must be timed perfectly.

Drill AS-7

1. Set up a chair with a broom or mop sticking up from its back on SS #16. With your back to the base line, begin dribbling toward the screen from a spot midway between SS #17 and the near sideline.

2. Six to ten feet from the screen use a head-and-shoulder fake, change-of-direction fake or stop and go maneuver, and accelerate toward the screen. Be sure your head is up and the ball is well protected.

3. Cut your steps and bend your knees as you approach the screen. Turn the toes of your left foot toward the basket on your last step, bounce the last

dribble hard, and stop, pivot, and jump all in one smooth, continuous motion. Make three in a row.

    4. Repeat steps 1 and 2 at SS #15, 14, 13, 12, 11, and 17.

    5. Repeat steps 1–3 dribbling from the opposite side of the screen so that you must dribble with your left hand and pivot off of your right foot for the shot.

    Important Note: As in the case of shooting off a screen when the ball is passed to you, you will have to practice this maneuver coming off of screens from almost every possible angle. Learn the angles that allow you to shoot most quickly and accurately.

    6. Repeat steps 1–4, but do not pick the ball up for a shot on the last dribble. Instead, give a good head-and-shoulder fake straight up, do a crossover dribble moving two or three steps back in the same direction from where you came and then hit your jumper.

POINTS OF EMPHASIS

- Be sure the last dribble before your jumper is in close to you and opposite the inside or pivot foot.
- Review the Points of Emphasis in Shooting Off a Screen with Quick Release.

Skill: Underhanded Layup with a Twist

The underhanded layup with a twist is an advanced move that many high school, college, and professional players use for added protection of the ball on their layups. This adaptation of the underhanded layup allows a player to use the right hand from the left side of the basket or the left hand from the right side. This maneuver should not be attempted until the standard and underhanded layups have been mastered and you are physically strong enough to execute the move.

This move requires a great deal of body control because you will be twisting the trunk of your body in the air on the takeoff. From the left side of the basket you will take off on the right foot with the ball held in both hands on your left hip after having dribbled with the left hand to the basket.

Your right hand is under the ball with your left hand on the side of the ball.

As you jump, your right knee drives up and across your body while your right elbow swings across your body. This pulls your right hip and shoulder, twisting your body perpendicular (sideways) to the basket as your right hand, palm up, reaches toward the basket and lays the ball into the basket softly off the backboard.

As the body twists, the ball is brought up over the right shoulder with both hands. The left hand is not released until the ball is at least at eye level, and the ball should be released from the right hand at the top of the jump with the right arm fully extended. The ball is well protected because the body position after the twist places your body between you and the defense.

Drill AS-8

1. Begin at SS #16, facing the basket without a basketball in your hands.

2. Run at half speed at a 45-degree angle to the basket as though you were going to take an underhanded layup with the *right hand* from the *left side* of the basket. This means that your last step will be with your left foot.

   a. Your head is up looking at the basket.

   b. Your last step is small enough so that your momentum will be straight up and not out and under the basket.

   c. As you jump off the left foot, swing your right elbow across your body and drive your right knee up and across your body.

   d. Your momentum on your jump should be up with a half twist so that your back is to the basket as your right hand, with the palm up, extends fully toward the basket.

3. Repeat this five times.

4. Repeat steps 1 and 2 with the basketball.

   a. Use one dribble with the left hand going to the basket.

   b. Be sure you bring the ball up to at least eye level before you release the left hand.

   c. Keep your eyes on the basket throughout the move to help keep your body balanced and in line with the basket.

   d. Release the ball at the top of your jump with the right arm fully extended and the ball rolling off the fingertips softly with a flick of the wrist and fingers of the right hand.

   e. Because the underhanded layup with a twist requires more body control than more conventional layups, landing on two feet under the basket may require more practice. After releasing the ball, spread your arms and legs comfortably to gain extra balance and try to land as softly as possible on the balls of both feet simultaneously with your knees bent.

   Important Note: There is a debatable point regarding the proper grip on the ball after the player has finished the dribble and prepares to take off on the jump to the basket. Because defensive pressure often comes from the side of the shooting hand, players should hold their hands on the sides of the ball with their elbows out for added protection.

   As the body twists and the arm and hand rotate in toward the body, the shooting hand naturally rotates under the ball. The danger here is the player must take extra care that after the hand rotates under the ball, he or she must take the ball straight up to the backboard and *not* continue to twist the hand. If the hand continues to twist, the ball will have a side/overspin that is more difficult to control.

5. Repeat step 4 until you can make five in a row.

6. Repeat steps 1–5 from the right side using the left hand and taking off on the right foot. As with most skills, learning this maneuver with the nondominant hand will take a great deal more practice.

WORKOUT, EVALUATION, AND PROGRESS CHARTS

Table 8-1   Advanced Scoring Workout—30 Minutes

Warmup

DRILL	INSTRUCTIONS
AS-1	Two-hand taps: Do three sets of 1-minute duration. One-hand taps: " "
AS-3 & 4	Make three in a row from SS #6, 7, 9, 10 front pivoting right and left from each spot. Follow each shot and use power layups to score on each missed shot.
AS-5	Make three in a row jump shots, hesitation and drive to the basket, and reverse dribble to the basket. Repeat on the other side.
AS-6	Make three in a row from SS #11–17, moving left to right and right to left.
AS-7	Make three in a row from SS #11–17, dribbling left to right and right to left.
AS-8	Make ten in a row from each side.

Cooldown

Table 8-2   Advanced Scoring Self-Evaluation and Improvement Test

DRILL	INSTRUCTIONS	SCORE
AS-1	Number of consecutive taps in 30 seconds	
	Two-handed	No. of taps
	One-handed	No. of taps
AS-3	Take five shots from each SS #6, 7, 9, 10, pivoting right and left from each spot.	No. of shots made
AS-5	Take five jump shots, hesitation and drive to the basket, and reverse dribble to the basket from each side.	No. of shots made
AS-6	Take five shots from each SS #11–17, moving from left to right and right to left.	No. of shots made
AS-7	Take five shots from each SS #11–17, dribbling from left to right and right to left.	No. of shots made
AS-8	Take ten from each side.	No. of shots made

Table 8-3 Personal Advanced Scoring Progress Chart

Drill	DATE							
AS-1 Two-handed								
One-handed								
AS-3								
AS-5								
AS-6								
AS-7								
AS-8								

CHAPTER NINE

REBOUNDING

Rebounding is a critical part of the game of basketball. Few games are won without a superior effort off the boards. However, the individual skills of rebounding are largely the application of footwork and jumping. This chapter will cover the theory of defensive and offensive rebounding and drills to develop and improve rebounding skills.

Every missed shot provides an opportunity for a rebound. If the team that shot the ball gets the rebound, it is called an offensive rebound, while a defensive rebound results when the defending team secures the rebound.

The importance of becoming as good a rebounder as possible cannot be overemphasized. Defensive rebounding keeps opponents from getting second and third chances at scoring. This encourages your team to play good defense, knowing that a missed shot will put you on offense. Poor defensive rebounding can discourage defensive effort.

Offensive rebounding can be likened to an eraser on a pencil. If your team misses a shot but can secure the rebound, it erases the missed shot, and you get another opportunity to score. A team cannot afford to allow a formidable opponent too many erasures in a game without losing. Teams that rebound well can either fast break or slow the tempo of the game to their advantage. In the final analysis, the team that controls the boards controls the game—and usually wins.

Rebounding is a combination of mental, physical, and skill-related components. The mental part involves your knowledge of positioning and desire and determination to get the ball. The physical refers to your size, balance, timing, and quickness. The skill-related component relates to your footwork, body position, and mechanical technique.

THE MENTAL COMPONENT

1. Assume that every shot taken will miss.
2. Be courageous. You must have no fear. Go for every rebound possible aggressively. Move your feet and try to get them under you in the best position as possible for the rebound. Jump off both feet with your arms up and land balanced on the balls of both feet.
3. Be aggressive and go for every rebound. A good rebounder is tenacious, hungry, and proud. He or she tries to get every rebound possible. Remember that the leading rebounder on a team will always play a lot of minutes regardless of his or her other skills.
4. Get into good position. Anticipate where the rebound most likely will come off. You must move on the flight of the shot into good position. On defensive rebounds, this means between your opponent and the basket, and on offensive rebounds, you must not let your defensive man screen you off from the basket.
5. Anticipate shots. Know your teammates' moves and favorite shooting spots and learn as much as possible about when and from where your opponents like to shoot.

THE PHYSICAL COMPONENT

Height, strength, amount of arm extension, quickness, and jumping ability—how high and how quick—are the important physical aspects of rebounding. The great rebounders:

1. Cover a large area. They can quickly get to the spot where the ball is going to come down and go up and get it. The ability to cover a large area depends on good anticipation, aggressiveness, quick feet, good footwork, and good balance. Lateral quickness is especially important.
2. Jump off two feet and grab the ball with two hands. The two-foot jump is more stable and allows you to jump up straight. The best way to get a rebound is to move on the flight of the shot into proper position—for the box out on defense and, on offense, to the spot where you anticipate the ball will come off the rim. You must go for the ball as soon as you know you can get it. Your success will depend on your balance, timing, and the quickness of your jump.

Surprisingly, the height of your jump is less important than the timing and quickness of the jump. Even in the professional game, three out of every four rebounds are grabbed below the rim. The best rebounders jump quickly and time their jumps so that they get their hands on the ball at precisely the top of their jumps.

You must learn to grab the ball with two hands. One-handed rebounders cannot control the ball well and often lose the ball on the way down because of poor balance or because an opponent bats it away.

It takes courage to leap with both hands in the air for a rebound. It exposes your body to punishment. The one-handed rebounder is unconsciously afraid of getting hit so he or she leaves one hand down for protection. Jumping off two feet with your feet about a shoulder width apart will enable you to ascend straight up with balance and stability and grab the ball with two hands. Practice it this way and it will become habit.

The one-handed rebound is only appropriate when you cannot get your feet under you to jump straight up for a rebound. This often occurs on an offensive rebound where you are boxed out or on the move toward the basket and the rebound comes off several feet from where you are. To "keep the ball alive," or tip it into the basket, you may have to jump off one foot, on an angle toward the ball, and tip the ball with one hand.

Important Note There is considerable debate in coaching circles concerning when a rebounder, offensive or defensive, should raise his arms up so that his elbows are up and out in line with the shoulders with the palms facing the basket. Very tall and strong players often pick up pushing fouls when they do not raise their arms up quickly on the shot even when they are not guilty of such an infraction. For this reason, many coaches drill their big players to raise their arms up immediately on the shot to avoid being called for a foul.

While this is a good idea for certain players, it may impede a player's ability to get rebounds. I suggest that most players raise their hands either as they move into defensive or offensive rebounding position and before they jump, or immediately after doing so. However, some large players, who are prone to picking up rebounding fouls, must be taught to raise their arms on the shot, or they will foul out very quickly.

Keep in mind that moving and jumping with quickness and agility is more difficult with the arms raised. It takes enormous upper- and lower-body strength and stamina that few players, especially young players, have. In addition, there are many players who will simply not be able to move or jump quickly with their arms up. (*Note to coaches:* It is very important that you evaluate each of your players individually in this regard and not teach every player the same technique.) (See Figures 9-1 and 9-2.)

THE ANGLE OF THE REBOUND

It is important to understand where the ball is most likely to rebound when a shot is missed.

1. Most missed shots will deflect out on the opposite side of the basket at a similar angle. This means that a missed shot from one corner will often rebound toward the opposite corner. A missed shot from a 45-degree angle from the right side will often rebound out on a 45-degree angle on the left. (See Figure 9-3.)
2. The second most common carom will be straight back in the direction of the shooter.
3. The farther out the shot is taken from the basket, the farther out the rebound is likely to carry.
4. Low and very high arced shots tend to rebound farther out than medium arced shots. This is also true of hard shots versus soft shots.

Figure 9-1 Jumping Position for the Rebound

Figure 9-2 Going Up Strong for the Rebound

5. You should be aware of the tightness of the rims, the resiliency of the backboards, and how "alive" the basketball you're playing with is. For example, if the ball is "alive," the rims are tight, and the backboards are resilient, rebounds will bounce out farther.

THE SKILL-RELATED COMPONENT

There are different theories on the best way defensively to block or box out your opponent after a shot. Certainly each approach has validity, and it is very likely that different systems are better suited for different players.

All the systems have the following general principle in common: When your opponents shoot, you should screen your opponent from going for the offensive rebound. Some coaches teach that you should make contact with your opponent as quickly and as far from the basket as possible, pivot to face the basket, and hold him or her out for as long as possible. Other coaches just want their players to step in the path of their opponents and then go for the rebound themselves. These coaches do not want you to make physical contact on the block-out because they feel this impedes the defensive rebounder as much or more than the offensive rebounder.

In addition, there are different strategies for blocking out de-

**Most missed shots (rebounds) deflect out on
the opposite side of the basket at similar angle.**

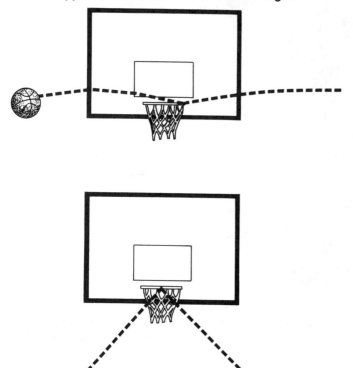

Figure 9-3 Rebounding Angles

pending on position—guard, forward, or center—and whether or not
your opponent took the shot. Which system is best for you will depend on
your physical characteristics. If you do not jump well, you should make
contact on your block-outs and then go for the ball. If you are not physically strong but are tall with good extension and jump well, it may be better for you to just step in front of your opponent and then go for the ball.

CONCEPTS OF DEFENSIVE REBOUNDING

Regardless of whether your team is playing man-to-man or zone defense,
you will have block out responsibility on the shot. The basic notions of
defensive rebounding are:

1. See your opponent and the ball at all times. If you have to lose sight of
   one of them, make it the ball. Then quickly get into position where you
   can pick up the ball again without losing sight of your opponent.

2. Move on the release of the shot to a position between your opponent and the basket.

3. Do not lose sight of your opponent on the flight of the shot. You must see him so you can step in his way and block him out if he goes for the rebound.

4. Depending on your position in relation to your opponent and the basket, you will front or reverse pivot, making contact with your opponent.

5. Make yourself big—as soon as the shot goes up, you should bend your knees and spread your feet more than a shoulder width and raise your arms up to the basket with the elbows out and the palms facing the basket.

6. If you are close to the basket when the shot is taken, you must create as much space for yourself as quickly as possible. In order not to get caught under the basket, a poor rebound position, aggressively go to your opponent and reverse pivot, making contact with him on the pivot. Your pivot should bring your lowered butt into contact with his legs. Your body will be directly between him and the basket.

7. As you get farther from the basket when the shot is taken, you must be careful how you approach your opponent on the block-out. If there is too much room, he will easily be able to go around your block. Depending on your quickness, his quickness, and the distance you are to the basket, you might retreat or advance to twelve to fifteen feet from the basket in the path of your opponent and block him out only if he goes for the rebound.

8. Your opponent is a dangerous potential rebounder when he shoots. If he is inside twelve to fifteen feet when he shoots you must block him out immediately on the release of the shot. If he shoots from outside that range, it is usually better to step in his path by retreating or advancing to twelve to fifteen feet and blocking him out only if he goes for the rebound.

9. The concept of the defensive rebound is that if every member of the team blocks out, you will get the rebound. Sometimes the opponent who did the least work on the defensive boards gets the rebound because other members of the team sacrificed themselves by blocking out the most serious offensive rebounding threats.

There are four parts to defensive rebounding:

1. The box- or block-out.
2. The jump.
3. Protection of the ball.
4. The outlet.

THE BOX- OR BLOCK-OUT

1. Move on the release of the shot to get the best possible position between your opponent and the basket. Do not take your eye off your opponent.

2. When you get into position you use either a front or reverse pivot and block your opponent from the rebound.

3. Your pivot should bring you into body contact with your opponent. Your feet are about a shoulder width apart, knees bent, butt low, back straight, elbows out, upper arms parallel to the floor, hands up, with the palms facing the basket and your head up.

THE JUMP

1. When the ball rebounds off the missed shot, you must hold your opponent off—stay between him or her and the ball—until you know that you can get the ball. If you jump or release too early, and your opponent is taller, quicker, or stronger, he or she may beat you or outjump you to the ball. So depending on your ability and who you are boxing out, you jump for the rebound at the earliest opportunity when you know you can get the ball.

2. You should "explode" off the toes of both feet with your legs spread on the jump, making your jump quick and taking up as much room as possible. Some players flair their legs even wider as they elevate to further discourage opponents. Do this only if it does not impede your own quickness and balance.

PROTECTION OF THE BALL

1. Always grab the ball with two hands and hold it firmly. You should not tip the ball on defensive rebounds unless absolutely necessary. Try to land as balanced as possible on the balls of both feet, with your feet spread at least a shoulder width apart. Pull the ball into your upper chest with the elbows out and your head up and knees bent. As you bring the ball into your chest, rotate one hand on top of the ball and the other under the ball for better protection.

It is an advanced maneuver to grab a rebound and turn and release an outlet pass all in one motion.

Important Note: As with other skills of this nature, some coaches teach a very tall player not to bring a rebound down into the chest area but to hold the ball high over the head, pivot, and outlet the ball. Either technique is valid, but if you hold the ball over your head, you must be very tall or defenders will knock the ball out of your hands.

The Outlet From the position where you have the ball protected after grabbing the rebound, you have several options. You will probably be facing your opponent's basket so you have to take a quick look over the shoulder toward the nearest sideline or away from the center of the court where most of the congestion is likely to be. If there is a teammate open for the outlet pass, you should front pivot out toward the nearest sideline and pass it to him. Use a two-hand overhead or baseball pass. If there is no one to outlet the ball to, fake a pass toward the middle and lay the ball out with one dribble toward the near sideline. Remember there is no five-second count in the back court, so there is no reason to rush this move.

CONCEPTS OF OFFENSIVE REBOUNDING

1. Constantly move into good position to receive the ball when your team is on offense. This puts pressure on your opponent to deny you the ball, enabling you to get better position on him when a shot goes up. Constant movement also creates "vision breakdowns" for your defender as he must take his eyes off either you or the ball. In either case, it gives you an advantage for the rebound. You should not remain in an offensive position where you cannot receive the ball and your opponent can see you and the ball at the same time.

2. Move on offense into a position where your opponent cannot see you and the ball. In many cases he will take his eyes off you, and, on the shot, you will be able to beat him to good rebounding position before he can locate you and block you out. A good offensive rebounding big man often takes his defensive man down low deep under the basket where the defensive player cannot see him and the ball at the same time. Depending on how the defensive man plays the situation, the offensive rebounder can either block him under the basket on the shot or, when the defensive man loses sight of him, move into good offensive position for the rebound.

3. Anticipate the shot and the angle of the rebound. You must know your teammates in terms of what shots they like to take, when, and from what positions. In addition, you should know who shoots a hard shot and who shoots a soft shot, and who tends to shoot long and who tends to be short.

4. Make your move during the flight of the shot. Do not hesitate. As soon as the shot goes up, you should anticipate where the rebound might go and make a move for that position.

5. If you can get in front of your defensive opponent, block him out. This can lead to an offensive rebound. This situation most often occurs when your opponent is fronting you in the post or trying to give weak-side help when you are on the side of the court opposite the ball. Seize this opportunity to block him out on the flight of the shot.

6. Screen your defender off other players, both teammates and defenders, when the shot goes up. In other words, as soon as a shot goes up, move; do not accept a block out. If there is a player or players near you either laterally or toward the basket, use them to cut your defender off from your pursuit.

7. Never accept poor position on a rebound. If your defender makes contact with you and boxes you out, you can:

a. Step back and go around him or her.
b. Spin off him toward the basket or into an open area.
c. Duck under him for better position.
d. Place a forearm on his back and make a move.
e. Tap him on one side of his tail and go the other way.
f. Fake or step one way and go the other.

8. Just as you make yourself big when you block out on a defensive rebound, make yourself small when moving into position for an offensive rebound. If you are not in good position when the shot goes up, crouch down low with your arms and legs in close and turn sideways. This will make you small and enable you to quickly slip into better rebounding position.

9. Never give up on a rebound. Go for every rebound even if you might only get one finger on the ball. This may keep the ball "alive" for a teammate or cause an opponent to make a mistake like losing the ball out of bounds, fumbling it, or committing a violation. There will be times when getting into good position for an offensive rebound will be impossible. Go for "a piece of the backboard." This means that you must look to get into the best position you can for a rebound and hold that position in hopes that the ball will come to you. Never accept a position on a rebound where you have no chance of getting the ball.

10. Use a variety of moves. Do not let your defender anticipate when, where, and how you will move for a rebound.

11. When you get an offensive rebound, protect the ball, hold it strong in both hands, collect yourself, and power the ball back up for 2 or 3 points. You may use a strong fake before you power the ball backup. Be sure your head is up and you do not walk.

12. If you cannot get two hands on the ball, tip the ball into the basket or away from your defensive player where maybe a teammate will have a chance of getting the ball.

Drill R-1: Jumping the Stick

1. Place two chairs or boxes three feet apart and at about a level six inches under your maximum vertical jump.

2. Place a stick across the two chairs and stand sideways with your right shoulder toward the stick.

3. Use a two-foot jump off your toes over the stick and land on the balls of both feet, flexing your knees as you land. Your left shoulder should now be facing the stick.

4. With as little pause as possible, jump back over the stick to the other side in the same fashion.

5. Jump back and forth over the stick ten times.

6. Do three to five sets of ten jumps each.

7. Each day increase the number of repetitions in each set by one, until you can do sets of twenty-five repetitions.

POINTS OF EMPHASIS

- This will increase jumping agility and stamina.
- Your form and quickness will improve by necessity.
- Keep your head up.
- Be careful. Place the stick at the very end of the chair or in some way so that, if you miss your jump, you will not injure yourself.

Skill: Blocking Out

You must always anticipate a shot when you are playing defense so that you are prepared to move into proper rebounding position. If the player you are guarding is within twelve to fifteen feet of the basket, you must block him or her out. Immediately on the release of the shot, you must make a quick decision concerning your footwork.

If you are close to your opponent, within three feet, it is best to reverse pivot quickly into block-out position. You will not have the time or room for a front pivot.

If you are farther than three feet away from your opponent when the shot goes up, you can either use a front pivot, which will cut down the distance between you and your opponent or use a quick slide or advance step and either a front or reverse pivot. The decision will depend on your quickness, your opponent's quickness, the angle and distance you are from your opponent and the basket, and your personal preference in terms of what footwork you can execute quickly and smoothly. (See Figure 9-4.)

Drill R-2

1. Begin at SS #1 with your back to the basket in a good defensive stance.

2. Reverse pivot on your right foot into the lane into good block-out position.

Block-Out Position:

a. Feet wider than a shoulder width.

b. Knees bent and weight forward on balls of feet.

c. Butt protruding with waist bent and back straight.

d. Arms up, elbows out in line with shoulders, and palms facing the basket.

e. Head up.

Important Note: Some coaches insist that their players raise their arms and hands immediately on the release of the shot and then move into block-out position so they will not be called for a pushing foul.

3. Repeat steps 1 and 2 reverse pivoting on your left foot toward the base line into good block-out position.

Figure 9-4 Blocking or Boxing Out

4. Repeat steps 1 and 2 front pivoting on your right foot into the lane.

5. Repeat steps 1 and 2 front pivoting on your left foot toward the base line.

6. Repeat steps 1–5 from SS #5, reversing the directions for hands and feet.

POINTS OF EMPHASIS

- The pivot into block-out position must be made quickly and smoothly. You should make contact with your opponent simultaneously with the completion of your pivot into block-out position.
- Your feet must be wider than a shoulder width with your knees bent and butt protruding into your opponent in a stable position with a low center of gravity. With your arms up and elbows out, this is called "making yourself big," and it will be difficult for your opponent to get around you without being called for a foul.

Drill R-3

1. Begin at SS #9 with your back to the basket in a good defensive stance.

2. Execute the following and be sure that you step first with the right foot when sliding right and step first with the left foot when sliding left:

   a. Slide step right and reverse pivot on right foot into the lane.
   b. Slide step right and front pivot on right foot into the lane.
   c. Slide step left and reverse pivot on left foot toward baseline.
   d. Slide step left and front pivot on left foot toward the base line.
   e. Advance step with right foot forward and reverse pivot on right foot into the lane.

f. Advance step with right foot forward and front pivot on right foot.

g. Advance step with left foot forward and reverse pivot on left foot toward the base line.

h. Advance step with left foot forward and front pivot on left foot.

3. Repeat steps 1 and 2 from SS #7 reversing the directions for hands and feet.

POINTS OF EMPHASIS

- These moves must be made quickly with a low center of gravity. If your opponent decides to move for the rebound at any time, you must be ready to respond with the appropriate pivot into block-out position.
- Never take your eyes off your opponent until you have made contact in block-out position.

Drill R-4

1. Begin facing the basket on SS #1.

2. Throw the ball off the backboard above the rim so that it rebounds on the other side of the basket. As soon as the ball leaves your hands, slide or run across the lane and using a two-foot jump, catch the ball at the top of your jump.

3. Repeat steps 1 and 2 throwing the ball from SS #5.

Drill R-5

1. Face the basket between SS #8 and 9 in block-out position.

2. Throw the basketball high off the backboard and "explode" off the toes of both feet, catching the ball at the top of your jump in both hands with both arms fully extended.

Did you collect yourself before you jumped?

Were your feet spread, knees bent, and head up?

How was your balance?

Were your palms facing the ball as you jumped?

Did you "explode" off both toes with your quickest jump?

Did you grab the ball strong with both hands?

Did you land balanced on the balls of both feet with your head up?

Did you flex your knees on your landing to soften the impact?

3. Pull the ball into your upper chest rotating your right hand on top of the ball and your left hand under the ball. Your elbows should still be out wide.

4. Without turning your head more than an eighth of a turn, take a quick look over your right shoulder. Front pivot out on the ball of your right foot toward the sideline so that you are facing the opposite basket.

5. Repeat steps 1–4, but fake a pass left (inside) before you pivot. After you pivot, lay the ball out and take one dribble toward the sideline pulling the ball securely into your body with your elbows out after the dribble.

6. Repeat steps 1–5 beginning from a spot between SS #7 and 8 and reversing directions for hands and feet.

Important Note: This drill can be modified into an advanced form by bringing the ball into the upper chest or turning while you are in the air and out-letting before you land. In addition, some coaches do not allow their taller players to bring the ball down on a rebound. In this case, land with the ball held high overhead with the arms fully extended.

POINTS OF EMPHASIS

- The ball must be well protected at all times.
- Your head is up.
- Every movement must be executed with authority.

Drill R-6

1. Begin facing the backboard on SS #9.
2. Throw the ball off the backboard, over the rim, so that the ball rebounds on the other side.
3. Run across the three-second lane and catch the ball in the air with two hands, landing with a solid two-foot jump stop. You must catch the ball outside the three-second lane and on as few bounces as possible.
   a. Feet are at least a shoulder width apart.
   b. Knees bent.
   c. Ball pulled into upper chest with elbows out.
   d. As you pull the ball into your chest, rotate one hand on top of the ball and the other under the ball.
   e. Head up.
4. Take a quick look over your left shoulder. Front pivot out on your left foot, raising the ball with both hands over your head and fake a strong two-handed overhead pass toward the hash mark.
5. Reverse pivot on the ball of your left foot into the same position as when you caught the ball.
6. Throw the ball off the backboard, over the rim, so that it rebounds on the other side and repeat steps 3–5 reversing the directions for hands and feet.
7. Repeat steps 1–6, but after taking the quick look over your shoulder toward the sideline, lay the ball out with one dribble toward that sideline with the opposite hand of the shoulder you looked over. After the one dribble, grab the ball in both hands in the same position described in step 3.

POINTS OF EMPHASIS

- This drill is excellent for developing agility, stamina, footwork, and timing.
- Do this drill aggressively, catching the ball strong, maintaining good balance with a low center of gravity, and keeping the ball well protected.

Drill R-7: Two-Handed and One-Handed Taps

1. Face the basket on SS #2.
2. Throw the ball high off the backboard. Using a two-foot takeoff, catch

the ball at the top of your jump with your hands fully extended and, as quickly as possible, throw the ball back off the backboard.

　　3. As soon as you land, jump again and catch the ball at the top of your jump with your arms fully extended. Repeat this five times and bank the ball into the basket.

　　4. Repeat steps 1–3 from SS #5.

　　5. Repeat steps 1–5 with two-handed taps.

　　a. Taps are an extension of the catch and throw.

　　b. Get all ten comfortably spread fingers behind the ball with the hands relaxed and slightly cupped.

　　c. Give with the fingers and relax your hands as the ball makes contact with the fingers.

　　d. Let the ball sit for just a split second in your hands and gently push it back up with the middle three fingers of each hand, concentrating on the spot on the backboard you are tapping to.

　　e. As you gain control of this modified two-hand tap, decrease the amount of time the ball remains on your fingertips as long as you do not lose control of your taps.

　　6. Repeat steps 1–5 with one-handed taps—right hand from the right side of the basket and left hand from the left side of the basket.

　　The one-handed tap is an advanced skill that requires considerable balance, timing, coordination, strength, and practice. A large hand is also advantageous.

WORKOUTS, EVALUATION, AND PROGRESS CHARTS

Table 9-1　Rebounding Workout—15 Minutes

Warmup

DRILL	INSTRUCTIONS
Backboard or rim touches	Begin with two sets of five jumps each, and increase the number of repetitions by one each day.
R-1	Begin with two sets of five jumps each at twelve inches, and increase the number of repetitions by one and the height of the stick by one inch everyday until you reach your maximum.
R-2	Do each pivot two times.
R-3	"　　　"
R-4	Do one set of 1-minute duration.
R-5	"　　　"
R-6	Do two sets of 1-minute duration.
R-7	
Two-hand catch	Do one set of 1-minute duration.
Two-hand tap	"　　　"
One-hand tap	"　　　"
Cooldown	

Table 9-2 Rebounding Workout—30 Minutes

Warmup

DRILL	INSTRUCTIONS
Backboard or rim touches	Begin with three sets of five jumps each, and increase the number of repetitions by one each day.
R-1	Begin with three sets of five jumps each at twelve inches, and increase the number of repetitions by one and the height of the stick by one inch everyday until you reach your maximum.
R-2	Do each pivot three times.
R-3	" "
R-4	Do three sets of 1-minute duration.
R-5	" "
R-6	" "
R-7	
Two-hand catch	" "
Two-hand tap	" "
One-hand tap	" "
Cooldown	

Table 9-3 Rebounding Self-Evaluation and Improvement Test

DRILL	INSTRUCTIONS	TIME	SCORE
Backboard or rim touches	Jump up and touch backboard or rim.	1 minute	No. of touches
R-1	Set stick at maximum height.	1 "	No. of jumps
R-3		1 "	No. of pivots
R-4		1 "	No. of rebounds
R-5		1 "	No. of rebounds
R-6		1 "	No. of rebounds
R-7	Execute two-hand catches.	1 "	No. of taps
	Execute two-hand taps.	1 "	No. of taps
	Execute one-hand taps.	1 "	No. of taps

Table 9-4 Personal Rebounding Progress Chart

Drill	DATE						
Backboard or rim touches							
R-1							
R-3							
R-4							
R-5							
R-6							
R-7 Two-hand catch							
Two-hand tap							
One-hand tap							

INDEX